OHIO STATE
FOOTBALL

Ohio History and Culture

Series on Ohio History and Culture

OHIO STATE FOOTBALL
The Forgotten Dawn

Robert J. Roman

The University of Akron Press
Akron, Ohio

All inquiries and permission requests should be addressed to the Publisher, the University of Akron Press, Akron, Ohio 44325-1703.

21   20   19   18   17   5   4   3   2   1

ISBN: 978-1-629220-66-6 (paper)
ISBN: 978-1-629220-68-0 (ePDF)
ISBN: 978-1-629220-67-3 (ePub)

A catalog record for this title is available from the Library of Congress.

∞ The paper used in this publication meets the minimum requirements of ANSI / NISO z39.48–1992 (Permanence of Paper).

Cover design: Amy Freels. Cover photo: The Ohio State football team in the spring of 1890. Photo courtesy of The Ohio State University Archives. The full uncropped image appears on page 97.

Ohio State Football was designed and typeset in Centaur by Amy Freels, with assistance from Tyler Krusinski. *Ohio State Football* was printed on sixty-pound natural and bound by Bookmasters of Ashland, Ohio.

This book is dedicated to my mother, Katherine Biggs Roman

Contents

Introduction

Almost as dear as the red, white and blue

In the fall of 1873, in the farmlands just north of Columbus, the state of Ohio opened a new school of higher education. At the time the school had only seven faculty members, and the faculty welcomed their first twenty-four students that September.[1] In the twenty-first century that same school, the Ohio State University, has nearly seven thousand faculty members and it averages nearly sixty thousand students every year.[2] The few men and women on campus in 1873 would have had difficulty recognizing the enormous institution that their school has since become.

Yet as surprised as those early students and faculty might have been to see so much growth, the faculty would likely have been even more surprised to discover a different modern development. Today the highest-paid faculty member at the Ohio State University—in fact, the highest paid employee of the state—is the university's football coach.[3] That coach is, to many, the public face of the school.[4] The faculty of 1873 would have had no framework to grasp this situation.

Even today some people question the priorities at the university that have led to the current preeminence of football there.[5] The students, however, even in those earliest days, might have understood.

*

The Ohio State University originally owed its existence to the Land-Grant College Act of 1862, a Congressional act that gave grants to states to fund colleges and universities. Prior to the Act, the best-known schools of higher education were intended to educate the social elites and were usually founded by religious sects. Princeton University had been founded by Presbyterians, Harvard University and Yale University by Congregationalists, and Columbia University by the Church of England. Other American colleges and universities across the nation followed a similar pattern. Sectarian campus chapel services were considered part of a student's training, and attendance was often a requirement of admission.[6] For these reasons, colleges and universities were traditionally the province of the wealthy, of religious clerics in training, or both.

The Land-Grant College Act led to a social revolution.[7] Less wealthy Americans found new opportunities for higher education, and new educational opportunities helped a more culturally and ethnically diverse group of Americans find opportunities for advancement. Those Americans included students who were not members of a specific, approved Christian denomination, or who for other reasons simply preferred to receive a secular education.

As with any revolutionary social change, the Land-Grant College Act also triggered passionate opposition. The backlash was particularly strong in Ohio, a state that was dominated in the nineteenth century by an unusually large number of sectarian religious colleges.[8] Critics from those sectarian colleges accused the new Land-Grant school of being godless, and they were quick to question the secular values of its students.

As a result, the Ohio State students felt under attack and they were constantly fighting for respect. To these students, the criticisms of their school felt like narrow-minded bigotry, and they developed much of their sense of self-worth from how well they competed with the sectarian schools. They began to advocate for toleration and freedom of conscience, and their confidence in that cause rose and fell based on their successes and failures in athletic contests.[9]

It was during this time that a new sport arrived on American college campuses. American "gridiron" football had originally been played on the East Coast by schools such as Princeton, Harvard, Yale, and Columbia, but national sports magazines quickly declared it a growing movement. By the 1880s that movement had come to Ohio. The sport offered the feel of gladiatorial battle, which made it attractive to students who wanted to measure themselves against their rivals.[10] To Ohio State students, football became a way to prove their self-worth while honoring the name of their school.

The defensive and wary Ohio State students also did not always see eye to eye with the administration of their own university. In the hostile social environment of the time, the university's board of trustees was often forced to act with deference to broader community attitudes, and the students often felt frustrated by conservative university policies. The trustees, in response, were often annoyed by the impetuous actions and attitudes of the students.

*

As the Ohio State students developed their athletic teams and were otherwise promoting their school, they were also telling their own story. They told that story as it unfolded, in their student newspaper and their school yearbook. For a modern audience looking back, reading that story can reveal who these early students were, at least as they saw themselves, and what issues were important to them. It was in the Ohio State student newspaper in 1887 that an editor pleaded with his fellow students to remember to wear their school colors—to hold the colors of scarlet and gray "almost as dear as the red, white, and blue."[11]

As the university trustees grew increasingly annoyed at the enthusiasm and perceived impetuousness of the students, they became particularly concerned with irresponsible student behavior in support of their football team. Eventually the university assumed control over that team, and as a result the true story of its early years was lost. Most of what is believed about the birth of Ohio State football is a myth. The truth was forgotten.

In the decades that followed, the true story of those early students and their football team has been waiting to be rediscovered. That true story, much more than the myth, allows us to understand the success that the team has achieved since. The patterns of support, established from the start, were continued by those who followed. The students' vision and enthusiasm, as well as their defensiveness, became the model for modern fans. Those who criticize Ohio State football today will see everything they find objectionable among its founders. Those who are fans of Ohio State football will see themselves.

Part One

Let us have a varsity team that would do honor to its name

Chapter One

Foot ball has suddenly made its appearance

Harry Hedges was a mountain of a man. His friends called him "Jumbo." He spent his childhood working as a field laborer in Urbana, a farm town in western Ohio, and after he enrolled at the Ohio State University the college yearbook described him as "Not pretty, but massive." By the spring of 1886 Hedges had become the president of the Ohio State sophomore class.[1]

On the morning of April 28 of that year, the sophomores were walking out of the university's chapel service when they saw a line of thirty men marching toward them double-file. One man in the formation waved the flag of the junior class. Another held the flag of the sophomores, and a third carried an oilcan, which they intended to use to burn the sophomore flag. Each of the thirty men also carried a fifteen-inch club to prevent anyone from stopping them. When the sophomores realized that these juniors were planning to burn their flag, they looked to Hedges. Hedges considered the situation but he could see only one option to stop them. Standing alone and unarmed, he placed himself in the path of the marching junior line and demanded the sophomore flag.[2]

*

Six months earlier Hedges had been elected vice president of his class. The student newspaper covered the election and noted, "All the persuasive power of Jumbo's muscle was needed to keep the various candidates from stuffing the ballot box or falsifying the returns."[3] Before the election Hedges had decided against being sophomore president, letting his roommate, Joseph Dyer, take that position. Hedges and Dyer both came from farming families but Dyer planned to apply to a law school after he graduated from Ohio State.[4] Hedges apparently agreed that the words "class president" would be more useful decorating his friend's student record.

The university was still young at this time, with an enrollment of only 330 students. That total included the four graduating classes, plus a grad school, a prep school, and various two-year professional schools, including dentistry, pharmacy, and veterinary. The sophomore class of Hedges and Dyer had an enrollment of only forty students.[5]

The forty sophomores, representing the graduating class of 1888, were dwarfed by the seventy students who immediately followed them—the freshmen from the graduating class of 1889.[6] When the university first opened in 1873, the school's total enrollment was only twenty-four students.[7] Year by year the enrollment steadily increased because year by year each new group of freshmen arrived at least a little bit larger than the one before it. The freshmen arriving in the fall of 1885 had almost twice as many members as any other class.

In October one of the freshmen attempted to use his class's size to their advantage. That freshman, William Morrey, organized a voting bloc, intending for his classmates to dominate a campus election.[8] When the three upper classes caught wind of what Morrey was up to, they responded with a united front, foiling the plot. "The freshmen attempted too much," the other classes gloated immediately afterward.[9]

Tensions remained high among the classes in the weeks that followed. A divisive feeling of rivalry filled the air. It was during this time that Jumbo Hedges and Joe Dyer challenged the freshmen to a football game.[10]

*

Football was a campus tradition. No one knew exactly when that tradition began. Sitting on the west side of campus was the North Dorm, the school's larger dormitory, and the students who lived there had played football on their grounds for as long as anyone remembered. The Ohio State student newspaper, the *Lantern*, had noted as early as April 1881: "Foot-ball is the order of the day at the Dorm, and nearly every evening witnesses a jolly game."[11]

Students had founded their newspaper in January of that same year, and the *Lantern* quickly began to hold a central position in campus life. It had a "local

The North Dorm, center of Ohio State campus life in the nineteenth century. (Photo courtesy of The Ohio State University Archives)

editor" in charge of campus news, a "personal editor" who published campus gossip, and an "exchanges editor" who let the students know what was happening on the campuses of other schools. The newspaper also had a "literary editor" who invited and published more scholarly submissions from the student body and an editor-in-chief who held the project together and offered, through editorials, a running commentary on life at Ohio State.

The *Lantern*'s first editor-in-chief seemed somewhat less enthusiastic than others about football. He noted in the spring of 1881 that the North Dorm students were still playing football even while everyone else had begun to play baseball.[12] It apparently took some time for everyone on campus to accept that football was played all year at the North Dorm.

The football that North Dorm students played was only informal pickup games but by the 1880s the students at major schools on the East Coast— Harvard, Princeton, Columbia, and Yale—had been playing football for several

The residents of the North Dorm assemble for a photo in 1885. (Photo courtesy of The Ohio State University Archives)

years with organized varsity teams. On some Eastern campuses the sport's popularity was rivaling even baseball. National sports magazines declared organized football to be a growing movement, and people across the country watched with anticipation, expecting that movement to spread west.[13]

At Ohio State, in the fall of 1885, the sophomores and freshmen agreed to organize formal class football teams. It seemed as reasonable a way as any to settle their differences. The *Lantern* celebrated Ohio State's step into organized football by cheering, "Foot ball has suddenly made its appearance."[14]

✳

Jumbo Hedges and Joe Dyer needed to build the sophomore team and their first task was to pick a captain. A captain in those days, in any sport, was a team's most important figure. He was the unquestioned leader on the field. In a role more like a modern coach, the captain in football trained his players, assigned them positions, and called his team's plays during games.[15]

Hedges apparently agreed that Dyer would be the better captain for their team. Dyer was a varsity athlete—he was the starting right fielder on the Ohio State baseball team.[16] Hedges participated in the pickup football games at the Dorm but, despite his mass and muscle, he had never played more organized campus sports.[17]

Hedges preferred to be his team's manager. A manager was in charge of all of the team's off-field leadership responsibilities: recruiting players, finding opponents, and negotiating a schedule.[18] Hedges already had an opponent so he focused on recruiting, inviting sophomore athletes with experience in the North Dorm games to join the class team.

One of the first people that he recruited was a sophomore named Fred Ball. Ball was a talented athlete. He was a member of the Ohio State tennis team, and he also was a member of a sophomore class tennis team that competed against the other classes.[19] In the coming spring he would be a member of a new varsity football team, playing a position in the backfield called a "three-quarter back,"[20] so it is most likely that Joe Dyer, as the sophomore football team's captain, also put Ball in that position that fall.

Ball, like Hedges and Dyer, had joined the sophomore class government that year—Ball was the treasurer of their class[21]—but he spent more of his energy as a campus leader on a different organization. As a freshman he had been the O.S.U. delegate to the state Y.M.C.A. convention, and the following fall the campus Y.M.C.A. elected him to serve as president of their branch.[22] Hedges and Ball each respected the campus achievements of the other.

Hedges next recruited a sophomore named Chester Aldrich. In contrast to Ball, Hedges's relationship with Aldrich seemed to be built on confrontation. Hedges and Aldrich were both born in Ohio but they came from separate worlds. Aldrich was a wealthy blue blood, known for his fine clothes and aristocratic manners.[23] He was raised on an estate near Ashtabula and before he arrived at Ohio State he had attended a prestigious prep school.[24] The patrician Aldrich thought that he deserved the kind of leadership positions that came to the gregarious Hedges naturally. The tension between the two came to a head late in the spring of their freshman year at the "Incognitus et Agnos," a campus end-of-year satirical event run by North Dorm students.[25] Aldrich objected to how Hedges wanted to use him in the show and he refused to perform, spoiling much of the fun for everyone.[26]

Despite their differences, Hedges wanted Aldrich on the sophomore football team. Swallowing his pride, Aldrich accepted. The evidence suggests that Dyer put Aldrich next to Hedges on the line.

✦

The freshmen were building their own class team and they were led by a student named Charles Cutler Sharp. Everybody called him "C.C."[27] In the era of J.P. Morgan, J.D. Rockefeller, and P.T. Barnum, men with business ambitions often preferred to be addressed by their initials. C.C. Sharp was a natural athlete and the leader of his class on almost any athletic field.

Sharp seemed most engaged at school when facing competition. He had earned a position on the varsity baseball team when he was still a prep student.[28] He also was a sprinter and he set a personal goal of winning the school championship in the 100-yard dash. He was listed as a member of the class of 1889[29] but he challenged the rest of the freshmen to join him in trying to graduate early.[30] He could not stand to see the class of 1888 have even that advantage over them.

Jesse Lee Jones was another North Dorm freshman but Jones had no interest in Sharp's early-graduation challenge. Sharp had already spent two years on campus, as a student in the O.S.U. prep school, but for Jones the experience of university life was completely new. He had worked in a factory the previous year in his home town of Martins Ferry,[31] and after he got to Ohio State he wanted to enjoy all that his school had to offer. He was elected sergeant-at-arms of the freshman class[32] and he participated regularly in the North Dorm football games.

In those informal games Jones and Sharp each brought out the competitive spirit in the other. Sharp was an established class leader and Jones wanted to dethrone a campus king. Sharp understood what Jones wanted and he was not willing to let it happen. In one Dorm game the two faced each other on opposing lines. Tempers flared, and as the game played out they nearly sent each other to the campus infirmary.[33]

Jumbo Hedges did not personally dislike most of these freshmen, and despite the rivalry between the classes most of them did not personally dislike him. He had known many of them since they were prep students. He had looked out for them as preps, even tutoring some of them when they needed help with Latin.[34] He had grown up the oldest of eight children in his family[35] and he continued to act like a big brother after he came to Ohio State.

During spring break one year earlier Hedges had put up a prep named Frank Raymund in his family home in Urbana, Ohio.[36] Raymund remained a loyal friend afterward. Their friendship, however, did not stop Raymund from joining the freshman football team.

*

The freshmen and sophomores finished forming their class teams and they seemed ready to schedule the challenge game, but there was a delay. Personal issues called Hedges off campus[37] and Joe Dyer refused to play without him.[38] The two teams agreed to postpone their game until he returned.

While they waited, a bigger delay occurred. Winter arrived early as heavy storms rolled down from Canada. The campus grounds, covered in a deep layer of snow, had become impassable. Outdoor activities were cancelled. Snowbound students turned their competitive impulses toward playing poker in the dormitory,[39] and the freshmen and sophomores agreed to postpone their football game until the weather cleared up in the spring.

Some people began to fear that the game would never be played. All through the winter the *Lantern* published articles on the topic of football to keep people thinking about the sport. The articles covered football at Harvard, football at Yale, football at Princeton, etc.[40] In March a *Lantern* writer named Emma Boyd reminded her readers directly that "the Sophomore and Freshman classes are to have a foot ball contest this Spring."[41] She then offered her hope that the game would inspire others on campus to play and "promote a legitimate indulgence in what is already THE college game of America."[42]

Chester Aldrich then began to promote a more ambitious idea. In January the managing editor of the *Lantern* had put Aldrich in charge of the newspaper's "Local Notes" column. In February Aldrich argued in his column that the time had come to form a varsity football team—a team of students who would compete against other schools and represent the entire university. The Ohio State students had only ever faced intercollegiate athletic competition with their varsity baseball team but Aldrich argued that football offered the same opportunities. "There is also plenty of good metal out of which can be formed a foot ball team that would do credit to the O. S. U.," he said. "Let us have a Varsity team that would do honor to its name."[43] He repeated his call for a varsity football team in another column one month later.[44]

Varsity sports were usually under the authority of a student organization named the Ohio State University Athletic Association. The Athletic Association had intended to field a varsity football team from the start but they had never succeeded in forming one. In 1881 the Association established three standing committees—one for baseball, one for football, and one for general athletics.[45]

That first year no football team was formed. The following year the committee did no better, and the *Lantern* asked, "Where is the foot-ball? What a
grand game could be had on the campus."[46] When no progress was made in the
third year the *Lantern* began to plead that "a first-class foot-ball team be organized at once.... We ought to challenge our neighbors to measure their ability
with us in that line. It would be a splendid advertisement for the university."[47]
After that year, the ineffectual football committee was dropped. By the time
Chester Aldrich began calling for varsity football during the winter of 1886 the
Association had long since given up on that plan.

Over the years Ohio State students had tried to establish varsity teams in many
sports—baseball, bicycling, rifle, rowing, and more.[48] Other than baseball none of
these teams lasted more than a season. Students always formed their teams while
caught up in the excitement of each new project but by the following year that early
excitement always cooled. No one was more frustrated than a student named
William Stowe Devol, a senior who had watched his cricket team, his archery team,
and his equestrian team disappear.[49] The Athletic Association's failure to maintain
varsity sports was a recurring topic of conversation throughout the 1880s.[50]

The loss of teams cost the students opportunities to compete against other
schools, and losing those opportunities hurt the school's ability to maintain any
intercollegiate rivalries. Ohio State students did have rivalries with other colleges
in the state but their interactions with those schools were fairly limited. With
few opportunities for intercollegiate competition, the students identified most
immediately with their various campus organizations—their clubs, their frater-
nities, and, especially, their graduating classes. The feelings of rivalry for Ohio
State students were most often directed toward other Ohio State students.

As a result, the students did not have much school spirit.[51] With varsity
sports struggling there was little spark to keep the fires of school spirit burning.
Only class spirit thrived. Aldrich spoke for many students who wanted a more
intense emotional connection to their university. They wanted to feel pride in
Ohio State as a way to feel pride in themselves. They wanted to feel superior to
their college rivals. "Let us have some college spirit,"[52] Aldrich pleaded.

Jumbo Hedges saw the value in Aldrich's varsity football solution.

*

In January 1886 a local Columbus attorney offered Joe Dyer an apprenticeship.[53] A legal apprenticeship was a path to law school that was quicker and surer

even than college. Dyer accepted the offer and withdrew from school. He later became a city prosecutor, and he eventually returned to Ohio State as a faculty member in the O.S.U. School of Law.[54]

More immediately, however, Jumbo Hedges needed a new roommate. He offered Dyer's spot in his dorm room to a prep student named Charles Wey-brecht. Weybrecht seemed not to have many other friends on campus. He weighed two hundred pounds and was saddled with the nickname "Fatty."[55] Chester Aldrich joked that when "Fatty" began rooming with "Jumbo" the school would have to empty the room below them, or at least add new building supports.[56] Weybrecht got even by dumping a bucket of water on Aldrich from the second-floor dorm room that he now shared with Hedges.[57]

Dyer's withdrawal also meant that Hedges inherited the class presidency. "Jumbo now rules the Sophomore class meetings with an iron hand," read the news.[58] The sophomores held a special election and chose Aldrich as their new vice president.[59] These changes in leadership guided the events of the rest of the school year.

*

In April the long winter finally ended and students who had been cooped up in their dormitories were anxious to stretch their legs.[60] They had spent months together with just each other to look at. The female students who attended the university were not permitted to live on campus[61] and, with spring fever in the air, young men needed an outlet to release their pent-up high spirits.

On April 28, at just after 2 a.m., a group of sophomores snuck out of their dorm rooms and gathered in the darkness outside. Then they snuck into University Hall, the tallest building on campus, and climbed up into its tower. Above the tower they raised a flag—cherry and lavender, the sophomore class colors.[62]

Under their flag they added a message directed to the junior class. The university's thirty juniors were the graduating class of 1887. Two years earlier, as freshmen, they had tried to raise their own flag above University Hall.[63] They had been stopped in the act, so for the new prank the sophomores—the class of '88—hung a banner with a message to remind everyone of that failure: "Wanted to but couldn't—'87."[64] Beneath that banner they hung an effigy of the junior class, wearing the junior class colors of olive-green and pink.[65]

The juniors woke up the next morning to find the sophomore flag and taunting message flying together over the campus. Halbert Edwin Payne, the junior

University Hall as it would have looked just before the class of 1888 hung their flag.
(Photo courtesy of The Ohio State University Archives)

class president, was the best pitcher on the varsity baseball team. He was 5'11"
and the *Lantern* described him as having the physique of Apollo.[66] Payne was not
the type to back down from a challenge, and he knew that he would never hear
the end of it if he let the sophomores get away with a prank this good at the
juniors' expense. So he prepared a response.

At 8:00 a.m. the University Hall janitor took down the material hanging from
the tower, and by 8:30 the juniors had the sophomores' cherry and lavender flag. At
a quarter to noon the men of the class, clubs in hand and an oilcan ready, lined up
double-file for a march across campus. At the front of their line was H.E. Payne.
Just as they started their march, however, they found Jumbo Hedges blocking their
path and shouting at Payne, demanding the return of the sophomore flag.[67]

Students gathered around Hedges and the juniors, waiting to see what would
happen. Fatty Weybrecht shook with a "passion for war" but he understood that
as a prep student this was not his fight.[68] Chester Aldrich and Fred Ball both
watched from a few yards away, Aldrich wearing his most expensive Victorian

three-piece suit. The juniors attempted to march around Hedges. Hedges reached out to them trying to take back the sophomore flag. As he extended his arm one of the juniors clubbed him across the face. Hedges staggered and his face was bloodied, but he managed to stand his ground. Then, as he regained his bearings, he began fighting back.[69]

Hedges's classmates were too stunned to react until Fred Ball jumped into the fray. Ball quickly took a shot to the face similar to the one that struck Hedges. Ball fell, and on that cue the others sophomores swarmed. The juniors franticly swung their clubs at the charging sophomore bodies. The sophomores began wrestling the juniors to the ground. Chester Aldrich's fine clothes were left in tatters.[70]

The two sides tugged at the sophomore flag until it ripped apart. The sophomores then turned their attention to the juniors' flag. The junior flag-bearer ran. That retreat disgusted H.E. Payne, who later said that if he had a rope he would have hung the coward.[71] The sophomores chased the flag-bearer and the fighting stretched across campus. In the end the junior flag was also ripped apart and Hedges grabbed the largest piece to finally wipe the blood from his face.[72]

A few days later, in his "Local Notes" column, Aldrich attempted to capture the moment:

> The Seniors and ladies on the steps, and the professors from their windows, like the old men sitting on the walls of Troy, too weak to fight, watched the combatants on the campus below, asking who is this or that. He that towers above the others—can that be Hector? Yes, but they call him Jumbo.[73]

*

Diverse reactions to the campus battle soon appeared in the Columbus city newspapers. The *Columbus Dispatch*, a local daily, published the story that evening with an outraged headline: "Terrific Conflict Between the Juniors and Sophomores at State University: Bloody Faces and Bruised Heads."[74] The two classes "met in deadly conflict," they reported.[75] The *Dispatch*'s competitor, the *Ohio State Journal*, took a much more cavalier, boys-will-be-boys tone the next morning: "Students At Play: State University Pupils Tumble Over One Another in Struggle for Colors."[76]

The Ohio State students were inclined to embrace the second interpretation. After all, they did not see themselves as savages. The *Lantern* took the *State Journal*'s interpretation a step further and proclaimed the incident a bonding experience and celebrated it as a highlight of the year. They wrote that events of this kind give college life its "spice" and "seasoning," and as a result of such skirmishes,

> men come to know each other; to know another's worth, and see their own failings; to have the corners rounded and ugly prominences knocked off; and, more than all, to learn what the English boys learn at Rugby and Oxford, to forget the individual and to feel and fight for the community.[77]

The freshmen were impressed by how well the battle turned out and wanted a piece of the action. Chester Aldrich even dared them: "The Freshmen have had an example set to them of the way they should go when they arrive at the proper age."[78] A few days later Jesse Lee Jones and Frank Raymund led a group of their classmates up the tower to raise their own class flag.[79] Their colors were garnet and light blue. Jones and Raymund wanted to add a taunting message as part of their fun so they challenged the seniors. Then they signed their own names under their note to make sure that C.C. Sharp did not get the credit.

In the days that followed, the twenty members of the senior class, including William Stowe Devol, were tempted to respond, but by then the faculty had begun watching over the campus with increased scrutiny. With graduation only weeks away, the seniors had the good sense to try to keep their noses clean. The sophomores scoffed that the freshman prank had failed to steal their class's spotlight.[80]

Yet everyone had grudging respect that the freshmen ringleaders had been bold enough, or foolish enough, to personally sign their work.[81] True to the prediction made by the *Lantern*, the classes were never closer.

*

For Jumbo Hedges and Chester Aldrich this moment of campus unity felt like an opportunity, and they used the opportunity to form a varsity football team.[82] Hedges became the varsity manager and Aldrich became varsity captain, so Hedges recruited players while Aldrich ran the team's practices. Hedges invited H.E. Payne from the junior class and Fatty Weybrecht from the prep program. Dominating the lineup, however, were the football players from the freshman and sophomore class teams. Among the freshmen were C.C. Sharp, Jesse Lee Jones, and Frank Raymund, as well as William Morrey, the leader of the freshman voting-bloc plot the previous fall. This football team was the first united under the colors of the university.[83]

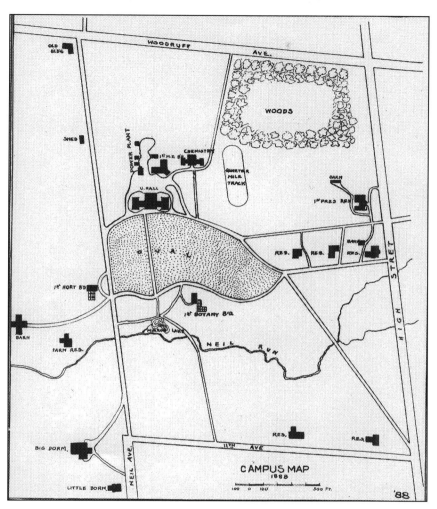

The Ohio State campus as it looked in the 1880s. (Photo courtesy of The Ohio State University Archives)

As manager, Hedges also had the responsibility of finding an opponent. This task proved much harder. No other school in central Ohio had a varsity football team. The only varsity football teams that were widely known at that time were those at the major schools in the East—Harvard, Princeton, Columbia, and Yale—and none of those established teams were likely to accept a challenge from an upstart like Ohio State. Even if an Eastern school might have accepted, the cost for an O.S.U. team to travel so far just to play a game would have been prohibitively expensive. As a result, the O.S.U. students continued to practice for a game that they did not really expect to play.

Within a few weeks the enthusiasm that had united the football team faded, just as it had faded for so many Ohio State teams before. Frank Raymund suffered an injury in one of the practices,[84] and his hobbling across campus for the next few weeks looked like it would be the only lasting consequence of varsity football's existence. Aldrich and Hedges hoped that their work would prove to be the start of something bigger but for the moment it had hit a dead end.

*

Meanwhile the freshman and sophomore class football teams never played their challenge game. In the short-term excitement of forming a varsity team the class game was forgotten. Early the next fall the *Lantern* remembered the challenge and tried to revive interest in the game, but the moment had passed.[85]

Chapter Two

Integrity, ability, energy, earnestness, and true worth

Jumbo Hedges and Chester Aldrich remained friends after the events that inspired the 1886 varsity football team.[1] When they became juniors the following fall, Hedges chose not to run for reelection as class president, letting Aldrich take a turn in office. Hedges participated in student government afterward as class sergeant-at-arms. A sergeant-at-arms maintained order in meetings and kept the members in line, and the position may have been the best use of his imposing presence. The *Lantern* described Aldrich's election as conducted "under the tender care of the fatherly 'Jumbo'."[2]

The North Dorm students continued to play pickup football that fall. Most of the students that Aldrich and Hedges had brought into their short-lived varsity team continued to participate in the more informal games on the North Dorm field. Fred Ball, Frank Raymund, C.C. Sharp, and Jesse Lee Jones all returned.[3] Only a few members of the spring team were no longer playing football.

One was the former voting-bloc leader William Morrey. Morrey did not usually play football because he lived in the South Dorm.[4] The South Dorm, or Little Dorm, was only a block away from the North Dorm but it had a separate culture. Ohio State's football tradition remained specific to the North Dorm.

*

In most places at that time someone like Hedges was unlikely to interact with someone as wealthy as Aldrich, and the two were less likely to become friends, but Ohio State students took pride in how their school was able to mix people from any background. One of the seven members of the university's board of trustees was Peter Humphries Clark, an African American political activist.[5]

William Morrey, middle row, wearing a boater (second from right), poses with his fellow Sorth Dorm residents. (Photo courtesy of The Ohio State University Archives)

The students bragged that the social categories that usually held people apart meant nothing to them. "Here the rich and poor mingle together," wrote the *Lantern* in 1884, "with no other distinctions than those of integrity, ability, energy, earnestness, and true worth."[6]

Like many members of his generation, Hedges had been the first in his family to go to college. The Ohio State University owed its existence to the Land-Grant College Act of 1862, a Congressional act that gave grants to states to fund colleges and universities. Less wealthy Americans found educational opportunities through these newly opening Land-Grant colleges.[7] Ohio's Land-Grant College did not even charge tuition. Ohio residents needed only a high school diploma and a qualifying exam score to enter. The state legislature established the school in 1870, just north of the state capital, with a focus on scientific training, and the school's faculty first welcomed students in 1873.[8] Hedges enrolled for a degree in agriculture, with a career plan in agricultural technology.

Not every student who entered the university was successful. A freshman named William Beatty was a very good campus athlete but he was a poor student.

Peter Humphries Clark, of the original Ohio State board of trustees. (Photo courtesy of The Ohio State University Archives)

Like C.C. Sharp, he had played on the varsity baseball team as a prep student, and he had been recruited to the varsity football team in the spring.[9] He also held the school record in the 100-yard dash and had held that record for many years.[10] He originally had been a member of the class of 1887 but he failed enough coursework as a freshman that the faculty set him back, first into the class of 1888 and then into the class of 1889.[11] His father was General John Beatty, a decorated Civil War hero, former United States Congressman, and long-time supporter of the university. General Beatty had helped his son stay in college but after a third unsuccessful freshman year the general arranged for his son to get a job.[12]

Congress required states accepting funds from the Land-Grant College Act to provide training in "the agricultural and mechanical sciences," but the education offered beyond farming and technical training was left to the discretion of each state. Different states made different educational choices. Ohio's farming community had wanted to use the funds to build a narrow agricultural and mechanical college but the state's professional educators pushed for a broader and more comprehensive curriculum modeled on the research universities of Europe.

Ohio's governor in 1870, Rutherford B. Hayes, had hoped to appease both sides in the debate but his own position was closer to the educators'. He thought that Ohio lacked a college that was inclusive enough to represent the entire state, and building one became his primary consideration. He insisted that Ohio's new Land-Grant college should become the state's flagship school.[13]

When Ohio State was founded the state of Ohio already had thirty-four colleges and universities—more than any other state, more in fact than all the nations of Europe combined.[14] Almost all of those schools were established with religious affiliations, each representing one of various specific sects. Ohio had once been at the heart of the early American frontier, as close to the Deep South as it was to New England. After the Revolutionary War, when the new government opened the Ohio Territory for settlement, settlers arrived there from throughout the nation. They were as diverse a people as found anywhere in the United States at that time. They were Baptist, Methodist, and Congregationalist. They were Presbyterian, Episcopalian, and Unitarian. They were Lutheran, Mennonite, Evangelical, Roman Catholic, Quaker, Pentecostal, Jewish, and on and on, varying from one city or town to the next.[15] The first item of business for a new community was to build a house of worship. The second was to build a college, and the colleges usually reflected the sectarian religious affiliations of their founders.[16]

Governor Hayes envisioned a different purpose, and a different philosophy, for his state's new flagship school. Hayes had been baptized a Presbyterian and had attended an Episcopalian college, and more recently he had begun attending Methodist services with his wife, but he personally claimed no religious denomination.[17] He believed that sectarianism was unnecessarily divisive.[18] His goal for Ohio's Land-Grant College funds was to establish a school that would unite the state's people, to let them rally around their common bonds rather than be separated by their differences.[19]

For Hayes, this school was his chance to leave a lasting legacy as governor, and he became the guiding force behind the principles that he wanted it to represent.[20] After the school was founded he became its leading promoter.[21] For his leadership some called Hayes the "Father of the Ohio State University," and he kept a paternal eye on the school's development even after he became the President of the United States.

The students echoed President Hayes's ambition that Ohio State be recognized as the state's flagship school. In fact being considered a flagship became a cornerstone of the Ohio State self-image. The students bragged about their school—mostly about the quality of its academic offerings compared to other schools in the state, especially in the sciences.

They similarly bragged about their level of religious tolerance. Non-Christians were not warmly embraced by the state's sectarian schools but Ohio State, by charter, welcomed any qualified applicant. A spirit of ecumenicalism became an explicit point of campus pride, just as President Hayes had hoped it would. The students emphasized that their school gave an education to "Gentile, Jew, all mortals great and small."[22] They believed that broad-minded religious acceptance was part of what made them special and distinct. They believed it because President Hayes had said it was so.

An example of that acceptance was the friendship of Fred Ball and a student named Samuel Oppenheimer. Oppenheimer was well liked on campus for his quick wit and musical talent.[23] He also was the university's first Jewish student.[24] Like Ball, Oppenheimer was a member of the tennis team—he played as half of the team's featured doubles pair.[25] Also like Ball, he had been a member of the 1886 varsity football team. He had been the three-quarter back on the side opposite Ball. Even more than Chester Aldrich and Jumbo Hedges, Ball and Oppenheimer were unlikely friends in their state and in their era in many places outside their school. While Oppenheimer was an observant Jew, Ball was the devout president of the campus Young Men's Christian Association. Ball, however, did not believe that religion should ever be imposing or judgmental. As he put it, he thought churches should "teach more and preach less."[26]

*

The boastful self image that defined Ohio State's students also influenced how they approached sports.[27] As much as they wanted to be respected for their academic offerings and broad-minded values, they equally wanted to be considered the state's leader in physical activity and athletic prowess. Opportunities to participate in intercollegiate sports were rare, but the students saw those opportunities as yet another way to prove their flagship status.

Despite the North Dorm's passion for football, the most popular sport at the university overall had always been baseball. The North Dorm was home to a quarter of the Ohio State student body but baseball was "the national pastime" and "America's great sport."[28] Back in the 1870s Ohio State students formed a campus Baseball Association, and that Baseball Association then formed the school's first varsity team.[29] When students formed a broader Athletic Association in 1881, the new Association needed to annex the baseball team in order for anyone to take it seriously. The *Lantern* asked everyone to support the Athletic Association by forming teams in as many sports as they could, but it also made a point of assuring the baseball purists that the focus of sports at Ohio State would always "be centered on the base-ball nines."[30]

Ohio State's first intercollegiate athletic competition was a baseball game in the spring of 1881. The opponent was Capital University, a Lutheran school in Bexley, a suburb on the east side of Columbus. Ohio State won 8 to 5. It was the last time the students used a nickname that they had used during the 1870s: the Ohio State Franklins.[31] The name referred to the fact that their campus was located in Franklin County. When the team started to compete against other colleges, however, the students insisted that their flagship State University should never be portrayed as local.

*

Because student pride at Ohio State was based on attending the state's flagship school, the students became defensive whenever anyone seemed to look down on their university. They feared being thought of as just an agricultural college—as merely a trade school for farmers.[32] Students from other schools often gave the O.S.U. students opportunities to feel defensive. Those students found the bragging at Ohio State insufferable, demonstrating an inflated self-image that they saw as totally unearned.

The students from those schools particularly resented Ohio State's funding. Although the university's funding originated from the federal government, its continuing endowment officially came out of the state treasury. The resentment was greatest at Ohio University in Athens, Ohio, (where they had been expecting the Land-Grant funds for themselves[33]) but it was also seen at other older, established colleges throughout the state. Among the most vocal critics of Ohio State were the students at the University of Cincinnati, founded in 1819. The University of Cincinnati student newspaper, the *Academica*, wrote of Ohio State in 1885, "It may be jealousy on our part to say that we do not see any reason why this institution, whose courses of study are not more than a year or two in advance of those of our High Schools...should continue to receive appropriations in the future."[34]

The editor-in-chief of the *Lantern* in the fall of 1885 was a junior named Vernon Emery. Early in 1886, after Emery discovered what the *Academica* had written, he responded with an angry 500-word essay. By this time a new student had taken the reins as the newspaper's editor-in-chief, but Emery's name was put back in the masthead for one more issue in order to put the full weight and authority of the *Lantern* behind his piece.

Emery insisted that the *Academica* writers had their facts wrong. He said that they must have confused Ohio State's collegiate programs with its prep school. He explained that "graduates of the High Schools of Cincinnati are able to enter our Freshman class provided their High School work has prepared them for the course they wish to pursue" but high school graduates who are not properly prepared "must make up their back work in our preparatory department." He emphasized that, unlike the University of Cincinnati, no one had ever graduated from Ohio State in less than four years. He then added that the *Academica* writers must have had their thinking clouded by all of the breweries in Cincinnati, and concluded, "If you ever should get outside the limits of Cincinnati, if you will come to Columbus we will show you what a university is like."[35]

The defensiveness of the O.S.U. students was still on display one year later. In the spring of 1887 the university held a campus event, featuring distinguished state dignitaries making lofty speeches to celebrate its mission, and the *Lantern* promoted the event with a call to action. A new editor-in-chief, named J.A. Wilgus, wrote, "It is time to dispel the notion which so many people have that the O. S. U. is a third rate agricultural college away back in the woods."[36]

Meanwhile Ohio's farming community, which had been upset with the state government for allowing the university to have a mission that was broader than farming education, continued to be upset even after the university was founded. They had never embraced President Hayes's plan to establish an academic flagship and they criticized the university for swindling funds that they still argued had been allocated specifically for the agricultural and mechanical sciences. The O.S.U. students defended their school against those attacks as well.[37]

The most hostile criticism of Ohio State, however, came from the state's religious institutions.[38] Many wanted Ohio's colleges to continue to maintain clear sectarian designations and they denounced the new secular state university as "atheistic."[39] Ohio State students regularly described such critics as "theologues" who demanded that all of life be viewed through the narrow prism of religion and ecclesiastic study. Far from fulfilling President Hayes's dream of uniting the state, in the early years of the university few issues in Ohio were more divisive.

Ohio State students claimed that all of these criticisms arose from small-minded intolerance and bias. In reaction they re-emphasized their own claims of tolerance and broad-mindedness. In addition to bragging that their school had no religious qualifications or divisions based on social class, they congratulated themselves for their lack of prejudice when "colored" students first arrived on campus, brought in by the trustee Peter Humphries Clark.[40] They also ridiculed the more conservative schools struggling with the issue of women's education, noting that Ohio State had been chartered from the start as coeducational.[41]

They especially enjoyed mocking the "theologues" who accused them of impiety. Ohio State's first athletic fight song dated from the 1870s and the only accomplishment that it bragged about was the amount of swearing done by the baseball team.[42] The school yearbook, the *Makio*, was named after a mythical Japanese pool that was supposed to reveal a viewer's fate in its reflection,[43] and the yearbook staff occasionally illustrated the *Makio* with a smiling devil welcoming their fellow students to Hell.[44] The Ohio State students may have felt dismissed as mere farm school apprentices "away back in the woods," but they prided themselves as the most intellectually free men in the state.

The most explicit statement of the student credo would be written for the *Makio* in 1897:

> The University has been a seat of intellectual freedom. Thought has breathed here the inspiring air of liberty. The University has no political or religious tests; applies none, acknowledges none. For students the criteria have been moral soundness and a power and willingness to work. Its teachers have been elected because of their qualifications, without regard to their ecclesiastical or political affiliations. This atmosphere of freedom has been a principal condition of the strong and constant progressive spirit that has always pervaded the institution. True intellectual and moral progress is possible only where liberty prevails. To nothing else is freedom so essential as to thought.[45]

*

After the game against Capital in 1881, Ohio State's next three intercollegiate baseball games were all in 1882, against other schools with sectarian religious

Image from the front of the 1887 Makio. (Photo courtesy of The Ohio State University Archives)

affiliations. Two were against Otterbein University, an Evangelical school in the nearby town of Westerville.[46] The third was against Ohio Wesleyan University, a Methodist school in the town of Delaware, twenty miles north of Columbus.[47] The two games against Otterbein rotated home fields, the first in Westerville and the second at Ohio State, but Ohio Wesleyan always had to play their games at home in Delaware. The Wesleyan faculty were extremely strict and protective, never letting their students participate in sports off campus. They believed that visits to non-Methodist campuses offered unacceptable temptations.[48]

The Ohio Wesleyan students always presented themselves as pious and serious-minded. The school's official student newspaper, the *Transcript*, featured religious sermons on the front page and other theological observations inside. They also had an alternate newspaper, the *Practical Student*, but it was no less devoted to religious content. Ohio Wesleyan students generally regarded the Ohio State students as blasphemous sinners and reprobates. Ohio State students generally regarded the Wesleyan students as self-righteous prigs. The two schools were natural rivals.

*

The irreverent attitude of the Ohio State students had put them at odds with the school's board of trustees almost immediately. In 1881 the board was under pressure from political interests in the state who were upset over the school's alleged offenses against God and farming. Those political interests had leverage in the state government to block the university's funding and the board was anxious to appease them.

As part of that appeasement the board required students to attend daily chapel services, including the reading of scriptures and a faculty-led prayer. This chapel policy was to be enforced through a demerit system. Each missed service would lead to one demerit and a student would be expelled after he or she reached the maximum demerits allowed.

The students saw the new chapel policy as an unacceptable change to the mission of the university. A *Lantern* editorial stated, "Our former policy was one of strict neutrality upon all religious matters. Each student was left to use his own judgment as to whether he should recognize religion in any of its forms."[49] The article concluded, "Certainly it would be hard to improve on such a policy."[50]

The students were most annoyed that the action of the board pandered to a stereotype that they saw as demeaning. The only valid reason for a chapel

A mandatory Ohio State chapel service, held in University Hall in the 1880s. (Photo courtesy of The Ohio State University Archives)

requirement at Ohio State, the *Lantern* argued, was if the moral character of the students was defective. They said that their school actually had a higher moral tone than other schools in the state: "We have been comparatively free from drunkenness and rowdyism, and all those petty meannesses that we see chronicled of the students of other colleges."[51]

The students were supported in their complaints against the chapel policy by most of the faculty. Many O.S.U. professors believed that compelling students at a public institution to attend religious services violated the Constitutional separation of church and state. Edward Orton, a geology professor, had been president of the university since it opened its doors in 1873. His namesake Orton Hall has since become the centerpiece of the Ohio State campus, with generations of alumni holding nostalgic memories of the chimes ringing from its tower.[52] Orton resigned as president in 1881 rather than administer the chapel rule.[53]

The trustees quickly hired Walter Quincy Scott to replace Orton as president. In addition to being a professor of political economy, Scott was also a

Presbyterian minister. The change had little effect, however. Where President Orton had actively refused to enforce the chapel policy, President Scott simply took no action on it.[54]

President Scott became a popular figure among the O.S.U. students but he became a problem for the trustees. Even worse than his indifference to the chapel policy, the trustees discovered that he advocated a radical theory of property. He argued that property rights should be limited entirely to the goods that an individual produces. No property should be inherited, he said, and land and other natural resources should be owned communally. This position outraged the farming community and the trustees fired him in the spring of 1883. The firing stirred passionate protests from the students but the board had already hired a replacement.[55]

When students returned in the fall of 1883 they discovered a new president: William Henry Scott. The new President Scott (no relation to the first) was a Methodist minister, and he insisted that the school offer Christian values. He had six children and he intended to send them all to Ohio State.[56] This President Scott finally authorized the enforcement of the chapel rule.

Many members of the faculty still believed that compelling students at a state university to attend religious services was unconstitutional, and they sought the advice of Ohio's attorney general. The United States Supreme Court would ban compulsory prayers at state-funded schools in 1962 but in 1883 there was no such precedent. The attorney general assured the faculty that the trustees were entirely within their rights.[57]

Students arguing the issue took a different approach. A letter published in the *Lantern* that fall called on the board to look beyond the law and respect the principle that guided American separation of church and state. "We do not undertake to discuss the question as to whether the introduction of religion into the public schools is constitutional or not, but merely as to whether it would be advisable or not even if constitutional."[58] The letter went on:

> When we call our schools public, we mean that they are for all, and not for any particular class. The introduction of religion will certainly drive one class away. It is not a conjecture, but a well known result, that has occurred over and over again, and may be expected just as to-morrow's sun is. For this reason, and this reason only, should religion be kept strictly out of the public schools; but it is a sufficient one in itself.[59]

The first four presidents of the Ohio State University. (Photo courtesy of The Ohio State University Archives)

On campus this argument was considered well-reasoned, thoughtful, and eloquent, but if any of the trustees read it, it did not move them to change their minds. For them, the only relevant issue was their belief that the chapel policy assured the continuation of the university's funding. For others off campus, the outraged response at Ohio State only confirmed the reputation of the students there as godless.

*

After the three baseball games in 1882 the Ohio State team did not play another intercollegiate game until 1884. The opponent in that game was the University of Wooster. Wooster was a Presbyterian school founded in the town of Wooster, Ohio, and their students, led by a good pitcher named Kinley McMillan, fielded the best amateur baseball team in the state. The Ohio State students thought that their most ambitious sports goals were suddenly within reach when such a respected opponent agreed to come down to Columbus for a game.

The game was scheduled for Decoration Day (as Memorial Day was known in the nineteenth century) and was set to be played at Recreation Park in downtown Columbus. Recreation Park was the home field of the Columbus Buckeyes, the city's professional baseball team. The pro Buckeyes would be in Baltimore playing the Orioles on Decoration Day, so the Park would be empty. The manager of the Ohio State team decided to rent it for the game.

Ohio State lost to McMillan 11 to 4,[60] but more significant than the score was the aftermath. The team had overestimated how attractive the game would be to ticket-buying locals from the city, and they lost most of the money that they had spent in renting the Park. They asked for help to pay for the losses but the Athletic Association turned them down. The team was furious and they began to question the value of their affiliation with the Association. Soon afterward they seceded.[61]

That decision led to disaster. The team reestablished a separate Baseball Association and moved back under it, but the baseball association that they founded was not up to the challenge of supporting an intercollegiate schedule. In the spring of 1885 Wooster invited Ohio State up to their campus for a rematch, but Wooster was 100 miles away and the travel was too expensive for the team to make the trip. In fact the team could no longer afford to travel at all. Everyone recognized the source of the problem but they could not find a solution. In October 1885 the Athletic Association and the Baseball Association tried to renegotiate a merger, but they were unable to come to terms.[62]

The only baseball played by the Ohio State team during the 1884–85 school year were a pair of games against the soldiers from a Columbus military barracks.[63] The team's sole game the following spring was on May 30, 1886, again facing the same barracks soldiers.[64] The Baseball Association also began sponsoring class teams that year, and the games played by those class teams were generally considered more interesting than the games played by the varsity. To play against a military barracks did not inspire much passion but when class teams faced each other every contest was a rivalry game.

Chester Aldrich attended the May 30 game but his primary interest was seeing an old friend from Ashtabula named Scott Webb play second base. Aldrich had once been a member of a North Dorm baseball team but by 1886 he had become more interested in football. It was during this time that he was forming the varsity football team with Jumbo Hedges.

During the following school year, 1886–87, the Baseball Association was not able to schedule any varsity baseball games at all. The students saw their situation as ridiculous. They had an Athletic Association that could not hold onto any varsity teams and a Baseball Association that could not schedule any varsity games. The seniors who were preparing to graduate in the spring of 1887 had not seen Ohio State face another school in any athletic competition since the Wooster game in the spring of 1884, when they were freshmen.

Frustration was growing. The failure to compete in intercollegiate sports left many feeling impotent. The feeling was especially gnawing given the students' vision of their school as the state's flagship. The 1886 varsity football team might have helped ease that frustration if it had survived, or even if it had ever faced a single intercollegiate opponent.

✻

In the fall of 1886, Jumbo Hedges's friend Fatty Weybrecht was among the students who was no longer playing football at the North Dorm. Weybrecht had not returned to school that year. His father had become ill and Weybrecht had stayed home in Alliance, Ohio, to take care of his family.[65] Reports appeared in the *Lantern* over the next few months discussing whether he was likely to return, and those reports as often as not included jokes about his weight.[66] During Christmas break that year Hedges visited Weybrecht in Alliance instead of returning to his own home in Urbana, and he convinced his friend to return to school.[67] Weybrecht enrolled at the start of the 1887 winter term and the *Lantern* welcomed him back by joking, "We are happy to say that he still retains his beautiful form."[68]

Hedges and Chester Aldrich were the co-leaders of the junior class, regardless of what titles they officially held.[69] As leaders they felt obliged to express their opinions on campus issues, including the chapel policy. They each made a point of missing just enough chapel services, and earning just enough demerits, to approach the threshold of expulsion.[70] Their protest was purely symbolic, however. Even they did not dare cross that final line.

Chapter Three

A little more regard for the rules

J oseph Frederick Firestone was a former Ohio State student. He had entered
the O.S.U. collegiate program in 1883 after graduating from the O.S.U. prep
school.[1] He was a member of the class of 1887—the class of H.E. Payne—
but in 1885, before his junior year, he transferred from Ohio State to the Stevens
Institute of Technology.[2] Stevens was a school in Hoboken, New Jersey, set on
the peak of a cliff above the Hudson River overlooking New York City. It was a
young school but developing a reputation by applying scientific principles to the
field of business management. The program attracted students from across the
country, including Firestone.[3]

Firestone still had family ties in central Ohio. His immediate family lived
in the Akron-Canton area but his extended family owned the Columbus Buggy
Company. In the nineteenth century, Columbus Buggy was the nation's largest
manufacturer of horse-drawn carriages and the city of Columbus was known as
the "buggy capital of the world."[4] Firestone's younger cousin Harvey would later
join the family business and use that start to become one of the wealthiest men
in America. Joe Firestone wanted a similar opportunity.

Firestone had developed into a stocky man while still at Ohio State. Some
people started to call him "Fatty."[5] The nickname might have stuck if it had not
at the same time become attached to the prep student Charles Weybrecht. Firestone also developed into a formidable athlete. As a sophomore in the spring in
1885 he won the school championship in the shot put.[6]

He remained a formidable athlete after he arrived at Stevens, and he eventually joined the Stevens varsity football team. In the first two games of the 1885

season Stevens lost to Princeton 94 to 0 and to Yale 55 to 0, and the left guard in particular was criticized for poor playing.[7] Soon afterward the Stevens football players invited Firestone to try out at that position.[8]

At Stevens Firestone discovered radical changes made to the rules of football. At that time any school could play football according to its own unique version of the rules. Football at root is a very old sport, and it once had as many versions as there were communities that played it. Ancient Rome brought a version to England. England spread versions to the New World. Most everybody in the English-speaking world knew the basic idea of the sport, although specific rules developed locally, varying from one community to the next. Rules in that era could differ on such details as the size of the field, the number of players per team, how the teams scored points, and so on. Out of early football's diversity, various sports evolved, and some of those sports eventually came to be codified more explicitly. They included soccer, rugby, and the sport that Joe Firestone discovered at Stevens—"gridiron" football.[9]

*

The version of football played at Ohio State's North Dorm was an evolutionary mutation, with elements that otherwise were rarely found together. Their games featured backfields with slots for halfbacks, three-quarter backs (a position usually seen only in rugby), and a goalie (as used in soccer). Most of the students who were members of Ohio State's varsity football team had lived in the North Dorm, so the North Dorm's version of football served as the blueprint for the varsity team.[10]

During the same school year that Jumbo Hedges and Chester Aldrich were working to bring varsity football to Ohio State, the students at two schools in southern Ohio were forming their first varsity football teams as well. One of those schools was Marietta College, on the southeastern edge of the state, at the meeting point of the Muskingum and Ohio Rivers. The other, to the southwest, was the University of Cincinnati.

If either of those teams had challenged Ohio State in 1886, Jumbo Hedges, as the Ohio State manager, almost certainly would have accepted, but neither school was even aware that Ohio State had a team. Ohio State, Marietta, and Cincinnati were each at least one hundred miles away from the others and communication between the campuses was minimal, limited mostly to family relations or to previously-established friendships. Few students on any of these campuses kept up with such faraway sports activity.

Outing, a national sports and recreation magazine, learned of the team at Marietta and contacted them to ask about their attempts to bring varsity football to the state of Ohio. Ohio was the third-most populous state in the country but all that many Americans thought about it was that political parties pandered to it during presidential elections. *Outing* thought that a feature on Ohio football would inform their audience. The Marietta team thought that their record to date was more embarrassing than worth celebration, and they turned down the interview.[11]

If either Marietta or Cincinnati had agreed to play Ohio State, the first step in scheduling a game would have been to negotiate a common set of rules. For Ohio State to play Marietta, for example, a representative from Marietta would have met with a representative from Ohio State—either Hedges himself or a delegate from the Athletic Association—to hammer out "concessionary rules."[12] Negotiating concessionary rules was once the standard approach to football competition. Students at British schools such as Cambridge and Oxford originally played under local rules, and to be able to play each other, they each made compromises. Princeton played Rutgers in 1869 in the first American intercollegiate football game, and student representatives met beforehand for the concessionary prep work. The sport took firmer root in America in the 1870s as Columbia, Yale, and other Eastern colleges began to compete, and savvy rules negotiation was considered as important to victory as the actual play on the field.[13] Ohio football teams beginning intercollegiate competition would have expected to do the same.

The new American "gridiron" football developed after teams introduced elements that were previously unique to the rugby version. It was at the Rugby School in England that players were first allowed the use of their hands to carry the ball instead of only kicking it with their feet. Traditionalists considered such an extreme change to the rules heresy and the school found itself shunned by most opponents. In relative isolation the football played at Rugby became a separate sport, named for that school. In America, Harvard played a variation of rugby football, and that choice left Harvard also with few likely opponents, yet the pressures of rivalry eventually grew so strong that in 1875 Harvard and Yale agreed to a game. Walter Camp, an eighteen-year-old prep student, was curious to see how the two schools would pull off the necessary concessions.[14] Equally curious were students from other schools throughout the Northeast.

The rules that Harvard and Yale developed allowed the players to carry the ball but limited their scoring opportunities to kicking goals. A "touch," which involved carrying the ball across the goal line and literally touching it to the ground, merely entitled a team to a "free kick" try for a goal—a rule derived from some versions of rugby. The game also used the oblong ball from rugby, instead of the round ball used in traditional football, and included rugby-styled running, tackling, and fighting for field position. The heart of the sport, however, was still the goal kicked from the field, as the sport was traditionally played. The game between Harvard and Yale was a success, and other schools wanted to play what they saw as an entertaining new version of the sport. In 1876 Princeton hosted a meeting of the major Eastern schools to codify the new rules.

Representatives from those schools met for many years afterward at an annual rules convention, and at the conventions football continued to evolve throughout the early 1880s. It was Walter Camp who offered the most revolutionary new ideas. Camp had joined the Yale team as a freshman in 1876 and he became Yale's convention delegate as a medical student in 1880. Yale had long advocated using eleven players, instead of fifteen, to allow a more open game, and the 1880 convention finally agreed to make that change. Camp saw an opening to introduce a more radical innovation. He argued that, instead of players fighting for the ball in a scrum, the sport would be more strategic if one team held possession of the ball at the start of each play. Action would begin when an offensive lineman snapped the ball to a player in his backfield who would then lead the team's attack. Those offensive players would face defensive players from the other team at what Camp called the "line of scrimmage." This "scrimmage plan" marked the beginning of a unique and entirely American version of football.

Teams adjusted the roles of their eleven players to best fit Camp's innovation. They began to use a player alignment with four men running plays in the backfield behind seven men blocking on the line. The player in the backfield who guided the offense was called the quarterback, named for how deeply he was set relative to the three other players in the backfield: behind the quarterback were two *half*backs; further back stood the *full*back. The halfbacks and fullbacks became the primary ball carriers. The lineman who snapped the ball to the quarterback was positioned at the center of the line, so he was called the center. The players on either side of the center guarded the snap, so they were called guards.

The players next to the guards did most of the tackling on defense, so they were called tackles. Finally, the players at each end of the line were called ends.

Both Ohio State and Marietta had made the transition to eleven-man teams but neither school used the new Eastern alignment. Ohio State's version of football featured five players in the backfield (two halfbacks, two three-quarter backs, and a goalie) and six players on the line (with no more specific designation). Marietta's version of football also featured six players up front on the line, but behind that front line were three players on a "back line."[5] Behind the back line were two goalies.[6]

In the East, after the scrimmage plan revolutionized how football was played, Walter Camp continued to develop the sport as a troubleshooter. His most significant innovation in that role came at the 1882 convention, after teams had discovered a strategy of stalling after taking a lead. There was no rule at the time compelling the team in possession of the ball to ever give it up, so Camp said that a team would lose possession after being tackled, or "downed," a specified number of times unless they moved the ball a specified number of yards. This idea of downs and yards-to-go proved nearly as revolutionary as the scrimmage plan itself. Teams began painting lines across their fields to measure their yards-to-go. The lines formed a "gridiron" pattern that gave the sport its informal new name.

In 1883 the focus of the convention was a growing concern over tie games. Camp responded with an idea called "variable-point scoring" that made different achievements worth different point values. For the first time a goal-line touch—now called a touch*down*—was itself worth points, instead of simply providing an opportunity to kick a goal. The free kick after a touchdown was still attempted and could add "extra points" to the play. A tackle behind a team's own goal line was called a "safety" and gave points to the defense. In 1884 the point values settled as four for a touchdown, two for a goal-after-touchdown, and two for a safety. A goal from the field, or "field goal," was still considered the heart of the sport and was worth five points.

Ohio State students were aware that a new form of football was being developed and codified in the East, but few of those students bothered to learn the new rules. The campus football players did not even care to try. In 1886 the *Lantern* complained about how far out of touch the games played at the North Dorm were with the latest developments in the East: "It is to be regretted that foot ball is not played with a little more regard for the rules by which it is generally governed."[7]

The Ohio State and Marietta teams did not use the same rules even to deter-mine the winner in their games. Most rules of football declared the winner to be the team holding the higher score at the end of a specified time period, but the games played at Marietta did not use a clock and instead the winner was the first to score six goals.[18] Princeton, Rutgers, and Columbia had briefly used a similar six-goal rule back in 1869 and 1870.[19] Any concessionary rules between Ohio State and Marietta would have had to be unique.

✻

The first school to play gridiron football in Ohio was the University of Cincinnati. In the early 1880s young men from the city of Cincinnati attended Eastern colleges and returned with gridiron football experience. Back home they joined a local fitness organization named the Mount Auburn Athletic Club and there they formed a club football team. In the fall of 1885, with the goal of having someone to play, they helped the students from a local school form a team. That school was the University of Cincinnati.

The experience of the Cincinnati students was typical of how gridiron football usually spread to the Midwest. The annual football rules conventions in the East included no schools from across the Appalachian Mountains, so news of the changes made at the conventions was slow and inconsistent in moving west. In the early 1880s the University of Minnesota hired a Princeton graduate to be their new professor of philosophy, and the students asked him to coach their football team. Taking guidance from that Princeton man and from a physics professor from Yale who followed him, the Minnesota students stayed up-to-date throughout the decade as Walter Camp continued developing his rules. The Minnesota students in turn taught the sport to other nearby schools in order to have someone to play.[20]

The University of Michigan, in Ann Arbor, Michigan, followed a different path to learn how to play the gridiron version of football. The students there turned directly to the Eastern schools for guidance. Michigan had long billed itself as the "Harvard of the West" and they made a point of mirroring Harvard's football transitions—first to rugby and then to the later versions. In the early 1880s Michigan challenged Harvard and other rising Eastern powers. Those schools were still looking for new opponents themselves and they sometimes accepted. Michigan always lost to such top-tier Eastern competition but through those games Michigan ended up as the most experienced and formidable football team west of the Appalachians.[21]

The earliest attempts to keep up with the rules of football within Ohio had been isolated efforts that were never complete. Oberlin College was a nationally respected school in Oberlin, Ohio, a village west of Cleveland, and students from Eastern states enrolled there in 1881 with football on their minds. Those students wanted to form a varsity team but the faculty stopped them. Oberlin had been founded by Congregationalists, and its faculty considered football to be a brutally unchristian sport. The Oberlin students were allowed only to form class teams, and those class teams were not allowed to face off-campus opponents. As a result, their students could not keep up as the gridiron rules developed.[22]

Cincinnati was the largest and most populous city in Ohio, and the size of the city allowed it to indulge in the less respectable excesses of American life. It was known for an unusually large number of breweries and for a correspondingly large number of street riots.[23] It also became the first place in Ohio to embrace gridiron football. In October and November 1885 the Mount Auburn Athletic Club and the University of Cincinnati played the first games of gridiron football within the state.

Ohio still had no intercollegiate football, however. Over the next two years the Mount Auburn team remained the University of Cincinnati's only opponent.

*

The football team at the Stevens Institute of Technology was not of the caliber of the elite Eastern teams but they did brag that they were "better than any college of her size in the country."[24] The highlight of their 1885 season was a 162 to 0 victory over City College of New York.[25] As at Ohio State, the students at Stevens commented on Joe Firestone's size and heftiness. "He has the fatness of twenty boys, he has,"[26] their yearbook joked. But size itself provided an advantage in football as it was played in the East. A guard's role in a football offense was to protect the snap from the center to the quarterback. On defense the guard's role was to try to down the quarterback before he could deliver the ball to a ball carrier.[27] Firestone grew increasingly comfortable in this role and he became a respected member of the team.

In the spring that followed, in 1886, as Jumbo Hedges and Chester Aldrich were forming Ohio State's first varsity football team, Firestone was winning the Stevens campus championship in the shot put.[28] That same spring Firestone was elected president of the Stevens athletic association.[29]

Chapter Four
What shall be done with the challenge?

W illiam Stowe Devol had graduated from Ohio State in the spring of 1886 and despite his efforts with cricket, archery, and riding horses, he had never had an opportunity to play intercollegiate sports. He originally came from the city of Marietta but he remained in Columbus after his graduation, accepting a position as superintendent of the university's Agriculture Experiment Station.[1] The following fall Devol's younger brother James began attending Marietta College.[2] It was most likely through this family connection that the news of Ohio State's varsity football team finally reached Marietta.

*

After the collapse of the Ohio State baseball team following the Wooster debacle in 1884, the O.S.U. students were looking for any means to prove themselves in intercollegiate competition. They played tennis but tennis was not a varsity sport. The tennis team was a club team, organized in 1882 by a professor named William Rane Lazenby.[3] Lazenby served as club president, and as president he chose not to schedule matches against other schools. He believed that intercollegiate sports brought out the worst in students.[4] He had previously attended Cornell University, where students were banned from playing intercollegiate games. The Cornell president had described the purpose of such competition as "merely to agitate a bag of wind."[5] When Lazenby's tennis team played outside opponents, those opponents were independent club teams from the city.

No one complained because Lazenby was the only reason that the tennis team survived at all. As a club sport, tennis was not under the authority of any

Professor Lazenby leads his botany class. (Photo courtesy of The Ohio State University Archives)

student association, and while the other sports on campus fell apart, Lazenby's "Lawn Tennis Association" thrived. The *Lantern* had commented in 1882, "Lawn Tennis flourishes every evening on the campus, Professor Lazenby's Club having attained great proficiency under his able direction."[6] Chester Aldrich added in May 1886, "Base ball is sadly on the decline, but lawn tennis, under the guardianship of Professor Lazenby, is all the rage."[7]

In 1886 Lazenby played tennis as half of the team's doubles pair—he was Sam Oppenheimer's doubles partner.[8] That year Oppenheimer took some words from Professor Lazenby as preaching and asked him to stop. He said that he got enough sermons from President Scott.[9]

Professor Lazenby did not blame the Athletic Association for the sagging state of O.S.U. sports. Instead he pointed to what he saw as a more systematic problem: the school's lack of adequate playing fields. Students improvised makeshift fields for every sport that they played and the lack of proper facilities was Lazenby's explanation for why the teams never lasted. Every year Lazenby lobbied the board of trustees for a one-time gift of between $150 and $200 so that "all grounds needed for field sports be put in the best possible condition for the use of the students."[10] Maintenance of those athletic grounds would afterward

Ohio State cadets after winning a competitive drill in 1890. (Photo courtesy of The Ohio State University Archives)

be left to the various teams that used them. Yale University had recently spent $30,000 on their athletic grounds,[11] but the board of trustees at Ohio State always turned down Lazenby's $200 plan.

∗

The only physical activity for O.S.U. students that provided intercollegiate competition was military drill, and that kind of competition excited almost no one. Military training was another requirement of the Land-Grant College Act, and male students were required to march for one hour every day. Ohio State's faculty commander would sometimes drill his cadets competitively against military departments of other schools,[12] but those intercollegiate drills did not arouse a fraction of the enthusiasm produced by an intercollegiate baseball or football game. Few people wanted to buy a ticket to watch students marching.

The most entertaining aspect of military drill was not even part of its official curriculum. In the early 1880s a cadet named Joseph Nelson Bradford organized a fife and drum corps among the student troops.[13] Later the corps added brass instruments, and still later their band came to be called "the pride" of the university and trademarked as "The Best Damn Band in the Land."[14] The band, however, had no role in those intercollegiate drill competitions.

*

Chester Aldrich and Jumbo Hedges were both members of a student organization named the Alcyone Literary Society. Alcyone competed in campus oratory contests against Browning and Horton, Ohio State's two other literary societies.[15] Hedges had held many Alcyone leadership positions over the years—vice president, treasurer, sergeant at arms—but it was Aldrich who was elected president of Alcyone in the fall of 1887.[16]

One of Aldrich's ambitions at Ohio State was to participate in the State Oratory Contest. The State Oratory Contest was an annual event where students, representing their schools, would compete to give the best speech. It was the best-organized intercollegiate competition in the state. The 1887 contest, hosted by Ohio Wesleyan, was scheduled to be held on February 17, in Delaware, Ohio.

An organization named the Ohio Intercollegiate Oratorical Association (O.I.O.A.) ran the State Contest. The O.I.O.A. was a confederation of local organizations, each run independently by the students at the participating schools. Ohio State's local organization was the Ohio State University Oratorical Association; it was responsible for choosing an orator to compete at the State Contest. The O.S.U. Oratorical Association was run as a confederation of the three campus literary societies. Jumbo Hedges, of Alcyone, was elected vice president of the O.S.U. Oratorical Association that year.[17]

The three campus literary societies also together published the *Lantern*. When Hedges had joined Alcyone as a prep student, he did not join to be an orator. He joined because he wanted to work on the student newspaper. When J.A. Wilgus took over as the new *Lantern* editor-in-chief in the winter of 1887, Hedges was elected managing editor.[18] The editor-in-chief was ultimately responsible for the content of a newspaper but Hedges, as managing editor, assigned the staff to their positions.

*

Chester Aldrich's growing personal relationship with Hedges began to be reflected in the political views that he expressed in his speeches. Aldrich still wore expensive clothes, and people still commented on his blue-blood manners, but during his junior year he publicly embraced more egalitarian values and positions. He began advocating for the workingman against entrenched financial power.

Every year, just before the State Oratory Contest, the O.S.U. Oratorical Association held a local contest. The winner of the local contest moved on to the state contest. Aldrich had first competed in the local contest two years earlier, as a freshman. The *Lantern* commented that year, "Mr. Aldrich was unfortunate in the choice of a subject, but he showed a true oratorical style."[19] He finished in fourth place out of six orators. He was determined to deliver a more crowd-pleasing speech as he approached the contest as a junior.

The local contest in 1887 was held on the evening of February 4, in the auditorium of a Methodist church just south of campus.[20] Three students were scheduled to speak: Aldrich, the *Lantern* editor J.A. Wilgus, and a freshman named Hugh Laughlin. The O.S.U. Association always invited prominent figures from the community to serve as judges, and that year they invited three: a state Supreme Court justice, a minister, and a state Senator who was formerly a United States Congressman. These three were authorized to select the Ohio State orator to send to Delaware on February 17.

In the auditorium on February 4, Aldrich rose first to speak. His speech addressed a growing problem that he said threatened the entire nation. Titled "Our National Permanence—Its Strength and Its Dangers," it argued that liberty itself was being threatened from within by growing conflicts between the American social classes. He began, "Political liberty is the boon for which man has ever contended. Its realization has been the mighty instrumentality of progress, the prime factor of civilization, the conveyor of national honor," but he said that the health of the nation was threatened by growing economic polarization:

> Today labor and capital stand staring at each other like two enraged combatants. The middle class, which maintains our state of equilibrium, is rapidly disappearing because the rich are becoming richer and the poor poorer.

As Aldrich spoke he could feel his control over the audience. His rhetoric was soaring, his delivery was flawless, and his gestures effectively accented his points. All of his practice at Alcyone appeared to be paying off. Nearing the end of his speech he reached out to the listening crowd and asked, "Must this nation, with its starry possibilities, after a few centuries of splendor go down in ruins?"[21] As he finished the audience exploded with applause.

J.A. Wilgus took the podium following Aldrich. Wilgus's speech was titled "Boycotting, No Remedy."[22] As Aldrich listened he could not help noticing how well written it was. Wilgus was lucid and logical and he used appropriate statistics to support his points. Wilgus's delivery, however, was flat and halting.[23] Aldrich watched with relief as the audience's eyes glazed over.

As Wilgus finished to polite applause, Aldrich could imagine moving on to Delaware. The winner of the State Oratory Contest the previous year had been Howard H. Russell of Oberlin College, who had won with a speech titled "Mob and Law" which argued that those who participate in labor strikes are anarchists who need to be brought to justice.[24] Russell would later form the Anti-Saloon League, a powerful political lobbying organization that in 1919 would bring prohibition to America nearly single-handedly.[25] Oberlin had an enrollment that was four times larger than Ohio State and Aldrich dreamed of taking on their next representative.

The final Ohio State orator was Hugh Laughlin, who gave a speech on "Goethe and His Fatherland."[26] Laughlin's thesis was that the celebrated German writer perfectly represented the spirit of his people. Aldrich noticed that Laughlin made a few freshman-level errors in his pronunciations but overall he appeared knowledgeable and passionate about his subject. For the student audience, however, a literary lecture did not seem worthy to represent them in intercollegiate competition.

When Laughlin sat down the judges compared their scoring. The three criteria for evaluating speeches were Thought, Composition, and Delivery. Aldrich took the top score in Thought from one judge and the top score in Delivery from another, but the judges' favorite overall was Laughlin's more scholarly speech.[27]

To the student audience the scores made no sense. Aldrich's speech had seemed ready to take on the world. A disgusted *Lantern* writer later noted that "Senators and Judges think they know more about such worldly subjects"[28] and don't like to be lectured to by a student. "Men of the world have a sort of contempt for school boy opinions and methods of reforming the world." Such men, he went on, are more swayed by academic lectures, such as about Goethe, "which they do not know so much about." J.A. Wilgus felt a need to distance himself from those dismissive comments. As the *Lantern*'s editor-in-chief he offered an apology in the next issue. He assured the distinguished judges that the writer's words did not represent an official position of the newspaper.[29]

People soon began calling Aldrich "the Daniel Webster of Alcyone,"[30] and although he would not represent Ohio State in the State Contest, the campus Oratorical Association selected him to serve as their delegate at the next O.I.O.A. organizing convention.[31] Aldrich rewarded that selection by bringing back a commitment that Ohio State would host the 1888 Contest. The *Lantern* noted, "No mistaking now. C. H. Aldrich was cut out for a senator."[32]

Some students lost their taste for the State Oratory Contest that spring. They concluded that such a subjectively judged competition could never satisfy as a replacement for sports. One student was heard complaining that he would "rather bet on a horse race than an oratorical contest."[33]

Chester Aldrich, later that year, briefly took up boxing.[34]

*

Compared to oratory, intercollegiate sports in Ohio were not well organized at all. Unlike the State Oratory Contest, which was supported by the O.I.O.A., baseball had no central organization to provide administrative structure. Neither did any other sport. Every college sports manager in the state acted independently in scheduling opponents for his team.[35]

Many college students in Ohio enjoyed competing in track and field but they competed in their events only against others from their own schools. At Ohio State the Athletic Association held a competition every spring and fall called "field day," crowning the campus champions. In the spring of 1887 the *Lantern* expressed hope that the upcoming field day "will surpass all previous ones, and make us all feel a deeper pride in the results."[36] Most field day events were serious (the distance races, the broad jump, the shot put, and so on) and some were novelties (Jumbo Hedges dominated the "fat man's race"[37]). With Will Beatty gone, C.C. Sharp finally reached his goal of winning the school championship in the 100-yard dash.[38]

On a few occasions throughout the 1880s, students from various Ohio schools tried to create an intercollegiate organization that could mount a State Field Day. The best athletes in the state wanted to compete against each other. Those plans never lasted.[39]

*

In January 1887, six years after he left the White House, Rutherford B. Hayes returned to Ohio State to join the board of trustees. The arrival of a former U.S. President boosted the national profile of the school. William Henry Scott even

Field day competition at Ohio State, in 1886 and 1895. (Photo courtesy of The Ohio State University Archives)

offered to step down as president of the university to let Hayes have his job.[40] That possibility left the campus buzzing.[41] Hayes thanked President Scott for the offer but politely declined. He believed that he could do more for the university that he founded as a member of the board.[42]

The students understood the significance of the arrival of President Hayes[43] but many of them were equally concerned with their own leadership issues. In March the Athletic Association held their annual elections. Association officers were elected for terms roughly spanning a calendar year, rather than for a school year like most student positions. The Association recognized that other students saw their organization as failing and they hoped that new leadership could help them restore their reputation.

Two names put forward for consideration were Fred Ball and C.C. Sharp. Ball was still a respected campus leader. He was both the treasurer of the tennis club and the sergeant-at-arms of the Alcyone Literary Society. He was no longer president of the campus branch of the Y.M.C.A. but he remained the campus representative to the state Y.M.C.A. convention. Sharp did not have a list of leadership titles on his record but his informal reputation as an athletic leader was just as secure as Ball's. As a good baseball player Sharp understood the sports frustrations on campus as well as anyone. The Athletic Association elected Sharp as their new president and Ball as vice president. Their terms would last for the rest of 1887.[44]

*

Another newspaper, competing with the *Lantern*, was also published on campus. It was called the *Critic* and it traditionally appeared only during the spring term. Unlike the *Lantern*, which was run by the campus literary societies, the *Critic* had a much less formal or stable organization. It had always been taken on as a new project each spring by that year's junior class. The *Lantern* never gave their competitor much respect, referring to it as "the *Cricket*."[45] They also occasionally printed their own corrections to *Critic* errors, as though concerned that such a heavy chore would be too much of a burden for just one newspaper.

Early in 1887 the current junior class, which included both J.A. Wilgus and Jumbo Hedges from the *Lantern*, announced that they would not be taking up the *Critic* that spring. Jesse Lee Jones was only a sophomore but he did not want to see a campus tradition die. He announced that he would revive the *Critic* personally. Jones was the secretary of the Horton Literary Society but he had never worked for the *Lantern*, or any newspaper, so he stayed on campus throughout the 1887 spring break.[46] He was determined to learn the ropes of publishing and make sure that the newspaper would be ready by the start of the spring. Even the *Lantern* seemed impressed with Jones's efforts in support of the *Critic* that year.

*

A few weeks after the State Oratory Contest, the O.S.U. Athletic Association received a challenge from the Marietta football team.[47] Hedges was ready to accept but the decision was not in his hands. Unlike Marietta, Ohio State's varsity football team had not survived beyond the spring of 1886, so Hedges could not claim in the spring of 1887 to still hold the position of manager. Authority over Ohio State's response belonged to the Athletic Association. From C.C. Sharp's perspective the Marietta challenge had arrived a year too late. He and Hedges appeared to disagree on how hard it would be to revive the football team and make a respectable showing.

As the managing editor of the *Lantern*, Hedges used his position to try to pressure the Association. He placed his friend Frank Raymund in charge of the "Local Notes" column. "What shall be done with the challenge?" Raymund demanded to know.[48]

The interest of most students was in fielding a team—any team—that could represent them in competition against other schools. After the Marietta challenge the students began to take the idea of varsity football more seriously. With hopes for reviving varsity baseball fading, the students started to think that a football team might take up the fallen mantle.

*

Sam Oppenheimer left school at the end of the 1886–87 school year. The chapel policy was still in place and Oppenheimer confided to friends that the requirement to attend Christian sermons had been a burden.[49] A full year later another student began complaining about some perceived mistreatment from the administration. The *Lantern* suggested that he should put his troubles in perspective: "He should rejoice that he is not Mr. Samuel Oppenheimer."[50]

Frank Lawton Olcott Wadsworth was a member of the class of 1888, a classmate of Aldrich and Hedges. Wadsworth was a serious student, with a systematic and careful approach to his academic work. He studied physics and mechanical engineering, combining the passionate curiosity of a good scientist with the practical attitude of an engineer. His personal demeanor was equally serious and even getting him to crack a smile was considered an achievement.[51] Some friends tried to give him the nickname "Waddy" but he always preferred to be addressed as "F.L.O."[52]

Wadsworth was also a talented athlete. He was 6'2" and at the 1887 spring field day he won the school championships in the running high jump and in the mile and quarter-mile runs.[53] His approach to sports was just as systematic and careful as his approach to his studies. He joined the varsity baseball team when he arrived on campus in the fall of 1884[54] but he quit when he recognized that the team had no future. As a sophomore he helped form the bicycling team and served as its captain.

He turned to tennis that same year when he saw that Professor Lazenby offered the most stable team on campus.[55] There he found his most successful niche in sports. "Who can beat Wadsworth playing tennis?"[56] asked the *Makio*. He eventually replaced Sam Oppenheimer as Professor Lazenby's doubles partner.[57]

Chapter Five

Foot ball is to reign supreme in this period

I n the spring of 1887 Joe Firestone graduated from the Stevens Institute of Technology. He returned to Columbus soon afterward to take a management position with the Columbus Buggy Company.[1] His cousin Harvey Firestone took a job around the same time as a Columbus Buggy salesman,[2] but Joe wanted a position that would use his new business training to climb the company's corporate ranks.

Firestone then decided to form a football team among his coworkers. He had no trouble finding players for the team but he knew that finding an opponent would be a bigger challenge. He thought that he would find more takers if his men could claim to be the official team of the Columbus Buggy Company, and for that he had to convince management to endorse his project.

Later that fall it would be Joe Firestone who would first bring gridiron football to Ohio State.

✻

Jumbo Hedges held a number of student leadership positions in the fall of 1887 when he entered his senior year. In student government he was re-elected class sergeant-at-arms.[3] He also was elected president of the North Dorm.[4] As president he headed the North Dorm Governing Board, which could put on trial any resident accused of violating dormitory rules and was even authorized by the university to evict those found guilty.[5] The leadership role that Hedges put the most work into, however, was succeeding J.A. Wilgus as the editor-in-chief of the *Lantern*.[6]

Chester Aldrich did not return to the North Dorm when the new fall term began. Second-baseman Scott Webb, his old friend from Ashtabula, needed a roommate and Aldrich moved with him into the South Dorm.[7] Aldrich would not hold any major campus leadership positions during his senior year.

Fred Ball was also a senior and preparing to graduate in the coming spring. More surprisingly, so was C.C. Sharp.[8] Heavy course loads taken every term had made Sharp eligible for early graduation, fulfilling a competitive goal that he had set for himself as a freshman. That fall Sharp and Ball remained the leaders of the Athletic Association.

✻

As the fall term began, Jumbo Hedges was still fanning the flames for a varsity football team. Under his authority as editor-in-chief, the *Lantern* regularly accused the Athletic Association of failure to accomplish anything.[9] Hedges's friend Frank Raymund remained in charge of the "Local Notes" column, and in the first issue of the new school year Raymund joked dryly, "If the Lawn Tennis Association wishes to die of stagnation, it should join itself to the Athletic Association."[10]

The Association's failure to meet the Marietta challenge in the spring remained a topic of conversation across the campus that fall. Attention to football was so pervasive that the *State Journal* reported that the sport was the new Ohio State "rage."[11] The various classes formed teams and challenged each other. Some students meanwhile were petitioning the Association to form a new varsity team.[12]

C.C. Sharp bristled at the continuing pressure but he actually wanted to play intercollegiate sports as much as anyone. Seven students remained on campus from the 1886 varsity football team and, like most of them, Sharp saw varsity football as a glaring loose end in his athletic record. At a meeting of the Athletic Association in early October he established a committee for the purpose of forming a new varsity football team.[13]

Six of the members from the 1886 team were preparing to graduate that year. In addition to Hedges, Aldrich, Ball, and Sharp, there was also Frank Raymund and William Morrey.[14] Sharp had challenged his class to join him in trying to graduate early and both Raymund and Morrey met that challenge. These six seniors recognized their approaching graduation in June as a deadline to ever face intercollegiate competition.

Of the other members of the 1886 team, H.E. Payne had graduated with his class in 1887, and Will Beatty, Samuel Oppenheimer, and Fatty Weybrecht had all left campus for other reasons. Although Weybrecht had returned to campus in January 1887, he finally left for good just a few months later.[15] He had previously sent an application to West Point,[16] and after it was rejected he decided to take a job with the U.S. Postal Service.

Jesse Lee Jones was still a junior and of all the members of the 1886 football team, only he remained on campus as an underclassman.

*

Others on campus had also taken an interest in the work being done by the football committee. F.L.O. Wadsworth was another senior, as was his friend named Frederic Brown. Wadsworth and Brown had been teammates on the tennis team until Brown gave up playing tennis earlier that year. Both Wadsworth and Brown decided to try out for the football project.

Despite the work of the football committee, a few students continued to hold out hope of playing varsity baseball. A student from Youngstown named Jesse Hall Allen enrolled that year into the university's two-year veterinary program. "Pete" Allen, as his friends knew him, was a good pitcher and an even better hitter, and in 1893 he would play professional baseball with the Cleveland Spiders. In 1887 he wanted to play college baseball at Ohio State. Friends must have explained to him that neither the Athletic Association nor the Baseball Association could field a baseball team until they settled their lingering dispute over ownership.

*

By that fall, Rutherford B. Hayes had taken his seat on the board of trustees. Among the responsibilities of the board was to set the university's budget, and the trustees had a pressing need to meet to discuss appropriations for the upcoming fiscal year. The board deferred to President Hayes in the scheduling of that meeting.[17]

Hayes would be coming to Columbus from his home in Fremont, Ohio, near Sandusky, traveling by train more than one hundred miles. He proposed holding the meeting during Thanksgiving week. The board could work Monday through Wednesday and Hayes would still be home in time for his Thanksgiving dinner on Thursday afternoon.

*

Joe Firestone reappeared on the Ohio State campus in early October. He still had friends on campus, including Jumbo Hedges, who had served with Firestone three years earlier as an officer of the Alcyone Literary Society. Firestone was hoping to meet the latest leadership of the Athletic Association.

Former U.S. President Rutherford B. Hayes as he looked as a member of the Ohio State board of trustees. (Photo courtesy of The Ohio State University Archives)

Firestone offered the Association help in forming a varsity football team. He explained that modern football—gridiron football—was an entirely new sport. If C.C. Sharp resented an interloper taking charge of the Association's plans, he would have changed his mind when Firestone explained that the new sport was the wave of the future. The first local schools to ride the wave would hold a strategic advantage over their rivals.

With Firestone's guidance the football committee began forming a varsity team consistent with the latest rules from the East. Firestone even helped paint a gridiron pattern on the North Dorm grounds to mark yards-to-go.[18] He also served as the referee overseeing the team's scrimmages.[19] He did not have a formal title but he became, in effect, the first Ohio State football coach.

✳

The football committee finished recruiting but Sharp decided that the Athletic Association still needed to maintain its control over the team. Sharp arranged for the football committee—under his supervision—to continue acting as manager. The committee selected an acting captain, a North Dorm football player named Charles Barnes.[20] That choice raised some eyebrows. Barnes was familiar with the sport but he was just a first-year prep student.[21] Such a young captain would need a mentor like Sharp to make his more challenging leadership decisions.

Barnes finalized a lineup, but a few key names from the 1886 team were noticeably absent when the Association announced it in late October. The lineup included Sharp at right guard and Fred Ball at quarterback. Chester Aldrich was the team's left end.[22] Missing, however, were Jumbo Hedges and Frank Raymund, the students who had been criticizing the Association all year in the *Lantern*. Also missing was Sharp's class rival, Jesse Lee Jones.

Hedges soon wrote a front-page editorial in the *Lantern* endorsing the new team. "Foot-ball," he began, "has long been a favorite game in all of our eastern and most of our western colleges."[23] Ohio State had taken longer to embrace football as a varsity sport, he said, but its time had finally arrived:

> Diversity in athletic games is not the hobby of O. S. U. students. We can recollect when base-ball was all the rage. This was exhausted some two or three years since, and it dropped out of sight almost entirely. Then followed tennis, and now is another period of transition. Foot ball is to reign supreme in this period.[24]

*

Joe Firestone next went to Columbus Buggy management to suggest a promotion. The company was always looking for new publicity. A few months earlier they bought a carriage that had once been owned by George Washington and were currently exhibiting it on their grounds. Firestone told management that the Columbus Buggy employees had recently formed a football team and he suggested that the company sponsor a game. He mentioned that the local State University had also recently formed a team and he suggested that a Columbus Buggy football game against a college team would grab the attention of the local newspapers.

The most effective strategy, Firestone said, would be to play the game on Thanksgiving. Thanksgiving had become the most important day on the football calendar. Eastern schools considered it football's rivalry day, and every team wanted to schedule an attention-grabbing holiday game. Lehigh University and

Lafayette College were both regular Stevens opponents but their annual Thanksgiving game had established their rivalry as one of the best known in the East. Princeton played Yale on Thanksgiving, except on those years when Yale decided to play Harvard instead. The Thanksgiving game between Yale and Harvard in 1887 was projected to be such a draw that they arranged to play it at the massive Polo Grounds in New York City. Columbus Buggy management endorsed Firestone's football plan.

Firestone then went back to the football committee of the Athletic Association to officially offer his challenge. For Ohio State, a company team was not an ideal opponent, especially for such a seemingly historic game. The students would have preferred to face a football team from another college, particularly from one of the sectarian colleges that had always put Ohio State down, but C.C. Sharp responded to the challenge pragmatically. He knew that finding an intercollegiate opponent would have been as unlikely that fall as it had been eighteen months earlier, but a well-publicized game against a well-known company had the potential to open the door to intercollegiate competition in the future. Sharp accepted Firestone's challenge.

*

The Ohio State players then began preparing for the game, and in one of their first acts as a team they elected a new captain. All sports teams were entitled to choose their own leaders and Sharp had not expected his protégé Charles Barnes to hold the position permanently. The players chose as their new captain F.L.O. Wadsworth.

Sharp had an idea to create excitement for the Thanksgiving game and he approached Wadsworth to discuss it. The fall field day was scheduled for November 2, and Sharp thought that a football exhibition should cap the festivities. He wanted the new varsity team to play a game in front of the entire campus against a team of eleven alternates.[25] Wadsworth recognized the value of Sharp's plan but he said that the varsity team first needed more time to practice. Sharp arranged for field day to be postponed for ten days.[26]

Wadsworth continued holding scrimmages to help identify the best players for his lineup.[27] The Association had announced its original lineup with some fanfare but Wadsworth did not feel bound by the decisions of Charles Barnes. He said that each position was still open for competition. The first change that

Wadsworth made was to add his friend Fred Brown to the lineup. The second was to add Jumbo Hedges.[28]

When Jesse Lee Jones saw that Hedges had been added to the team, he decided to try out again himself. Jones had been a halfback on the 1886 team, and the halfback position was the weakest spot in the new lineup. Jones, however, told Wadsworth that he wanted to try out at right guard. Right guard was C.C. Sharp's position. At the next scrimmage, Jones and Sharp competed head-to-head, and Jones came out on top.[29]

The halfback position that Jones had chosen not to pursue was still available and a sophomore named Joseph "Jo Jo" Large tried out for it. Despite his name, Large was a small man—barely five feet tall.[30] He attempted a run around the right side of the line, and Chester Aldrich, playing at left end, stopped him. The collision annoyed Aldrich because it left him with a black eye and forced him to cancel plans for the evening.[31] He had been invited to a party thrown by Professor Orton but he said that he did not want to show up looking like a ruffian. Jo Jo Large took the worst of the hit, though, and was "rendered insensible."[32] He did not make the team.

C.C. Sharp meanwhile seemed to be considering how he could win back some pride after he lost his original spot on the team. F.L.O. Wadsworth played center, but challenging him would clearly be a losing proposition. Challenging Jumbo Hedges at right tackle would likely also not end well. The most satisfying option was to challenge Chester Aldrich at left end. After another position battle, Sharp took Aldrich's spot.[33]

That change triggered a domino effect in the lineup. Aldrich needed a new position and he challenged Sharp's protégé Charles Barnes at left tackle. He won. Barnes then challenged Fred Ball and took over at quarterback. Ball then ended up with the halfback position that Jesse Lee Jones had decided not to try out for originally.[34]

Wadsworth finalized his lineup in mid-November. On the left side of the line were Sharp at end, Aldrich at tackle, and a big prep student named Edwin Pedlow at guard. On the right side were Jones at guard, Hedges at tackle, and Fred Brown at end. Wadsworth remained at center. In the backfield were Barnes at quarterback, Fred Ball and a prep student named Samuel Morrison at the two halfback spots, and a prep named William Hain at fullback.

Field day finally arrived on Saturday, November 12. The football exhibition held that day was the first look at modern football that most of the students on campus had ever seen.[35] As Sharp had hoped, the exhibition sparked campus enthusiasm for the upcoming Columbus Buggy game.

*

Thanksgiving week began two weeks later. The board of trustees arrived on campus on Monday morning. On Tuesday morning the local newspapers began promoting the game. The students were excited by their historic step into varsity football but the game had little meaning for the trustees. If any member of the board was even aware that a game had been scheduled he had no comment on it. The administration monitored student academics but did not pay attention to their leisure activities.

On Tuesday afternoon dark rainclouds were filling the sky and the students began fearing the worst. The *Lantern* had for years been calling for someone to pave the roads surrounding campus: "Every person who has had occasion to walk to the college from down town, when it is muddy weather, knows how wretchedly ugly and bad both High Street and the path across the field are."[36] President Hayes had a similar thought as he looked at the heavy overcast sky. He envisioned a storm trapping him on campus through the holiday. On Wednesday the *Dispatch* printed a note advertising the football game to be played on campus the next morning, but added as a caveat the phrase "if the weather permits."[37]

The rain began falling on Wednesday morning. Hayes had the meeting of the board adjourned. The board's decisions were not settled but Hayes took the paperwork with him back to Fremont to fill in the final numbers himself.[38] By Thursday morning, as everyone had feared, rain had washed out the dirt roads surrounding the campus. For the administration the storm was an annoyance. For the students it was worse. The Columbus Buggy team could not travel even the short distance from downtown and the teams were forced to postpone the game.

*

It was a different case outside of Columbus. In southern Ohio, on that Thanksgiving Day, the University of Cincinnati faced its first football opponent other than the Mount Auburn Athletic Club. They played a game against a newly formed team from a local Cincinnati high school.[39]

In the East, meanwhile, college football was becoming a lucrative business. Yale defeated Harvard in their game at the Polo Grounds, and the game attracted twenty-four thousand spectators. At the time it was one of the largest crowds ever to attend a sporting event. Wealthy alumni supporting their alma maters mingled with New York City laborers simply searching for novel entertainment during their spare leisure time. The next day, in Columbus, the *State Journal* carried a wire service account of the game and at fifteen-hundred words it was the most detailed description of a gridiron football game ever published in central Ohio.[40]

*

Over the next few days the management of the Columbus Buggy Company decided that they had no interest in sponsoring a football team without the showcase of a Thanksgiving game. Without management approval Joe Firestone was not able to reschedule the game with Ohio State. The Ohio State team was frustrated. The football momentum, which had been building ever since the Marietta challenge in the spring, stalled.

Jumbo Hedges was dejected and his mood was obvious in the *Lantern*. He reminded his readers of an old saying: "Man proposes, God disposes."[41]

*

In 1890 Fred Ball would be living in Montgomery, Alabama. He moved there after his graduation and became a lawyer's apprentice. He still remained active in the Y.M.C.A. and joined the local chapter. By 1890, while he was preparing to establish his own law firm, Ball organized a Montgomery Y.M.C.A. football team using the training that he had learned at Ohio State. That team would help bring gridiron football to the American Deep South.[42]

Part Two

The long looked-for boom
in athletics has come at last

Chapter Six

Class colors fade into insignificance

I n the spring of 1888 the *Critic* was due for its annual revival but Jesse Lee Jones did not have a role in the new project. The Engineering Association arranged to take over the newspaper that year.[1] They even changed its name to the *"Engineer and Critic."*[2] The result for Jones was that he was blocked from the newspaper, despite the fact that he had personally kept the tradition alive the year before.

C.C. Sharp turned out to be among those doing the blocking. F.L.O. Wadsworth was the president of the Engineering Association and Sharp was his vice president.[3] An engineering student named Lucius Hine was serving as the newspaper's new editor-in-chief, and both Sharp and Wadsworth found spots on Hine's staff.[4]

Jones was not worried about finding something to do that spring. He had always found campus projects to keep him busy. As a freshman he had served as class sergeant-at-arms.[5] As a sophomore he had been both class vice president and secretary of the Horton Literary Society.[6] Most recently, as a junior, he had become the new president of the campus Y.M.C.A.[7] Over the years he also indulged a growing interest in birds. Years later, as a much older man, he would be recognized by the Audubon Society as an amateur expert in bird behavior. He never took formal classes in ornithology but he was often found climbing the campus trees to study their nests.[8]

Before Jones started at Ohio State he had apprenticed at a steel factory in his home town of Martins Ferry, and after he started at Ohio State his primary goal was to study for a career in metallurgy,[9] although he always found time to explore other academic interests. He took classes in ancient history, and he took

Curtis Howard, center, among the first Ohio State graduating class in 1878. (Photo courtesy of The Ohio State University Archives)

a series of classes in Greek and Latin where he read classical texts in their original languages.[10] His study of metallurgy apparently seemed more heroic when he pictured Bronze Age warriors first developing the craft.

Jones had also participated in both attempts at starting a varsity football team. His teammates accepted that their chance to play the sport was over but Jones, as a junior, assumed that he still had time.

✵

Jumbo Hedges and Chester Aldrich were both turning their attention to life after graduation. Hedges recently had accepted a position with the Champion Reaper Works, an agricultural machinery company in Springfield, Ohio.[11] He had been working for that company every summer while he was in school.[12] Aldrich meanwhile accepted an offer from a school district in Ulysses, Nebraska.[13] He would be helping to establish a new high school there, serving as both principal and superintendent.[14] The graduation ceremony for Hedges, Aldrich, and the rest of the Ohio State class of 1888 was scheduled for June.

Exactly ten years earlier, in the spring of 1878, Ohio State had held its first graduation ceremony. In the days leading up to that first ceremony the faculty asked the students what color the ribbons tied around the diplomas should be. The students realized then that they had never chosen school colors, so they selected a "colors committee," composed of students named Curtis Howard, Harwood Pool, and Alice Townshend. Those three committee members went downtown to a fabric store to look at ribbon samples, and they agreed that their diplomas would look nice decorated in orange and black. When they got back to campus to report their choice they were told that those colors were already used by Princeton. The Ohio State students wanted unique colors that were original to their school, so the committee rushed back down to the fabric store to make another selection.[15] This time they chose scarlet and gray. Of the three colors-committee members, the choice of colors held greatest sentiment for Curtis Howard—the only student among the three who would be graduating that spring. The fabric store had given sample ribbons to the committee, and Howard cut the scarlet and gray samples to divide among them. He said that, as Ohio State alumni, these colors would always be a part of their identity.[16]

It was a sentiment shared by the university's graduates for decades to follow.

*

After the Thanksgiving rainout in 1887, the future of varsity football at Ohio State was unclear, but the possibilities that football had represented further whetted the campus appetite for varsity sports. The students wanted to have a team and that team's sport was less important. Field day events, played only among themselves, no longer satisfied. On that point the *Lantern* spoke for most. A junior named William Crawford succeeded Jumbo Hedges as *Lantern* editor-in-chief, and in his first issue, at the start of the spring term, Crawford wrote an editorial pleading for something new. "We are tired of talking about general athletics," he wrote. "Let us see if something cannot be done in the line of football, base-ball, or tennis, which will be an honor to the University."[17]

Professors Lazenby (center) and Lord (right) play a game of cards. (Photo courtesy of The Ohio State University Archives)

The Athletic Association did not answer Crawford's plea. A junior named Julius Floto had by then replaced C.C. Sharp as Association president. F.L.O. Wadsworth replaced Fred Ball as vice president. Hugh Laughlin, the Goethe fan, was the new treasurer.[18] This new leadership team did not accomplish anything that spring other than organize a field day.[19]

Some students joined a fencing team. Nathaniel Lord, a professor of mining engineering, organized a fencing club on the model of William Rane Lazenby's tennis club. Among the students testing their skills as fencers were C.C. Sharp, F.L.O. Wadsworth, Fred Brown, Chester Aldrich, Scott Webb, and the Athletic Association president Julius Floto.[20]

✻

Pete Allen still hoped to play varsity baseball. For five years a dispute over ownership had gotten in the way of Ohio State fielding a baseball team but Allen suggested a plan to sidestep the problem. His idea was to revive varsity baseball not under the Athletic Association (which had disputed rights to the team) or the Baseball Association (which existed only in name) but instead as an independent baseball club.[21] He would let either the Athletic Association or the Baseball Association claim the team afterward, if they ever sorted out the rights.

Allen approached F.L.O. Wadsworth and C.C. Sharp looking for support. Wadsworth and Sharp were the leading figures in the recent football project, and when they backed Allen's plan they gave the new project legitimacy. The three installed themselves as a baseball committee. Sharp claimed a spot on the team in the outfield. Wadsworth grabbed third base. Allen made himself the team's pitcher. The three agreed that Allen would serve as both team manager and acting captain.[22]

A student named John Bownocker was the new *Lantern* "Local Notes" editor.[23] Bownocker had lived in the South Dorm ever since he was a prep student,[24] and as a long-time South Dorm resident his interest in sports had always been firmly with baseball. In his column he started keeping a close eye on the revival of the team.[25]

Other students on campus were also watching the baseball revival but most of them waited see what kind of opponent Allen could schedule before they were willing to embrace the new team. Capital University, the Lutheran school in Bexley on the east side of Columbus, had been Ohio State's first intercollegiate baseball opponent in a game seven years earlier. Allen sent them a new challenge. The Capital manager accepted, agreeing to bring his team up to the Ohio State campus on Friday, April 20.[26] With an intercollegiate opponent scheduled, Allen was able to recruit enough players to finish building the team.

A freshman named Frank Rane was one of Allen's recruits. Rane had come to Ohio State from Ann Arbor, Michigan, intent on preparing for a career in forestry.[27] His father was a cousin of the botany professor William Rane Lazenby. Rane had tried out for the football team in the fall, and he had even been Charles Barnes's choice to play right tackle before Wadsworth gave the spot to Jumbo Hedges. Since then Rane had developed a reputation as one of the school's best all-around athletes. He would go on to win multiple events at that year's spring field day, including winning the 100-yard dash and the running broad jump, and he set a new school record in the standing broad jump.[28] Pete Allen picked Rane to be his catcher.[29]

Ed Pedlow and Fred Brown also both tried out for the new baseball team. Both had been members of the football team in the fall. Pedlow was a good slugger and Allen put him at first base.[30] F.L.O. Wadsworth meanwhile looked out for Brown. He arranged for his friend to play third base, Wadsworth's usual position, in the Capital game.[31]

In the afternoon of April 20, Ohio State students began to gather at the North Dorm grounds. The Capital players walked from their campus in Bexley to downtown Columbus and from there they took a horse-drawn streetcar up to

Ohio State. The Ohio State baseball players met their guests at the local street-car stop and escorted them to the field.[32]

Capital took a three-run lead in the early innings but Pete Allen kept the score close by throwing eleven strikeouts. Capital exploded with five more runs in the sixth inning but, according to the coverage in the *Lantern*, "The boys soon waked up to the necessity of maintaining the honor of the O. S. U."[33] Ohio State answered with nine runs in the bottom of the sixth and then won the game 18 to 10. Allen led the team in hits and tied C.C. Sharp for most runs scored. William Crawford raved optimistically, "It is evident that we have some base ball players in our midst who can bring the O. S. U. up to a high position."[34]

Following the game the team called for an election to officially choose their leaders. Allen assumed that he had earned the right to keep both of his leadership positions but Frank Rane campaigned to be elected captain. With backing from Sharp and Wadsworth, Allen held onto the job.

Allen then moved Rane to first base, making Ed Pedlow his new catcher. Rane afterward began complaining about some of Allen's leadership choices.

*

By this time Jesse Lee Jones had found a project to keep him busy that spring. He helped a student named Emma Scott establish a campus Missionary Society, and he became the society vice president.[35] Jones had never previously expressed an interest in missionary work and his friends wondered why he had joined. Some joked that membership in a Missionary Society must look good on letters home asking parents for money.[36]

Emma Scott was the daughter of William Henry Scott, the university president, and she did plan to become a missionary. The *Makio* described her by borrowing a line from Samuel Taylor Coleridge: "Her very frowns are fairer far, than smiles of other maidens are."[37] Jones seemed to find her passion for the project compelling.

*

A few weeks passed after the Capital game and no further intercollegiate baseball games were scheduled. Pete Allen was only able to schedule a game against a "picked team" from Columbus. That Columbus team was composed mostly of alumni of the university but it was not officially affiliated with any institution.[38] Wadsworth returned to third base for the game, although games against such opponents had always bored him. Ohio State won 10 to 4. William Crawford complained in the *Lantern* that the team was already "resting on its laurels."[39]

Pete Allen eventually offered a challenge to students at Kenyon College, an Episcopalian school in the town of Gambier, Ohio. Ohio State students were acquainted with Kenyon students because Ohio State's most frequent opponent in military drill was Kenyon's Military Academy. The Kenyon Military Academy (K.M.A.) fielded a baseball team separate from the Kenyon College team, and it was the K.M.A. team that agreed to come down to Columbus on May 24.

In practices leading up to the K.M.A. game the Ohio State players began taking note of the slick defensive skills of a freshman named William Clark. Clark was a mixed-race, light-skinned African-American—or, in the language of the nineteenth century, a "mulatto."[40] To make room for Clark in the infield F.L.O. Wadsworth again gave up his position at third base.

C.C. Sharp respected Wadsworth's sacrifice for the team. Sharp then gave his position in the outfield to Wadsworth to play in the K.M.A. game. It would turn out to be Wadsworth's only intercollegiate baseball game.

Pete Allen wanted to buy uniforms for his players in time for them to wear in the game and he scoured the campus collecting donations. He ordered the uniforms in the school colors: gray pants with scarlet stockings, gray caps with scarlet bands, and gray jerseys with a scarlet "O S U" written across the chest.[41] No earlier Ohio State team had embraced the school colors so completely.

On the day of the game, the K.M.A. players took a train to Columbus. F.L.O. Wadsworth went downtown as Ohio State's representative to greet them at the station and escort them up to campus.[42] Some Kenyon professors were also on the train and Wadsworth was surprised to see college faculty showing so much support for their school's team.[43] Back on campus the Ohio State uniforms were late arriving from the tailor and the game had to be delayed for over an hour. The Ohio State team apologized to their guests but no one from Kenyon complained.

The game itself turned out to be a mismatch. The K.M.A. pitcher dominated. Ohio State had only two hits. Pete Allen batted 1-for-3 but he gave up nine hits and made five errors. F.L.O. Wadsworth batted 0-for-2. The K.M.A. team won 11 to 2.

Following the game the K.M.A. players needed to catch a 4:30 train back to Gambier and the Ohio State players escorted their guests downtown. At the train station, as the two teams separated, the K.M.A. team stood at attention and gave three cheers for Ohio State. When the Ohio State players got back to campus they spoke of their "privilege to meet so gentlemanly a crowd of fellows."

Afterward the *Lantern* offered extensive coverage of the game. One article tried to explain the loss with some grumbling about the umpire, a Kenyon student, but in the "Local Notes" column John Bownocker accepted no excuses. He wrote, "The fact was plainly demonstrated that our men need more practice."[44]

William Crawford had been thrilled merely to watch the team run onto the field wearing scarlet and gray. He challenged the entire campus to follow the players' example. He wrote an editorial arguing that it would be good for school spirit if every student wore the school colors "on all appropriate occasions, and whenever suitable." He noted, "We doubtless have among us some utilitarians who consider such things childish and foolish," but warned that they "should be careful about expressing such sentiments."

> By the same reasoning one could say that it was foolish for our troops in the war to lay down their lives for an old torn flag, or to cheer when Yankee Doodle was playing, but no one can prove this to patriotic Americans. To us as students of the University, the scarlet and gray should be almost as dear as the red, white, and blue.

Crawford added that the colors representing old campus rivalries need to be set aside: "fraternity, class, and society colors fade into insignificance before the college colors."[45]

The baseball team gave a spark to school spirit that the students had been waiting for. In May the *Lantern* observed, "Base-ball is our chief amusement just now."[46] In June the *Lantern* commented, "We don't come here simply to learn text books and attend lectures…athletics, tennis, base ball &c, go farther to bring a man out and make something of him than do large amounts of classroom work."[47]

*

George Cole was a student from Columbus, and in the spring of 1888 he was finishing his sophomore year. He had come to the university to study mechanical engineering. The university policy requiring chapel attendance had by then been enforced for nearly five years, but Cole began missing services. He missed so many services that year that he was expelled that spring.

Some students commented that Cole should have been more "careful" but others had a different interpretation of his motives.[48] They noted that Cole had previously been educated at a Quaker Friends School. There he would have learned to value freedom of conscience and been trained in the theory of civil disobedience. Cole's expulsion became the most discussed topic on campus that year, aside from sports.[49]

*

Word spread that varsity baseball was again played at Ohio State, and other schools began to send challenges.[50] One of those challenges came from Ohio Wesleyan University. Ohio State and Ohio Wesleyan had not played since 1882, but the Wesleyan reputation for pious claims of moral superiority still made them feel like a significant rival. They agreed to play on May 31, Decoration Day, as the finale of the baseball season.[51]

The game had to be played, as always, in Delaware. C.C. Sharp returned to the lineup but F.L.O. Wadsworth did not. The two had settled into a pattern of taking turns playing in games. The O.S.U. baseball players travelled to the Wesleyan campus, and as they arrived they saw that trouble was brewing. Two thousand rowdy Delaware townspeople had shown up for the holiday game and were already making themselves heard.

Wesleyan's playing field had no grandstand and the raucous crowd watched from a nearby hill. The crowd began throwing rocks when the Ohio State players took the field wearing their scarlet and gray uniforms. After the game began, the fans started threatening violence to the umpire. The Wesleyan players insisted that no one in the "howling mob" was a student,[52] but furious Ohio State players hissed that they had seen students egging on the crowd. They told the Wesleyan team that if they ever were allowed to leave their campus they would see how civilized fans acted.[53]

Nerves were fraying by the middle of the game when a left-handed pull hitter came to the plate for Wesleyan. Frank Rane was one of Ohio State's better athletes but for that at-bat Pete Allen did not trust his defense at first base. Allen ordered Rane to switch positions again, this time with third baseman William Clark. Rane decided then that he had had enough of Allen's leadership and he refused to make the move.

In the game Allen threw eleven strikeouts and hit a home run, but Ohio State lost 10 to 9. Following the game the primary discussion on campus was about the clash between Allen and Rane, and debate raged over who was to blame. Lucius Hine argued in the *Engineer and Critic* that Allen had abused his authority, and that the attempted move was an insult to Rane. In the *Lantern*, William Crawford in an editorial and John Bownocker in the "Local Notes" column both stated that a team must follow its captain without question and without giving in to personal jealousies.[54] The tensions revealed by the incident carried over even after the spring term ended.

*

The graduation ceremony for the class of 1888 was held on June 20, and Fatty Weybrecht made one last trip to campus to watch his friend Jumbo Hedges graduate. Someone asked Weybrecht whether he would ever return to school. He said that he might enroll that fall but he did not really mean it.[55] He had already decided to enlist in the U.S. Army. During World War One, twenty years later, he would be awarded the French Legion of Honor.[56]

On the day before each graduation ceremony, the Ohio State seniors traditionally held a ceremony of their own. The purpose was to symbolically hand the mantle of student leadership down to the junior class. A speech known as the "mantle oration" was the centerpiece, and the seniors of the class of 1888 selected Chester Aldrich ("the Daniel Webster of Alcyone") to deliver theirs. Aldrich's family came down early to attend the mantle ceremony, including his older brother who made a special trip from Buffalo.

Aldrich's mantle oration was written about the abolitionist leader William Lloyd Garrison, exploring the thesis that an individual must sometimes stand up to oppose the world's moral apathy. Aldrich argued that governing bodies, even when established specifically for the purpose of defending the greater good, occasionally let pragmatism get in the way of their ideals. The faculty previewed the speech and sensed an allegory to the controversy surrounding the expulsion of George Cole. They refused to let Aldrich deliver it, so William Crawford published it in the *Lantern*.

A month after his graduation Aldrich moved to Ulysses, Nebraska, to start his new job. Among his first responsibilities at the school was to select the school colors. He chose scarlet and gray.[57]

*

As the year came to an end, the North Dorm students gave Jesse Lee Jones a new project for the fall. They elected him to succeed Jumbo Hedges in the coming school year as the North Dorm president.[58] Jones meanwhile was mulling over what the football players could learn from Pete Allen's work in building a varsity team.

Chapter Seven

The reputation of the University is at stake

I n the fall of 1888 Jesse Lee Jones did not return as expected to begin his senior year. The *Makio* asked, "What wind has blown him hither?"[1] Jones had decided to spend a year away from school after reconsidering his priorities over the summer. He took a job teaching history at the high school in his hometown.[2]

The North Dorm students rushed to elect a new president.[3] If the Missionary Society or the football team were to return in the coming year, they also would have to get by without him.

✻

The football team seemed unlikely to return. The *Lantern* that year was praising baseball as "the great and only amusement."[4] John Bownocker advanced that fall from "Local Notes" editor to succeed William Crawford as the newspaper's editor-in-chief. Rallying the campus back to football was definitely not one of Bownocker's priorities.

The university hosted a series of lectures that fall by the poet and social activist Julia Ward Howe, best known as the author of "The Battle Hymn of the Republic." One of her lectures, given at the chapel, was on the topic of military training. Military drill, as taught by Ohio State, was laudable, she claimed. In an editorial Bownocker emphasized one specific point that Howe made: that military training was safer than playing football. "Foot-ball games seem to her more dangerous than O.S.U. artillery" because the artillery field leads to "fewer broken heads and ribs."[5] Bownocker suggested that Howe's condemnation of football might eventually come to be as well regarded as her earlier condemnations of slavery.

The North Dorm students still played football, but the version of football that they played was the same isolated, idiosyncratic version that the North Dorm had been playing for years.

*

Elsewhere in the state, the gridiron football movement continued to take root. That fall, to the southwest, in Oxford, Ohio, the students at Miami University formed a team. On December 8, 1888, that new Miami team hosted a game against the University of Cincinnati. It was the first game of intercollegiate football played within the borders of the state.[6]

In Columbus meanwhile Joe Firestone was still developing his own football plans. The management at Columbus Buggy had lost interest in sponsoring a company football team so Firestone had to find opportunities elsewhere. In 1888 he was introduced to Samuel Prescott Bush, another former football player from the Stevens Institute of Technology. Together the two formed a local community team under the name the "Columbus Foot Ball Club."[7]

Like Firestone, S.P. Bush had attended Stevens for the program in business management and the financial opportunities that it could bring. Bush graduated from Stevens in 1885, the spring before Firestone arrived, and then moved to Columbus as an executive with the Pennsylvania Railroad. His son would later become a United States Senator. His grandson and great-grandson would both eventually serve as Presidents of the United States.[8]

With the attention of the Ohio State campus turned away from gridiron football, the Columbus Foot Ball Club had to find other potential opponents. They sent challenges to newspapers throughout the state, addressed to anyone who would play them. One of those challenges was sent to the *Cincinnati Enquirer*.[9]

A Dayton organization named the Stillwater Canoe and Athletic Club read the challenge in the *Enquirer*. They had members with East-Coast football experience, so they formed their own club team in response. The new Stillwater team sent a letter to the *Columbus Daily Press* accepting the Columbus Foot Ball Club challenge publicly.[10]

A month later the Columbus team had not written back so the Stillwater Canoe and Athletic Club wrote to the *Daily Press* again. This time they offered their own challenge to any team willing to play them.[11] Not long afterward the Stillwater team played a game against Miami University.

*

F.L.O. Wadsworth had graduated from Ohio State in the spring, but before the ceremony the faculty told him that his application to return for a master's degree had been accepted.[12] As a graduate student he remained an active figure on campus, even continuing as a member of the tennis team. In the fall elections Professor William Rane Lazenby was chosen unanimously to be president of the Lawn Tennis Association. The Lawn Tennis Association had no vice president. Wadsworth was elected treasurer.[13]

Lazenby by then had come to accept that students want to play sports against other schools as a way to develop school pride. He still had mixed feelings about the issue, but even Cornell, his alma mater, had recently relented and allowed their students to play intercollegiate sports. Lazenby appointed a junior named Harry Mitchell to manage the O.S.U. tennis team,[14] and he allowed Mitchell to look for a suitable intercollegiate opponent.

Mitchell discovered that Ohio Wesleyan had a tennis team and he scheduled a match with them.[15] The match, in Delaware, on October 14, was to be Ohio State's first intercollegiate athletic competition in any sport outside of baseball. October 14 arrived but rain postponed the visit.[16] Over the next few weeks more bad weather postponed it even further. In early November the two sides finally cancelled the match altogether.[17]

Despite that cancellation, tennis at Ohio State had never seemed healthier. The membership of the Lawn Tennis Association was expanding. Professor Lazenby had been trying for years to get the campus woman interested in tennis and those efforts were rewarded as the club became fully coeducational.[18] F.L.O. Wadsworth had such a good time playing tennis that year that he did not even bother playing baseball.

*

George Cole missed the 1888 fall term and the board of trustees agreed to renew the debate over the chapel policy. Cole's expulsion had revived the issue but the trustees reconsidered their position due primarily to the presence of Rutherford B. Hayes. The policy had never been consistent with President Hayes's ecumenical vision for the university.

To revoke the chapel policy could create a public relations embarrassment, so the board decided to simply eliminate the demerit system. The requirement of compulsory chapel attendance was officially kept in place but by removing the demerit punishment they took the teeth out of it. In January 1889 Cole was quietly reinstated.[19]

*

John Bownocker was still worried about the tensions exposed on the baseball team during the previous spring, and he wrote an editorial in the fall proposing that the team ask a faculty member to coach them. A respected coach, he said, was the best hope to pull the squabbling players together. A coach's role in that era was limited to offering advice to help players train. The captain and manager, not the coach, were the direct leaders of the team. A coach merely provided a team with a mature voice of experience.

Everyone seemed to agree that Professor Lazenby would be an ideal voice of experience for any Ohio State team. Professor Lazenby, however, let it be known that he had no interest in the position. He said that he had his hands full just with tennis.

In February John Bownocker was still concerned about the state of the baseball team, and he wrote another editorial on the topic. He reminded everyone that the team "was crippled last year by petty jealousies" and he challenged the players to change their attitude:

> If any of the members are not men enough to put aside such a spirit when the reputation of the University, in this line, is at stake they should promptly be put out of the team and their places filled by other players.[20]

Bownocker asserted the importance of baseball success, and emphasized the problem created by not having it. "There is little doubt but that we lose students because of our weakness in athletic sports,"[21] he wrote. In contrast, he added that a "good ball club would be an excellent advertisement for the University."[22]

He also wrote, "If those who are to manage the team this year will begin work in earnest there is little doubt but that sufficient money can be raised to put the team in first class condition."[23] That spring the team elected Bownocker to be their manager.[24]

*

Outing magazine published an article that winter written by Walter Camp, intended to promote gridiron football. Camp had never finished medical school at Yale and was working as a sales manager, but in his spare time he also worked as a sportswriter—the first sportswriter dedicated exclusively to football.[25] His January 1889 *Outing* article, "Hints to Football Captains," served as a practical guide for anyone interested in starting a football team.[26]

In February the students at Denison University formed their first athletic association.[27] Denison was a Baptist school in the town of Granville, Ohio. Their new association put money into developing the Denison athletic grounds, with a plan to charge admission to athletic events—to their baseball games and to their campus field day. Flush with excitement over these projects, and with Walter Camp's recent *Outing* article fresh on their minds, the Denison students also developed a plan to form a varsity football team.[28]

The Denison athletic association then put forward another idea, but this idea would require the cooperation of other schools. They proposed establishing an intercollegiate athletic organization to make the scheduling of games between schools more organized and reliable.[29] Denison's best athlete was a student named Charles Bosler, and Denison's athletic association gave Bosler the task of promoting the plan. Bosler decided that the best opportunity "to agitate the subject"[30] would be at that year's State Oratory Contest. The contest was held on February 21, in Akron, and Bosler sent a Denison representative named Leonard Sutton to speak there with students from the various schools. Sutton found that no other schools were willing to make a commitment, however,[31] and the idea soon faded away.

The only immediate outcome of Bosler's work in Akron was to help Denison schedule some games. Ohio State agreed to play Denison in a baseball game that spring. The University of Wooster agreed to play Denison in a football game in the fall.

✳

Ohio State's baseball team seemed poised for a successful season. Pete Allen was reelected captain that spring[32] and John Bownocker, as manager, recruited enough players that Allen was able to establish a first and second team, the first practicing against the second.[33]

Among the members of the second team were Charles Bradfield "Caesar" Morrey, the younger brother of William Morrey, and Hobart Beatty, the younger brother of Will Beatty.[34] Morrey was a junior, studying biology, with a goal of either becoming a medical doctor or pursuing an academic career. He had first been called "Caesar" when he was a child, and it was his brother that made sure that the nickname followed him to college.[35]

The season got off to a promising start that spring. A student named Samuel Bennett became the team's new pitcher.[36] Pete Allen had met Bennett in the university's veterinary program. Allen then moved himself to catcher. Allen also moved Frank Rane from first base into the outfield, and Rane did not complain. On April 12 the team claimed a victory over the soldiers from the Columbus military barracks.[37]

On April 27 the team traveled to Granville for their scheduled game with Denison. Charles Bosler was Denison's pitcher but Samuel Bennett, pitching for Ohio State, had the better day. Ohio State won 10 to 4.[38] The Denison students took some solace when the Ohio State players expressed admiration for the new Denison athletic grounds.[39]

Ohio State's third game of the season, three days later, was a setback. The team lost to Capital University, 14 to 3. The *Lantern* acknowledged that "the Capital boys outplayed our club in every respect."[40] After the game some of the Capital players celebrated downtown, and the police had to be called in the middle of the night to break up a drunken brawl.[41]

*

The O.S.U. Athletic Association had by then elected new leaders. Harry Mitchell, Professor Lazenby's tennis manager, became the new president. George Bloom, a student from Xenia, Ohio, was his vice president. Frank Rane was elected secretary and Ed Pedlow was elected treasurer.[42]

After the setback against Capital, these Association officers claimed that the students needed a fresh influx of school spirit. They held a contest in early May to create a "school yell."[43] School yells were another new trend in college sports that had come to Ohio from the East.[44] Kenyon College had taken the lead locally with their widely admired yell of "Heike! Heike! Heike! K-E-N-Y-O-N! Kenyon! Kenyon!"[45]

William Clark, the slick-fielding third baseman, wrote the winning entry: "Wah Hoo, Wah Hoo! Rip, zip, bazoo! I yell, yell, yell! For O.S.U!"[46] Over the following few months it became:

Wahoo, wahoo!
Rip, zip, bazoo!
I yell, I yell
For O.S.U![47]

*

On May 5, 1889, the Ohio State baseball team returned to Delaware to face Ohio Wesleyan. The welcome that they received that day was even more hostile than the one from the year before. The O.S.U. players first noticed that something was wrong when no one from the Wesleyan team met them at the train station, a violation of established college baseball etiquette. When they arrived at the Wesleyan campus they were asked to change into their uniforms not in a campus locker room but instead in the back room of a local saloon. They interpreted this arrangement as a Wesleyan joke mocking the supposed moral deficits of the Ohio State students. Meanwhile a concert band played lively music on the campus to draw a raucous crowd. During the game, the catcalls, the rocks, and the threats on the umpire matched the atmosphere in 1888.[48]

The tension came to a head in the fifth inning. The Ohio State shortstop, J.J. Shaw, was on first base, took off to steal second, and ended up all the way at third. The Wesleyan players claimed that Shaw had never stepped on second base and asked the umpire to call him out.[49] The umpire had not had a good view of the play and refused to make the call.[50] The Wesleyan captain led his players off the field in protest. The Wesleyan student newspaper, the *Transcript*, reported, "When our boys saw the determination on the part of the umpire to sustain such illegal plays they wisely, quietly and in a gentlemanly way withdrew from the field."[51]

The umpire declared a forfeit and the crowd erupted in anger. The Ohio State players were left to fend for themselves as they made their way back to the train station.[52] The *Transcript* afterward seemed to revel in the bedlam: "From start to finish we had our own way and demonstrated the ability of our local preachers to 'do' the O. S. U. team at any and all times."[53]

John Bownocker, disgusted, promised that his team would never return.[54]

*

The people in downtown Columbus were also focused on baseball that spring but the fans downtown were not watching baseball at Ohio State. The Columbus professional baseball team, the Buckeyes, returned to the American Association after four years as an independent. On April 28, 1889, the Philadelphia Athletics came to Recreation Park. It was the first major league game that the Columbus fans had seen since 1884, and afterward they had little interest to spare for any college team.[55]

The owners of the Columbus professional team wanted to highlight the fact that they played in Ohio's seat of government, so they said that the name of their team should be changed that year to the "Columbus Solons."[56] A "solon" was an archaic term for a senator. Team names in this era were just nicknames and not legal trademarks, and the Columbus fans immediately ignored the new suggestion. The local newspapers continued to call the team the "Columbus Buckeyes."[57]

*

F.L.O. Wadsworth graduated with a master's degree in June. He accepted a fellowship to work with Professor Albert Michelson at Clark University, designing the laboratory apparatuses for Michelson's astronomical and spectroscopic research.[58] Wadsworth ended up with over seventy patents to his name. Some of those patents were for the equipment that helped Michelson win the 1907 Nobel Prize for physics. Others were for improvements to the design of the bicycle.[59]

Wadsworth eventually accepted a faculty position at the University of Chicago.[60] While there he helped oversee the university's tennis team[61] and also accepted opportunities to compete in professional tennis tournaments.[62]

*

Jesse Lee Jones had spent that year working as a high school teacher. Martins Ferry, Jones's home town, was located 120 miles directly east of Columbus, along the Ohio River, near West Virginia. It was the oldest surviving community in the state, and Jones would have made sure that his students were aware of their city's role in settling the West.

During the last days of colonial America the British Empire had refused to let settlers move onto land along the Great Lakes known as the Northwest Territory. The British feared that spreading west would make their unruly colonists even more unmanageable. For colonial frontiersman crowded against the Ohio River, the American Revolution was largely fought over elbowroom. When the Revolution began, the British formed military alliances with the tribes native to the region, united by a common interest in blocking further western expansion.

A pioneer named William Zane had settled with five sons and a daughter in the area that would later become Wheeling, West Virginia, and at the start of the war Zane's son Ebenezer joined the patriot cause. Ebenezer Zane was one of forty-two soldiers stationed at the nearby base of Fort Henry. In the fall of 1782 a combined force of Delaware, Seneca, Shawnee, and Wyandot warriors, armed with British weapons, attacked the area's frontier community, and the men, women, and children there rushed to Fort Henry for protection. In the battle that followed the forty-two soldiers were reduced to just twelve men, and civilians from the community were needed to man the turrets. Soon gunpowder was running low and the fort was in danger of being overrun. Ebenezer Zane decided that he had to risk retrieving his personal stock of gunpowder, hidden in his home sixty yards away.

The story of what happened next came to be passed down proudly for generations in Zane family lore; in 1903 it served as the basis for *Betty Zane*, a romantic historical fiction by Zane Grey, her descendant and one of America's great writers of "western" novels.[63] Ebenezer's young sister Betty argued that she should make the first attempt to get the gunpowder. "If I die in the attempt, my loss will not be felt."[64] She burst from the fort toward Ebenezer's cabin and the opposing forces were initially too surprised to react. She gathered the gunpowder in her apron and started to rush back, and the enemy then began to fire. Bullets whizzed by Betty's head and through her petticoat, but she reached the fort, and the community held off the attack.

After the war the Fort Henry survivors founded Martins Ferry, the first American settlement within the Northwest Territory. Ebenezer Zane later blazed trails throughout Ohio but Betty Zane never moved beyond her new hometown. There she married a man named Jacob Clark and had a son who she named after her brother. Ebenezer Clark had a daughter named Martha, who married a barrel-maker named Levi Jones.[65] On October 17, 1866, Levi and Martha Jones had a son named Jesse Lee.[66]

In the spring of 1889 Jesse Lee Jones was growing tired of teaching high school students. Throughout that year he thought about the unfinished business that he had left behind at Ohio State. William Henry Scott was still the president of the university, so his daughter Emma also seemed likely to still be around. Jones began preparing for a return in the fall.

Chapter Eight

The O. S. U. can "Yell like Hell"

Jesse Lee Jones returned to Ohio State that September to finally begin his senior year.[1] A new course on Greek art was listed in the latest university catalog. Jones wanted to take it, but he first made sure that it did not interfere with an advanced lab that he needed to complete his metallurgy degree.[2]

As Jones explored the campus again, it seemed as though he had left no footprints behind. The *Critic* was gone. No one had bothered to revive it during the spring of 1889. Emma Scott was also gone, and her Missionary Society had left with her. Jones was told that she was studying medicine in Cincinnati. Varsity football was gone. The Athletic Association had not continued that work. Ed Pedlow had been a member of the 1887 football team and he had since become the treasurer of the Association, but like the others he was now focused on baseball.

Jones decided to take at least one of these issues into his own hands. Before he took his break from school he had watched Pete Allen sidestep the campus bureaucracy to reestablish varsity baseball. Jones planned to follow the same strategy. He would form a football team and let the Athletic Association decide afterward whether or not to claim it.

His first step was to get a ball. In 1889 the rugby balls that were used to play gridiron football were not available on the shelves of Columbus stores. Few people in central Ohio had even seen one. The North Dorm students still played football but the version of football that they played used a round ball. Jones knew by then that a traditional round ball was not right for the modern sport.

He found a possible solution by talking to George Cole. Cole's father worked in Chicago, and Chicago was home to Spalding and Co., a nationally known sporting goods store. Jones assumed that such a renowned store was sure to sell footballs. He took up a collection at the North Dorm, asking each resident to pitch in ten cents.[3] Cole then sent that money to his father. Cole's father purchased a ball and arranged for the store to ship it to his son.

The North Dorm students were burning with anticipation when a package from Chicago arrived. Cole opened the box and worried that the ball inside was defective. It was oblong, not round. Spalding guaranteed that their footballs would arrive "perfect in material and workmanship, and correct in shape and size,"[4] so Cole repackaged the ball, locked it away in his room, and planned to ship it back. Others in the Dorm were sure that the ball was shaped as it was supposed to be, so they broke into Cole's room and took it. Then they kicked it around for several hours until Cole conceded that it was too scuffed to return.

Jones's next step was to learn the rules. By 1889 Ohio State students understood that American football had changed beyond the sport that the North Dorm students played, but not so clear was precisely what those changes were. The 1887 team had learned the modern rules of gridiron football but those rules had never been incorporated into the more casual campus play. Jones had been a member of that 1887 team but even he was not confident in his knowledge of the gridiron rules. Joe Firestone had been the primary source of information in 1887 but two years had passed since then. By 1889 Firestone no longer knew any students on campus and no longer had reason to visit, and as no one on campus knew him no one contacted him this time.

Jones looked for a new source for information. Ohio State had recently hired a twenty-seven-year-old Princeton graduate, John Wahl Queen, to fill in for a professor of history and political science who was on a leave of absence.[5] Jones took a course that Queen taught in political economy. He discovered that he and his professor had some things in common. They both were Democrats. They both were Presbyterians. They both were interested in Greek history. Most useful was that Queen had been a student at one of the leading football schools. Jones seized the opportunity to pick the young professor's brain.[6]

Queen's most helpful piece of information turned out to be the recommendation of a book, *How to Play Football*, by Walter Camp. Camp's book was a complete manual for building a football program. It explained the rules, laid out plays and basic strategies, and described the roles of each position and the optimal skills of the player to best fill it.

Conveniently, the publisher of the book was Spalding sporting goods. Jones took up another collection at the Dorm and again sent the money to Cole's father in Chicago. The book arrived, and Cole looked through it and declared it indecipherable. "All Greek," he said. He handed it over to Jones. Jones then formed a "rules committee" to study the book made up of North Dorm football players.[7]

A North Dorm freshman named Hamilton Richardson took the job of communications secretary for the committee. When the committee became confused about the lessons that Camp offered they asked for clarification from Professor Queen. When Queen couldn't help, Richardson sent letters directly to the football schools in the East requesting the information that they needed.[8]

The 1889 fall term ended and the 1890 winter term began. During that time the rules committee continued to study gridiron football with the same attention and dedication that Jones had previously given to studying the bird nests of campus trees.

✱

The officers of the O.S.U. Athletic Association had been ineffective in 1889, even compared to the leadership team that had served the year before. The latest officers had not even managed to organize a field day in the spring. "What has become of the Athletic Association?" the *Lantern* asked that fall. "It has had a precarious existence for the past few years and seems now to have disappeared entirely."[9]

Meanwhile, at Denison, the student newspaper, the *Denison Collegian*, published an editorial. The plan to form an intercollegiate athletic organization had been proposed during the previous winter but by that fall it was mostly forgotten. The *Collegian* revived the topic. "What is the matter with an inter-collegiate athletic association?" the editor asked.[10] It could coordinate a schedule for baseball, football, and even tennis, and crown state champions every year. "Such an organization would certainly put athletics far ahead of their present position. Let us hear from other Ohio colleges."[11]

The *Lantern* writers regularly read the *Collegian*, and the officers of the O.S.U. Athletic Association had contacts at the *Lantern*. Harry Mitchell read the Denison editorial and he liked the idea of an intercollegiate tennis tournament. He decided to help Denison with the plan. If nothing else, the project might quiet his own critics on campus. He contacted the *Collegian*, and they put him in touch with Charles Bosler. Mitchell and Bosler then contacted other schools, trying to bring them on board.

The students at Denison were preparing to play football that fall, as were the students that Denison had challenged from the University of Wooster. The Wooster students were learning the rules from one of their alumni. Kinley McMillan had been a good Wooster athlete in the mid-1880s. He had pitched the baseball game in 1884 that afterward caused so much trouble to Ohio State's athletic ambitions. After graduating in 1886, McMillan spent the next three years at the Princeton Seminary and was introduced to gridiron football through the Princeton team. He graduated in 1889 with a commitment to go to India as a missionary but he caught typhoid over the summer and his ship sailed without him. With no other responsibilities he went back to Ohio to consider his options. While home he discovered that the Wooster students had scheduled a football game and he offered to teach them what he knew.[12]

Denison and Wooster ultimately played two football games that year—one at Wooster and one at Denison. On November 23 the Denison team, with Bosler at center, headed to the Wooster campus. The coaching of Kinley McMillan seemed to serve as a secret weapon and Wooster embarrassed Denison, winning 48 to 0.[13]

The students at Oberlin College were also learning the rules of gridiron football that fall, and they were being trained by a student recently enrolled there. Frederick Bushnell Ryder had discovered gridiron football as a student at the Phillips Academy, a prep school in Andover, Massachusetts. He was the son of a Congregationalist minister, and after he finished his prep work he decided to attend Oberlin College, the Congregationalist school in his hometown. He still wanted to play football, so he taught the Oberlin students the latest rules and guided them in forming a varsity team.[14]

Ryder then contacted Wooster looking for an opponent for his new Oberlin team. They scheduled a game to be played on Thanksgiving, but the Oberlin faculty ordered it cancelled. The Oberlin faculty still considered football unacceptably brutal and unchristian, and intercollegiate football games were still banned there. Ryder found the faculty's perspective ridiculous, especially given that his own father, a Congregationalist minister, had no objection to the sport. He began to consider a transfer to another school.

Denison's rematch with Wooster was at home on December 6. Denison hoped to put up a better performance but the final score was 50 to 0.[15] The *Collegian* attributed their team's poor showing to not having someone like Kinley McMillan on their side. Gridiron football, they wrote, "is a recent game in the West, and our fellows were mostly inexperienced. The best that they could do with no 'coacher' was to get what suggestions they could from the rules, from an occasional magazine article, and from what they could remember of games they had seen."[16]

After their success in these games, Wooster was fully committed to the Bosler-Mitchell plan for an intercollegiate athletic association.[17]

✳

The 1890 State Oratory Contest was held on February 20. Wittenberg University hosted the event at the Grand Opera House in Springfield, Ohio. The State Contest had by then become a highlight on the academic calendar, and students from participating schools regularly attended the event, each loudly supporting the orator who represented them. Just one year earlier Wooster had impressed everyone by sending over 50 students to the contest in Akron.[18]

The O.S.U. Oratorical Association challenged the campus to beat Wooster's record,[19] and a quarter of Ohio State's four hundred students made the trip to Springfield. They arrived by train in a reserved car decorated with banners and bunting. They also each wore a badge trimmed with their school colors of scarlet and gray. The *Denison Collegian* commented on the size and enthusiasm of the Ohio State delegation.[20]

Students from various schools greeted the O.S.U. students by shouting their school yells. The O.S.U. students shouted their own yell in reply. The Ohio State yell had been written as, "Wahoo, wahoo! Rip, zip, bazoo! I yell, I yell, For O.S.U!" but in the year since it was written the students had begun shouting it as:

> Wahoo, wahoo!
> Rip, zip, bazoo!
> I yell like hell
> For O.S.U![21]

Students also shouted their yells in the Springfield opera house after their orator finished his speech, as if oratory were a sporting event.

Ohio State's orator in the contest was William Clark, the baseball third baseman and original author of the school yell. Some people seemed amazed by the choice. The *State Journal* reported, "For the first time in the history of the state a colored man will represent a college in the state contest."[22] A few paragraphs later the writer repeated the fact for emphasis. Ohio Wesleyan's student newspaper, the *College Transcript*, listed the orators in the contest and instead of provid-

Ohio State students prepare to ride the extensive train lines of the state of Ohio.
(Photo courtesy of The Ohio State University Archives)

ing Clark's topic (as they did for the other eight participants) stated only that he
was "a colored student from Middleport."[23]

Clark's speech was titled "Monopoly and Communism," and his thesis was
that the two competing socioeconomic models represented equally dangerous
threats to liberty. He argued that the old American aristocracy built on slavery
had been replaced with a newer corporate-based aristocracy: "Master and slave"
had given way to "plutocrat and proletariat."[24] The communist solution was no
better, he argued, as private property "is an essential condition of social progress."[25] Clark's proposed solution—expanded opportunities for education—flattered the academic values that had originally formed his university. His speech
finished second in the contest.[26]

An Ohio State junior named Carl Doney was pleased, both with Clark's
performance in the contest and with the level of support that the other students
gave him. Doney was the latest editor-in-chief of the *Lantern*, and he wrote in an
editorial, "Undeniably our yell was the loudest, our enthusiasm the greatest, and

our orator dangerously close to the best."[27] He added that when it came to showing school pride, "the O. S. U. is thoroughly in the lead."[28] The winning orator in the contest was a student from Buchtel College, a Unitarian-Universalist school in Akron. He delivered a speech titled "Democracy the Dominant Idea."[29] Another *Lantern* writer joked, "If the O. S. U. can 'Yell like ----' for second place, how should Buchtel yell for first?"[30]

The orator from Ohio Wesleyan finished fourth. His speech was titled "Puritan and Cavalier" and discussed contemporary American life as a reflection of the opposing religious factions that fought the English Civil War in the seventeenth century. The Wesleyan students were disappointed with the judges' scores, and many were disgusted by the entire evening. The coverage in the *Transcript* argued that the Wesleyan man "held the attention of the audience much better than any of the winners," and went on to criticize both the process used in rating the speeches and the "outrageous conduct" of the O.I.O.A. itself in failing to notify the participants in advance of the names of all the judges.[31]

Wesleyan's greatest scorn was directed toward what they saw as the scandalous behavior of the Ohio State delegation:

> The O. S. U. boys were the happiest students at Springfield. They came expecting to celebrate and with all the necessary appliances. Previous to the contest confidence characterized every action, and following the contest no ground was too sacred for them. The college yell was highly original and extremely *forcible*. In fact one line of it transcended common decency. We hope that hereafter if they have no respect for themselves they will respect those about them and confine their language within the bounds of what is proper.[32]

Carl Doney planned to become a Methodist minister but even he rolled his eyes at Wesleyan's blue-nosed reaction. He noted that the *Transcript*, "as is usual after defeat, vents its spleen in its characteristic manner."[33] Addressing the Wesleyan students directly, he goaded, "Whence comes this spirit? Throw off that long face worn at the contest; you surely have been defeated often enough to know how to graciously accept a Waterloo."[34]

Students from Wooster had also been annoyed with Ohio State's overbearing presence at the contest, and they were eager to take the Ohio State students down a peg. The *Wooster Collegian* was a monthly magazine published by the Wooster students and one of their writers complained about the conduct of the O.S.U. students in Springfield. He claimed to hope that the "hoodlum" element that had come to the

Ohio State's science facilities, such as this lab for electrical engineering, were a point of student pride. (Photo courtesy of The Ohio State University Archives)

contest "is not a fair representation of the Columbus student."[35] Even worse, he said, was the "concentrated egotism" that the Ohio State students revealed after returning home. He quoted the *Lantern* as bragging that "the O. S. U. is thoroughly in the lead" despite the fact that Ohio State did not win anything at the contest. He said, "They are obliged to misrepresent in order to get a shelf to stand their egotism on," but added that Wooster would be happy "to knock the shelf out from under them."[36]

Carl Doney saw the *Wooster Collegian* article as yet another ecclesiastical attack on his secular school. He called the criticism of the *Lantern* unworthy of any response, saying that the *Collegian* writer had clearly taken his words out of context, but he said that he wanted to defend Ohio State's other students from the "vilifying remarks which are so frequently poured forth by various envious journals."[37] As to whether Ohio State "hoodlums" were a worthy "representation of the Columbus student," he pointed out that, unlike the students from Capital University ("Theologues, too!"), no Ohio State man had ever been arrested downtown in a midnight brawl.[38]

He added that no school in the state could match Ohio State for training in the sciences, and that the university was the equal to any school in the state for a classical education. So if Ohio State students are egotists, Doney concluded, "'twill require more than words, simply words, in the *Collegian* 'to knock the shelf out from under' us."[39]

*

Doney supported the Mitchell-Bosler plan for an intercollegiate athletic association and he endorsed it in a *Lantern* editorial in early February. He claimed that a regular schedule of opponents was just what Ohio State's sports teams needed to survive. "Once in such an organization, there will be something for which to work," he wrote, "and our ball players and foot-ball men will work."[40]

On February 21, the day after the State Oratory Contest, representatives from various student athletic associations held a convention. The purpose of the convention was to form the intercollegiate athletic organization[41]—to write its charter and to establish its membership. The representatives met in Springfield, at the Arcade Hotel, taking advantage of the fact that so many of them would already be in town. The structure of the new athletic organization would be based on the Ohio Intercollegiate Oratorical Association: a confederation of local campus associations.[42]

The new organization was named the Ohio Intercollegiate Athletic Association (O.I.A.A.), and only the representatives from Ohio State, Denison, Wooster, and Buchtel entered the convention with authorization from their schools to join. It was decided that those four schools would form the nucleus of the O.I.A.A., around which others would be added. Harry Mitchell and Charles Bosler represented their schools. Bosler was elected president and Mitchell was elected vice president. The O.I.A.A. became Ohio's first intercollegiate athletic conference.

Other schools could be admitted with two-thirds vote of current members. Kenyon College wanted to join but first needed permission from their faculty. The Kenyon athletic association sent in an official application in late February. Ohio Wesleyan also sent in an application but the O.I.A.A. turned them down. Wesleyan did not have a campus athletic association, so they had no administrative body that could officially request an invitation or accept an offer. The fact that Wesleyan teams only played home games also made them unattractive to other schools. Oberlin also wanted to join but the Oberlin faculty set conditions on membership. Their students could play no more than three baseball games a season and could not compete in football at all. The O.I.A.A. refused to consider an application under those terms.

When Carl Doney announced the O.I.A.A. in the next issue of the *Lantern* he wanted everyone to recognize the significance of the opportunity. He called the students to action with an appeal to school pride: "As the first institution in the State in the point of mental education, let the University also be the first in such athletics as are considered by the State Association."[43]

*

On Monday, March 3, the O.S.U. Athletic Association held an emergency meeting.[44] At that meeting they ratified their membership in the O.I.A.A. They also adopted a new constitution, consistent with the O.I.A.A. model, bringing the Baseball Association and the Lawn Tennis Association under their authority. (Professor Lazenby had agreed to that decision a few days earlier.)[45] Then as an official O.I.A.A. member they cast their vote in favor of accepting Kenyon's application.[46]

At the meeting they also elected new officers. Many people considered Frank Rane the best athlete at the university and he was elected president. A junior named Edwin D. Martin became Rane's vice president.[47] With authority over both baseball and tennis, Rane and Martin would hold more power than any previous Association leaders had ever held. Rane was particularly interested in the O.I.A.A. plan to establish a State Field Day. He looked forward to the chance to test himself in various track and field events against the best athletes in the state.

The final item on the Athletic Association agenda was to accept sixty new applications for membership, approximately tripling the size of the campus organization. The "Local Notes" editor wrote, "After a sound and refreshing slumber of two years, the association woke to new vigor Monday."[48] Carl Doney added, "There is some hope that the long looked-for boom in athletics has come at last."[49]

In April the O.I.A.A. held its first meeting after the original organizing convention in February. The agenda for the April meeting was to finalize the baseball schedule and to make plans for the State Field Day and the State Tennis Tournament. The baseball schedule was designed to produce a legitimate state champion: each team was given a balanced eight-game schedule, with each team playing every O.I.A.A. opponent twice, once at home and once away. The State Field Day was scheduled for May 24, the State Tennis Tournament for June 14.

*

The arrival of the O.I.A.A. changed the situation for Jesse Lee Jones. On one hand, football would be an O.I.A.A. sport, so even without his help a slate of games would be available in the fall—or as soon after the fall as the Athletic Association could put together a varsity team. On the other hand, Jones was a senior, so a season beginning in the fall would arrive too late for him to play.

He needed to make a decision. He could step aside, taking pride in the contributions that he had already made to Ohio State football. Through his efforts the school had a Spalding ball and the students at the North Dorm were learning to play the gridiron version of the sport. Or he could press on that spring and build the team himself.

He was so close to finishing that he did not want to stop. The new Athletic Association officers were busy with baseball—football was still a lower priority. Jones made his decision. No descendant of Betty Zane could ask another man to finish the job that he had started.

With the Walter Camp book in hand Jones began holding football tryouts in early March.

Chapter Nine

We know too much of the Delaware boys ourselves

J umbo Hedges happened to return for a visit while Jesse Lee Jones was
holding his tryouts.[1] Hedges had been working for the Champion Reaper
Works since his graduation, developing the mechanized reaper market in
Iowa, Minnesota, and the Dakotas,[2] but business brought him back to Columbus
that spring. Jones was happy to see his former teammate, if only to get his bless-
ing for the new football project.

Jones, in addition to his work with football, also took on another project
that year. He was chosen to serve as the editor-in-chief of that year's *Makio*. As
the weather started getting warmer, both of his projects were coming closer to
their deadlines. Jones hoped that his final months of school would offer the yearbook something special for reminiscing.

✻

The baseball team had first claim on the use of the athletic field that spring
so Jones was forced to schedule football tryouts between baseball practices. Ed
Pedlow had been a member of the football team in 1887 but he had since become
a veteran baseball player. He could have helped with either baseball or football
but there was no question which team he would join. The "national pastime"
simply offered greater prestige.

Pete Allen was gone by then—his two-year veterinary program was complete—
so the baseball team needed to select a new captain. They chose the pitcher Samuel
Bennett. Bennett found a pitcher for the team that he trusted even more than
himself: a prep student with an impressive curve ball named Edward C. Martin.

People called the new pitcher "Kid" Martin to distinguish him from the older Ed Martin—Edwin D. Martin—who had recently become Frank Rane's vice president in the Athletic Association. Bennett also selected a new catcher: a freshman named George Pearce. Pearce and Martin made a good battery and people soon began calling Pearce "Kid" as well.[3]

Frank Rane arrived at the baseball practices that spring with new confidence and energy, and his attitude seemed to be reflected in a new power swing. He offered no sign of being disappointed that he had again been passed over as captain. He had more than enough authority over the team as the Athletic Association president.

Even without the involvement of any baseball players, Jesse Lee Jones was able to gather athletes to build a football team. The North Dorm students left their own football games behind and were ready to play the new gridiron version. A few prep students, who had never even known Jumbo Hedges, Chester Aldrich, or C.C. Sharp, were among them.

A prep named Richard TenBroeck Ellis was exploring as many campus projects as he could find that year. He joined the sketch club, the banjo club, the glee club, the smoking club, and the staff of the *Makio*, and he pledged to the Sigma Chi fraternity. When Jesse Lee Jones began forming a football team, Dick Ellis wanted to be part of that project as well.

A prep named Charles Foulk looked at football as an opportunity. Foulk was known on campus for his serious demeanor, and people sometimes asked him why he never smiled. Years earlier his parents had a baby that they named Charles, but that child had died after a single week. When Mrs. Foulk was forty-one she was surprised to become pregnant again, and when the new baby was born a healthy boy she named him after his dead brother. Foulk seemed to be looking for a means to prove himself worthy of his name.

Some students from the South Dorm also showed up to try out for the football team, and among them was a prep named John Buchanan Huggins. His family called him "Jack."[4] Jack Huggins had been born in Scotland as the son of an elderly American cotton merchant. He was four years old when his father died and his mother died seven years after that. He then bounced around the United States living among fifteen siblings and half-siblings,[5] and during those years he saw gridiron football played in the East. He eventually began living with a half-brother in Mansfield, Ohio, and after graduating from the local high school he decided to attend Ohio State. He arrived at the practice field claiming that he already knew how to play the sport.[6]

✴

Walter Camp had written in *How to Play Football* that a football team builds its offense to execute three types of plays: running the ball through the defensive line, running the ball around the defensive line, and the "wedge play" to crush the defensive line. The solution of passing the ball over the defensive line—the "forward pass"—was not legal. The players who ran with the ball most often were the halfbacks. "The half backs must be the ground gainers of the team," wrote Camp. "Such work calls for dash and fire—that ability to suddenly concentrate all the bodily energy into an effort that must make way through anything."[7]

Among those who tried out at halfback were Caesar Morrey and Jo Jo Large. Morrey had recently become the president of the senior class, and Large was his vice president.[8] Morrey was usually a baseball player, with a position on the second team, and he had once even played in a varsity game, filling in for Ed Pedlow in right field,[9] but he thought that he had a better chance of playing varsity sports if he joined the football team.

Jesse Lee Jones had previously been a classmate of Caesar Morrey's brother William, and he was a classmate of Caesar Morrey now, but he had never had much in common with either of the Morrey brothers. They were Republicans and he was a Democrat. They were free thinkers, while he was a devout Presbyterian.[10] The *Makio* had a tradition of using literary quotations to comment on the character of the students, and Jones continued that tradition when he took over the yearbook. For Caesar Morrey he found a quotation from the Revolutionary War statesman Richard Henry Lee: "Now with a giant's might; He heaves the ponderous thought."[11] But Jones appreciated Morrey's sharp mind, good field sense, and quick understanding of the rules of football. He made Morrey his right halfback.

Jo Jo Large had been new to the campus when he tried out for the 1887 football team. He had transferred that same fall from Ohio Wesleyan University. His goal in life was to design and build bridges, so he came to Ohio State to study mechanical and civil engineering. Jones remembered Large from that earlier tryout, when Chester Aldrich knocked him unconscious. Large was small but Jones liked seeing such a big spirit in such a little man (*Makio*: "What's in a name?"[12]—William Shakespeare). Large also proved to be the best kicker on campus. Jones made him the left halfback.

A fullback played as a running back but, in this era when all players played on both sides of the ball, fullbacks were more often selected for their defensive skills. When the opposing team had the ball the four backs were defensive backs, like safeties and cornerbacks in today's game, and as such they were the last defenders responsible for stopping the ball carrier. Camp emphasized that the fullback, playing deepest, should be the surest tackler of the four. "Other things being equal, it is eminently proper to select as a full-back an exceptionally strong tackler.... It usually means a touch-down if he misses."[13] The fullback, stationed deepest behind the line, also served as the team's punter. Jones selected Dave Hegler, an agriculture student from Washington Court House. Jones liked Hegler's attitude (*Makio*: "A man I knew who liv'd upon a smile; And well it fed him"[14]—Edward Young).

Selecting a quarterback was a football captain's most important decision. Walter Camp wrote, "The quarter is, under the captain, the director of the game. The importance of his work is therefore impossible to overrate."[15] A quarterback, after taking the snap from center, could either hand the ball off or pass it backward or laterally. Just as a forward pass was forbidden, so was the quarterback running with the ball himself immediately after taking the snap. He could carry the ball only if another player had taken possession of it during the play and passed it back to him (like an embryonic version of a flea-flicker play). Camp said of the quarterback, "He must be, above all the qualifications of brains and agility usually attributed to the position, of a hopeful or sanguine disposition. He should always believe the play will be a success."[16]

The vice president of the Athletic Association, Edwin D. Martin, tried out for the position. Martin was Frank Rane's right-hand man, and the Association could be counted on to recognize the varsity status of the spring football team if the Association vice president were its quarterback. Martin seemed confident in his abilities, even if no one else was. Jones made Martin the team's quarterback and hoped for the best.

In front of the backfield was the line. There was no rule at the time that explicitly required seven men on the line of scrimmage, but for most plays Camp recommended it. He wrote that the center, the man who initiated each play, was the key figure on the line. The position required both brains and brawn (or "sense and strength," as Camp put it[17]), but more important for success were the qualities of discipline and patience. The center would be the target of constant physical abuse, and the ability to endure that abuse without losing his head was the center's most essential quality. F.L.O. Wadsworth had been given this role in 1887. In 1890 Jones slotted it for himself.

Jones's position in 1887 had been at right guard. The guards, playing on either side of the center, needed both to protect their own quarterback and to attack the quarterback on the other team (combining the later roles of offensive guard and defensive tackle). They therefore must have a combination of size and quickness ("a heavy man who is not slow," said Camp[18]). Camp's words fit a new student named Paul Lincoln perfectly. Lincoln, a sophomore transfer from Cleveland, was the most athletic big man on campus. Jones made him the right guard. Jones wished that Ed Pedlow was still available to play on the other side. Instead he gave the position of left guard to Hiram Rutan, a freshman from Mechanicsburg.

Next to the guards were the tackles. On offense the tackles were responsible for opening holes in the line for the ball carriers to run through. This play was known as "bucking the line" (an early version of what would later be called an off-tackle play). On defense the tackles tried to down the running backs as they crossed the line of scrimmage. Jones gave these positions to two prep students: Charles Foulk from Warren, Ohio, and Walter Miller from Osage City, Kansas.

Outside the tackles were the ends. The role of an end on offense was to assist the ball carrier with runs around the line. His role on defense was to prevent those runs. He was "the sole guardian of that space between his tackle and the edge of the field."[19] When a ball carrier would try a run around the line, the defensive end would meet his progress and "force the man in."[20] Camp said the primary criterion for choosing an end was finding a man in condition because a player who tires easily cannot be effective in the position.

The prep student Jack Huggins had developed a friendship with a freshman named Arthur Holcombe Kennedy. "Mike" Kennedy was from New Holland, Ohio. Both Huggins and Kennedy were charming and handsome and fashioned themselves as ladies' men. Some coeds described Kennedy as the "handsomest man in college."[21] Others joked that he should be given "a little salt to reduce his freshness."[22] One day Huggins was heard saying, a bit too loudly, "I say, Mike, what is the name of that woman—the other day, you know?"[23] When Huggins tried out for the football team he convinced Kennedy to join him.

To describe Huggins in the *Makio* Jones quoted the English poet Nathaniel Cotton on the topic of vanity: "fantastic, frolicsome, and wild; with all the trinkets of a child."[24] For Kennedy he quoted the Swiss philosopher Johann Georg Zimmermann: "The more you speak of yourself, the more you are likely to lie."[25] Jones was impressed with both, however, as football players. He made them his ends.

Following tradition, the first act of the football team was to elect a captain. For months Jones had been acting as the team's captain as well as de facto coach. It was no surprise when the team officially elected him to the position. "The foot ball team is ardently at work under Captain Jones," the *Lantern* soon reported.[26]

✻

The team also needed to choose a manager. Camp wrote, "As a business requiring a broad grasp of a constantly changing situation, success can only be attained through the vigorous and fearless yet prudent course of the manager."[27] In football the convention was to give those responsibilities to a capable substitute on the team. The substitution rules at the time were the most rigid in the history of football. Any player leaving the field could not return during that game, so substitutes would expect to come into a game only in cases of injury or disqualification. A captain had on-field game responsibilities but the responsibilities of a manager were all off the field, and for that reason a team's manager was usually not an active player.

Ohio State elected as manager the substitute Dick Ellis. Ellis had entered the university as a prep student in the fall but he had advanced into the freshman class after a single term. Ellis's first task as manager was to take up a collection on campus and order the team uniforms. He ordered the same uniforms worn by the baseball team: gray pants with scarlet stockings, gray caps with scarlet horizontal bands, and gray shirts with a scarlet "O S U" across their chests. The purpose of a football uniform was not for protection. Its material was heavy canvas but it included no extra padding (and the football helmet had not yet been invented). The purpose of the football uniform was exactly the same as the purpose of a baseball uniform: to make individual players look and feel like a team.

The football players began to get more attention after their uniforms arrived. The team continued to share practice grounds with the baseball team through the end of the winter term, and as spring break approached, the *State Journal* mentioned both teams in their campus coverage: "The baseball and football teams are getting into fine shape for the coming season and much sport is expected."[28]

Jesse Lee Jones (holding ball) leads the Ohio State football team in the spring of 1890. (Photo courtesy of The Ohio State University Archives)

A manager's most critical responsibility was the scheduling of opponents. By then gridiron football teams existed at Denison, Wooster, Cincinnati, and Miami, but spring was well past football season and none of those teams were available. Buchtel and Kenyon also had football plans but those schools did not intend to form their teams until the fall.[29] Ellis had to find at least one team that would be willing to play a football game in the spring.

He found one at Ohio Wesleyan. While Jones was holding football tryouts at Ohio State, similar events were happening in Delaware. The Wesleyan students still had an ambition of joining the O.I.A.A.[30] and they had finally formed an athletic association in order to become eligible for admission.[31] They also decided to form a football team, assuming that it would strengthen their application.[32]

As a member of Sigma Chi, Ellis had come to know members of the Wesleyan chapter and through those fraternity contacts he learned of the existence of the Wesleyan football team.[33] In mid-April, the *Columbus Daily Press* discovered that "The foot ball team is looking for a game from Delaware."[34] Ellis tracked down the Wesleyan manager, a student named Fred Weaver, to offer Ohio State's challenge. The two managers began negotiations. The Wesleyan faculty had not removed their restrictions on student travel so Weaver insisted that the game be played on Wesleyan grounds. Ellis asked in return that the teams follow the rules specified in Walter Camp's book—neither side could ask for additional concessions. The two managers agreed to these conditions and they set April 19 as the date for their game.

*

Compared to the football team, the manager of Ohio State's baseball team had an easier task that spring. Harry Mitchell had already brought back a full schedule of baseball games from the April meeting of the O.I.A.A. The latest O.S.U. baseball manager was a student named Jack Niewvahner, and Niewvahner needed only to add a pair of games against Capital and another pair against community teams from Columbus. He ended up with the most extensive schedule that any Ohio State team had ever faced.

The spring term was scheduled to begin on April 14 after a two-week break, but the baseball players remained on campus to begin their season on April 12. That first game was against Capital. Kid Martin was sloppy in his debut but he showed potential. Frank Rane showed power from the plate. Ohio State won 16 to 7.

As the game ended the Ohio State fans who had not gone home for spring break gathered around the team to shout the school yell. The Capital students took offense, and that response amused the *Lantern*. "The O.S.U. yell created quite a consternation in the ranks of the East End theologues. May the yell resound in victories!"[35]

The football team returned to campus with the rest of the students on April 14, and they quickly returned to practicing for their April 19 game. On Friday, April 18, Fred Weaver sent a telegram stating that his team was not yet ready and needed a postponement. Weaver and Dick Ellis rescheduled, agreeing to play the game one week later, on April 26.[36]

April 26 was also the date of a scheduled baseball game, against Denison, but before that game the baseball team would play on April 21, against Kenyon. The O.S.U.-Kenyon game opened the O.I.A.A. schedule for both schools. Frank Rane had another strong performance, with three hits and four stolen bases. The rest of the outfield—Ed Pedlow in right field and a sophomore named George Schaeffer in left—was also effective. Ohio State won 14 to 2.

Meanwhile, anticipation for the football game was growing. The *Lantern* noted, "The fellows are in fine shape, and clad in their new uniforms present a fine appearance."[37] The *Journal* observed that the team "will go to Delaware next Saturday in style."[38]

On April 23, Professor Lazenby addressed the students at chapel on the topic of intercollegiate athletics. It was not the first time that Lazenby had used chapel services as a forum to discuss sports, but at this service he specifically addressed Jesse Lee Jones and Samuel Bennett as captains and mentioned their respective upcoming games against Ohio Wesleyan and Denison. Intercollegiate athletic competition was a worthy pursuit, Lazenby said, but it was known to create temptations for "tricky" and "unmanly" behavior. He asked the teams to remember that, when facing other schools, they represent the honor of their university.[39]

Lazenby also put in a word of support for the character of the Ohio Wesleyan students. The *Lantern* wouldn't have it: "We know too much of the Delaware boys ourselves."[40]

✣

The Ohio State faculty required all graduating seniors to write a final thesis on their major area of study. Caesar Morrey was graduating with a major in biology and chose the topic "A Study of the Brain of the Redbird." Jo Jo Large was studying civil engineering and wrote "A Study of the Fifth Avenue Bridge." Jesse Lee Jones combined his study of classical history with his metallurgy major by writing his thesis on "Ancient Arms and Armies."[41]

Chapter Ten

Our boys knew a little more about the game

Jo Jo Large had not been back to Wesleyan since he transferred to Ohio State. He did not hold strong religious convictions and he had never felt comfortable among the constant Wesleyan proclamations of piety. Some of the loudest proclamations came from students who formed a secret underground subculture. They knew the back exits of all the local saloons and had developed a system of warning signals when college officials were approaching.[1] Large was more comfortable at Ohio State where the vices were less colored by hypocrisy.

*

When the football players went to bed on Friday, April 25, they expected to take a trip to Delaware in the morning, but when they woke up on Saturday, April 26, they discovered another delay. Heavy rain had rolled in overnight and the game was a washout.[2] Jesse Lee Jones must have been reminded of the disappointment that he felt on Thanksgiving two and a half years earlier.

Dick Ellis contacted Fred Weaver to reschedule. The following Saturday was May 3 but Weaver said that the date presented a scheduling conflict for Wesleyan. The Wesleyan campus had only one athletic field, and the field was scheduled to be used for a baseball game against Denison that same day. Ellis and Weaver decided that their teams would play the football game at 9 A.M., giving the Wesleyan students time to restore the field before the baseball game that afternoon.

The rain on April 26 also washed out the Ohio State baseball team's scheduled game. Jack Niewvahner contacted William Carr, the Denison manager, to reschedule, but May 3 represented a conflict for both of their teams as well. Denison would be in Delaware playing Ohio Wesleyan that day, while Ohio State would be hosting Capitol. Carr suggested playing the game on Friday, May 2. Niewvahner said that the date might be available if he could convince the O.S.U. faculty to let the players skip their afternoon classes.[3]

With another practice week available, Jesse Lee Jones continued to tinker with his lineup. He decided that the left side of the line was not as strong as he wanted so he switched the positions of Jack Huggins and Charles Foulk, moving left end Huggins to tackle and left tackle Foulk to end. Then he benched the left guard Hiram Rutan and replaced him with Ham Richardson, the former communications secretary on the North Dorm rules committee.[4]

During practice that week, quarterback Ed Martin attempted a tackle, missed his man, fell on his shoulder, and began rolling on the ground in pain. The school infirmary confirmed that Martin had broken his collarbone and would be unavailable for the game.[5] As students spread the news, they consoled each other with the fact that the Ed Martin who was hurt was not Kid Martin, the talented baseball pitcher. Ed Martin, the vice president of the Athletic Association, asked Frank Rane, the Association president, to take his place on the football team. Rane agreed, and he took Martin's football uniform as well.[6] This substitution of the one Association officer for the other seemed to offer a substantial improvement for the team.

Jesse Lee Jones made Rane a halfback to take advantage of his sprinter's speed and he moved Jo Jo Large to the open quarterback spot. To put Large at quarterback instead of halfback was actually a better fit to the guidance of Walter Camp. Camp advised that smaller men should not be made halfbacks no matter how athletic they are. "In such a case, the very best advice that can be whispered in the ear of a coach or captain is to make quarters or ends of them."[7] Camp stated that at halfback a larger man was "better suited to the wear and tear of a season" but granted that at quarterback "a small man can be used to great advantage."[8]

As dusk arrived on the evening of Friday, May 2, injury struck again. Someone had left a piece of broken crockery on the field and Rane, at a practice, running full stride, cut a deep gash into his foot. As this latest news spread that night, some worried about how the injury would affect the baseball season.[9] The football players worried more about how they would play against Wesleyan in the morning. Their train was just a few hours away.

Jones was forced to shuffle his lineup again. He moved right end Mike Kennedy to take over at halfback. He kept Large at quarterback. He then replaced Kennedy at end with the right tackle Walter Miller and replaced Miller at tackle with a substitute named Herbert Johnston.[10]

*

On the morning of May 3 central Ohio awoke to drizzling rain but no one on the campuses of Ohio State or Ohio Wesleyan considered another postponement.[11] At six a.m. the Ohio State players took the horse-drawn streetcar from campus to Union Station downtown. From there they caught a passenger train to Delaware. The train pulled into Delaware Station at six forty-five[12] and the team was on the Ohio Wesleyan campus by seven.

The Ohio State players discovered that the Wesleyan athletic field was a wet and rocky mess. The turf was a layer of mud created by the morning rain, littered throughout with gravel. Then as they met the Wesleyan team they saw that they were outsized at nearly every position. The Wesleyan quarterback, Phil Saylor, would later be a professional athlete, getting a shot in 1891 as a pitcher with the Philadelphia Phillies.[13] Saylor introduced himself to the Ohio State players wearing a sleeveless shirt to show off his intimidating shoulders and biceps. The Ohio State players began girding themselves for a more painful challenge than they originally been expecting.[14]

A large group of Ohio State students had traveled with the team. Even some members of the baseball team found time to catch the morning game. They were soon joined on the Wesleyan campus by an even larger group of Delaware townspeople. Despite the weather, seven hundred people arrived to see the game. Wesleyan still did not have a grandstand and the fans all gathered on the hill overlooking the field. The new Wesleyan athletic association began calculating the money that they would have made if they had thought to charge for admission.[15]

Wesleyan would be playing Denison in baseball that afternoon, and the members of the Denison baseball team were already on the campus. Manager William Carr spotted Jack Niewvahner and approached in a huff. He asked where the O.S.U. baseball team had been the day before, May 2, when they were scheduled to play in Granville. Niewvahner was stunned. He replied that he promised to get back to them only if his faculty agreed to give his players the afternoon off. Denison's manager demanded a forfeit. Niewvahner spit back that Ohio State refused to lose a game over a Denison misunderstanding.[16]

Meanwhile the football managers had a final task to complete before they could start the game. They needed to select game officials: the referee, the umpire, and the timekeeper. The custom of the time was that each school would supply one official and the third would come from a neutral source, agreed upon by both sides. Ed Martin was still recovering from his collarbone injury but he agreed to serve as timekeeper. An Ohio Wesleyan student named Jack Andrews agreed to serve as umpire. The two managers then asked Charles Bosler to serve as referee. Bosler was the captain of the Denison baseball team, a member of the Denison football team, and the president of the O.I.A.A.

The teams took the field a little before nine. Ed Martin called the start of the game at 9:03, and Ohio State took the kickoff. Jesse Lee Jones, as captain, called his team's plays. He knew from reading Walter Camp that the most effective plays to run when facing a larger opponent were bucking the line and running around end.[17] These plays relied on technique as much as bulk and were considered finesse plays relative to the more physical wedge. Jones started the game tentatively, testing for weaknesses on the Wesleyan line.

Under the rules of the era the game would be a ninety-minute test of endurance, divided not into four quarters but into two forty-five-minute halves. Teams had to move the ball only five yards for a first down. (Ten yards for a first down would arrive in 1906 along with the legalization of the forward pass.[18]) To score, teams had to move the ball down a 110-yard field. (The modern sixty-minute game and 100-yard field were both established in 1912.[19])

When Wesleyan took possession of the ball they used a similarly tentative approach. They did not use the wedge either. The wedge was a "mass momentum" play, and the most brutal play in the history of football. Within a few years it would be banned. It began with a team's players all positioned several yards behind the line of scrimmage, and at the snap the linemen would lock arms, form a V-shape around the ball carrier as protection, and charge. In theory, the wedge was a surgical scalpel that carved through the opposing defensive line.[20] In practice, it was a hammer that pounded the other team. Walter Camp advised that using the wedge was an effective strategy when facing a smaller team, but Wesleyan did not seem aware of how to exploit their size advantage.

After a few changes of possession Ohio State found their first opportunity to score. Jo Jo Large, at quarterback, pitched the ball back to a teammate who then pitched it to another. After a series of such laterals the ball ended up back in Large's hands. By then a hole had opened in front of him and he rushed downfield, crossed the goal line, and touched the ball to the ground. His touchdown was worth four points.

Large then attempted the goal-after-touchdown to add two more points. By rule the extra-points try began from the spot on the goal line where the touchdown had been scored. From that mark a player would punt the ball to a team-mate who would try to drop kick it through the goal post. Large made the kick, and Ohio State took a 6 to 0 lead.

Wesleyan attempted to respond and seemed to have an opportunity on their next possession. Their fastest back broke through Ohio State's defensive line into open field. Caesar Morrey took off after him. By his own admission, Morrey then "jumped on his back and he came down hard."[21] The Wesleyan captain called for a "foul tackle." In earlier versions of football Morrey would have faced ejection for the play, but Jesse Lee Jones grabbed his copy of the Walter Camp rulebook and hurried over to the officials. Morrey's tackle was rough but Jones knew that there was no rule in the book against it. A foul tackle was specifically defined as a tackle around the neck or below the knee. Umpire Jack Andrews, the Wesleyan official, had final authority over the ruling but Jones successfully argued his case.

A few minutes later Ohio State had possession of the ball again. They drove down the field with ease and Morrey soon crossed the goal line for another O.S.U. touchdown. Large missed the extra-points try and the score was 10 to 0. Under the rules of football followed at that time, a team that scored a touchdown maintained possession of the ball, and the Ohio State team continued to move the ball with ease on the following drive. The Ohio State left end Charles Foulk soon appeared to score but this play brought a new protest. Foulk had crossed the goal line at a corner of the field, running out of bounds immediately afterward. He did not touch the ball to the ground beyond the line before leaving the field of play and the Wesleyan captain argued that the touchdown should not count.

The players rested as the two captains again huddled with the officials around the Walter Camp rulebook. Morrey was discovering that he had a talent for football—he was falling in love with the sport—but even he appreciated these repeated opportunities to catch a breather. Each captain presented his case. The rules as written were ambiguous, with inconsistencies appearing due to the quick evolution of the sport. One page in the book clearly stated, "A touch-down is obtained by touching the ball to the ground behind the line of the goal."[22] Foulk had not had a chance to touch the ball to the ground in the end zone before his momentum carried him out of bounds. Four pages later, however, the rules specified, "A touch-down is made when the ball is carried, kicked, or passed across the goal line and there held."[23] Jones argued that Foulk had clear possession of the ball while crossing the goal line.

Charles Bosler, as referee, was in charge of this ruling and he agreed with Jones. The *Lantern* later bragged that "our boys knew a little more about the game."[24] Jones made a mental note to thank Professor Queen in the *Makio* for his contributions to the university.[25] The Wesleyan fans were convinced that Ohio State must have played football before. The angle made the try for extra points difficult and Large missed again. The score was 14 to 0.

Ohio State appeared to have the game under control. Watching it from the nearby hill, C.E. Brown, the manager of Wesleyan's baseball team, approached Jack Niewvahner to discuss scheduling a game. Niewvahner was in such a good mood over the football game that he decided to drop the Ohio State boycott of the Wesleyan baseball team. He agreed to bring his team back to Delaware and they set a date for May 24.

As the football game approached the end of the first half, Wesleyan finally attempted a wedge. They picked up good yardage from the play, so they ran it again. And then again. Steadily they moved the ball downfield. Phil Saylor scored a touchdown just as the half ended. Wesleyan began to realize how they should have been exploiting their size advantage. Saylor made the kick and the teams rested through halftime with the score 14 to 6. The Wesleyan players paced like a tiger in a cage throughout the ten-minute break.

The rain had cleared and the sun was shining by the start of the second half. On the Wesleyan side of the field the mood matched the weather. Using the wedge exclusively Wesleyan began pushing Ohio State's defense down the field. Soon Wesleyan scored another touchdown. Saylor missed the kick and the score was 14 to 10. Play in the game grew increasingly physical. Tempers flared. Both teams began to be bothered by the rocky surface of the field. Phil Saylor's bare shoulders were shredded. Not long afterward, Ohio State end Walter Miller suffered the only serious injury of the game and Jesse Lee Jones replaced him with Hiram Rutan. Wesleyan scored for a third time with ten minutes left in the game. Saylor again missed the kick and the score was tied at 14.

The situation appeared grim but Caesar Morrey then delivered the most impressive individual effort of the game. Jo Jo Large tossed Morrey the ball and Morrey found a crack in the defensive line. He broke into open field and weaved through the defensive backs. As he worked his way down the field, the Ohio State fans stood. When he crossed the goal line, they roared.

But no one signaled the touchdown. Umpire Jack Andrews rushed downfield and claimed that Morrey had stepped out of bounds before crossing the line. Andrews marked the ball four feet out.

It was first-and-goal and Jesse Lee Jones had to reassess his strategy. Walter Camp recommended against trying finesse plays when facing a larger team at the goal line. With such a small field to protect, all the defenders would be stacked close to the line. An attempt to run around end would be too slow in developing and the ball carrier would be stuffed. An attempt to buck the line was likely to end with the ball carrier downed by the time he reached his tackle. Jones called for the wedge.

Guard Paul Lincoln was the only player on the Ohio State line whose bulk matched those on the Wesleyan side, so Jones set his wedge with Lincoln at the apex. Halfback Mike Kennedy carried the ball. On first down Lincoln pushed the wedge one yard and Kennedy was stopped short of the goal line. On second down Jones called for the exact same play. This time Lincoln inched over the goal line and Kennedy squeezed in for the touchdown. Jo Jo Large successfully made the kick, giving Ohio State two more points as insurance. The score was 20 to 14.

Four minutes were left to play in the game. Wesleyan went back on offense and began slowly grinding downfield. From the hill the other Ohio State students watched nervously as the outcome of the game again became in doubt. This time, however, it was the Ohio State team playing with renewed motivation. As time slipped away the defense held its ground, and the O.S.U. fans on the hill counted the seconds down.

Ed Martin called the end of the game and the Ohio State players jumped in celebration. The fans rushed down to the field to join the team. The Wesleyan fans looked on in disgust as the visitors shouted what the *Practical Student* called "the awful O.S.U. yell."[26]

✻

Two of the four Columbus daily newspapers covered the game. Neither covered it on their sports pages, next to the professional baseball games, boxing matches, and horse racing results. They covered it as a local curiosity. The *Columbus Daily Press* gave a brief summary that evening:

The foot ball game between the O. S. U. and O. W. U. college teams this morning was won by the O. S. U. team. Score 20 to 14. The game was called at 9 a. m. and was witnessed by a large crowd. No incidents.[27]

A report in the *State Journal* the next morning was even briefer: "DELAWARE, O., May 4. -- State university foot-ball team played the college team here Saturday, with a score of 14 to 20 in favor of the Columbus boys."[28] Neither the *Dispatch* nor the *Columbus Post* covered the game at all.

Coverage was heavier in Delaware. In the *Delaware Gazette* a four-paragraph article praised the Wesleyan team's effort and concluded with an observation that they had missed an opportunity: "Had our boys worked a little harder and displayed a little more head work in the first half of the game, there is reason to believe that the result would have been different."[29]

The Wesleyan campus newspaper, the *Practical Student*, had similarly rueful tone. Their coverage expressed an opinion that was beginning to be echoed across their campus:

> We would have won the game had our boys been as familiar with the rules as were the visitors, who have been playing the game. The visitors surpassed our boys in team work, but in individual rushing and running with the ball our boys played all around them.[30]

The coverage of the game was heaviest in the *Lantern*. It filled two full pages in the next issue, more than twice as long as the coverage of the baseball game—against Capital—played that same day. On the front page Carl Doney published an editorial to declare "This is a great year for athletics and enthusiasm at the University."[31] He celebrated the promise of a bright new future for the school, saying that "the foot-ball team is on top" and would soon silence the "harsh things" that Ohio State had come to expect from the students at other schools.[32]

*

Fred Weaver, the Wesleyan football manager, challenged Ohio State to a rematch.[33] Dick Ellis responded that he could accept only if the game were played in Columbus. For several days the Wesleyan students begged their faculty for permission to leave campus, but the Wesleyan faculty still refused.[34] Ohio State declined the challenge.

Dick Ellis attempted to schedule another opponent that spring but no other football teams were available. Charles Bosler suggested a possible game against his team, but bad feelings still lingered between Denison and Ohio State over the baseball misunderstanding from May 2, and nothing came of it. With no one available to play, Ohio State finished its first, abbreviated football season with a perfect 1–0 record.

*

The Ohio State baseball team finished their season with an 11–3 record. The "Kid battery," as Kid Martin and Kid Pearce were called, was on its way to becoming a campus legend.[35] The highlight of the season was a very satisfying victory over Wooster on June 6, and Ohio State finished in second place, behind Denison, in the O.I.A.A. standings.

The low point of the season was a loss to Ohio Wesleyan on May 24. After the game Harry Mitchell pulled aside Phil Saylor for a chat. He said that if Saylor hoped to compete in the O.I.A.A. in any sport his best chance would be to transfer to Ohio State.[36]

*

The injury that had forced Frank Rane to miss the football game also forced him to miss the campus field day just two weeks afterward. With Rane sidelined, Hobart Beatty, the prep student from the baseball second team, dominated the campus track events. Beatty was a son of General John Beatty and the youngest brother of William Beatty, the school's previous record-holder in the 100-yard dash. Hobart Beatty set new Ohio State records in the 50-yard dash, the 100-yard dash, and the 220-yard run.[37]

The inaugural O.I.A.A. Field Day was held the week after the Ohio State field day. The Athletic Association selected Ohio State's representatives and for many of the track events Rane, the president of the Association, represented the university. The Association selected him despite the fact that his foot was still healing and despite the fact that Beatty had surpassed his best times. At the contest Rane won state titles in the 100-yard dash and the hurdles.[38] The *Lantern* lamented, "Had Rane been in proper trim there is no telling what 'might have been'."[39] Both sprinters, Rane and Beatty, planned to play on the football team in the coming fall.

The O.I.A.A. also held its first tennis tournament in June. As expected, the Ohio State team dominated. Harry Mitchell, with his partner Robert Morrison, won in doubles play.[40]

✻

The *Makio* was released in June and Jesse Lee Jones opened the 1890 edition with an editorial. As if making a valedictory address, he looked back on the school year and ahead to the university's future. He boasted that college spirit had grown that year and went on to say that if college spirit continued to grow, it would lead to growth in the university itself, "for as an advertising medium nothing can equal an enthusiastic student."[41] The price for the growth of the university, Jones concluded, was for the administration to show more support for campus sports.[42]

Part Three

There is no reason why we should not have the best eleven in the state

Chapter Eleven

The indomitable Jack and the inevitable Mike

I n the twenty-first century, when two Ohio State football fans meet, the first might identify himself by shouting "O-H!" The second will respond "I-O!" The ritual began as a stadium chant and has since become a personal greeting. The greeting gives fans a sense of community and a way to show how far that community has spread.

In 1890 an Ohio State professor of paleontology was away on a dig when a group of young men approached his pit. From several yards away they shouted, "Wahoo Wahoo, Rip Zip Bazoo…" The professor stared back blankly while the men finished the Ohio State yell. When he got back to campus he asked his students what it meant, and as he told the story the room shook from the cheers and laughter.[1]

*

As the fall term began in 1890, football remained the story of the year. The new university catalog already mentioned the football team as a focus of student interest. New fans included George Schaeffer and Herbert Scott. Schaeffer was a standout left fielder on the baseball team, and he also worked as a clerk in the office of William Henry Scott, the university president. Herbert Scott was the president's son.

In his annual report to the trustees that fall, President Scott observed that the football team had aroused a "new and unprecedented interest in athletics,"[2] but he added that he had some concerns. He noted that football games are particularly violent, and that "it is apparently impossible to play them without more or less neglect of regular duties, not only for the time when they are played, but during the period of training for them."[3] He said that the example offered by Eastern colleges suggested that "some limits should be proscribed."[4]

On the other hand, President Scott offered a personal observation that college sports inspire loyalty among the students. "Some of the most loyal and earnest are members of the various teams, and others are zealous friends and supporters."[5] He concluded that, despite "the evils that already exist" as well as "those that seem likely to arise," the faculty "had adopted no plan for regulating these games."[6]

*

When the football team reassembled in September only four players from the May game were missing. Quarterback Jo Jo Large and center Jesse Lee Jones had both graduated. Fullback Dave Hegler had finished his two-year agricultural program and lineman Walter Miller had been a prep student who did not move on to the college. Everyone else was back on campus and eager to get back on the field.

Halfback Caesar Morrey had graduated but he remained on campus for postgraduate studies in the biology program. The faculty even gave him financial support—a job teaching Greek and Latin to the prep students. From just the one game in the spring football had gotten into Morrey's blood, but due to his new academic responsibilities he was available only part-time for football. Still, he hoped to be part of the team.

Halfback Frank Rane and quarterback Ed Martin had both missed the May game with injuries but both made a point of returning to the team that fall. The two also remained the leaders of the campus Athletic Association. The O.I.A.A. had scheduled a meeting to be held at Kenyon College in early October, so Rane called a meeting of the campus Association to select Ohio State's representative. The work to be done at the O.I.A.A. meeting would include negotiating each school's football schedule, a task traditionally performed by the teams' managers, so Rane and Martin decided to give their meeting representative the title "football manager." Martin took that assignment for himself.[7]

A few days later the team elected Caesar Morrey to be their manager.[8] They were, in effect, overruling the Athletic Association's selection. The Association still did not provide financial support to its teams so the football players saw no reason to give up their right to select their own leaders. Their election of Morrey was a direct challenge to the authority of the Association but the football team got away with it because, between the two organizations, the campus held the team in higher regard. The result was that Martin represented Ohio State at the O.I.A.A. meeting but Morrey was the manager.

The team elected Paul Lincoln to be their new captain. Lincoln was a big man who was popular, friendly, and easy-going. He had played particularly well in the Wesleyan game. At the most recent campus field day he had competed in the hammer throw and shot put. His father, an immigrant from England, had instilled the idea that education was the path to success in America. As a freshman Lincoln had attended Adelbert College in Cleveland, but he transferred to Ohio State before his sophomore year to study electrical engineering. He was also a member of the Horton Literary Society and at the first Horton meeting in the new fall he gave a speech in praise of football.[9]

The residents of the North Dorm elected Lincoln to be Dorm president as well. A classmate later reminisced, "The 'Big Dorm' was governed entirely by the boys. Some husky upper classman, with enough muscle to bluff the freshmen and enough character to control the others, was elected President. 'Jumbo' Hedges, Jesse Jones, Paul Lincoln, and E. B. Pedlow were typical occupants of that office."[10]

The responsibilities of a manager included recruiting new athletes to the team, and Caesar Morrey was able to gather a promising collection. George Schaeffer came from the baseball team. Horace Whitacre came from the tennis team. James Hine and Walter Landacre were both campus field day champions: Hine in the standing broad jump and Landacre in the pole vault and high kick. Of all these recruits the most exciting was the speedy track athlete Hobart Beatty. The football team that had won its only game in the spring was beginning to be thought of as unbeatable.

The responsibilities of a captain included selecting a starting lineup. Paul Lincoln built his backfield around Beatty and Frank Rane. The two champion sprinters seemed likely to be the fastest halfback duo in the state. Lincoln then placed the pole vault champion Walter Landacre at fullback. Landacre was another good runner and an excellent tackler. The weakest link in the backfield was Ed Martin returning at quarterback, but Lincoln counted on Martin to be adequate with so much talent surrounding him.

On the line Lincoln mixed three newcomers with four veterans. George Schaeffer and James Hine both made the starting lineup—Schaeffer at right end and Hine at left guard. Dick Ellis, the manager of the spring team, earned a position at right tackle. To complete the line Lincoln moved left guard Hamilton "Ham" Richardson to left tackle, left tackle John "Jack" Huggins to right guard, and halfback Arthur "Mike" Kennedy to left end. Lincoln followed the example of Jesse Lee Jones by making himself the center.

Some fans focused most of their attention on the charismatic Huggins and Kennedy. The first issue of the *Lantern* of the new school year offered a guarantee: "Our foot ball team, with the indomitable 'Jack' and the inevitable 'Mike' at the head, will, without a doubt, prosper."[11]

*

George Cole was not talented enough to earn a position in the lineup, and he felt left out after the Wesleyan game when no one recognized his contributions to forming the team. He tried helping at the team's practices but he quickly grew dissatisfied there. Playing on the practice squad felt like being a piece of equipment, meant only to be knocked around the field. The practice players did not even get uniforms. Cole wore painter's overalls, padded with blanket scraps for protection.[12] Cole soon decided that his connection to the team was too significant to simply be a tackling dummy. He then came upon another idea.

Cole had a friend with college football experience named Alexander Spinning Lilley.[13] Lilley was the son of Mitchell Campbell Lilley, a prosperous central Ohio merchant. The M.C. Lilley Company was one of the country's leading providers of ceremonial goods: military swords, Masonic accessories, replica Civil War uniforms, and so on.[14] The company also regularly advertised in the *Lantern*, selling fraternity regalia and graduation robes.[15]

When Al Lilley turned fifteen in 1885 his parents decided that he needed to attend a prestigious Eastern prep school. His choice was the Lawrenceville School, a feeder school for Princeton in New Jersey. A boy named Knowlton Ames, from Chicago, was already a student there, and the Lilley and Ames families had long-standing business and social ties. The Lilleys arranged for Knowlton Ames to write a letter of recommendation for their son. In his letter Ames mistakenly referred to Lilley as "Albert"[16] but his error did not cause a problem. Lilley was admitted to the school, and the next year the two boys became roommates. They also became close friends.

Ames was a gifted halfback on the Lawrenceville football team and when he moved on to Princeton in 1886 he became a sensation. In four years at Princeton he scored sixty-two touchdowns (a total not exceeded in college football for another hundred years). He also was an accurate kicker, and through a combination of touchdowns, field goals, and goals-after-touchdown he scored 730 career points—a point total that has never been matched. Along the way he picked up the nickname "Snake" for his elusive open-field running. Caspar Whitney of *Harper's Magazine* named an "All America team" in 1889, the first list of its kind, and Snake Ames easily made the lineup. Ames would be posthumously inducted into the College Football Hall of Fame in 1969.[17]

In 1888 Al Lilley followed Ames to Princeton. He also followed Ames into football, although not with the same success. Lilley was the quarterback on the Princeton freshman team and as a sophomore he became a substitute fullback for the Princeton varsity team.

In June of 1890, following his sophomore year, Lilley returned to Columbus for his summer break. While home a local coal company offered him an executive position. The company was partially owned by Miner T. Ames, a Chicago oil magnate and Snake Ames' father. Lilley accepted the position, and in October 1890 he sent a notice of withdrawal to Princeton.[18]

George Cole had been a friend of Lilley when they were children, and when Cole learned that Lilley would not be returning to Princeton he went downtown to ask his old friend if he would coach the Ohio State football team. Lilley was flattered by the offer and immediately agreed. Cole then went back to campus to tell the team that he found them a coach with Eastern football experience.

✳

On October 4 Ed Martin and the other O.I.A.A. representatives met at Kenyon. Various items were on the agenda. First, they standardized a ball. Each team would use the "lily-white #5," a 27-inch circumference rugby ball. Second, they clarified the obligations of each team in staging games. Home teams would provide the referees and visiting teams would provide the umpires. Visiting teams would pay their own travel costs but the home teams would host their visitors with a meal and a place to sleep.[19] These obligations were adapted from the traditions of intercollegiate baseball.

Finally, the representatives needed to respond to a crisis in scheduling. Buchtel College had recently announced that they did not intend to play football. They had lost money playing an O.I.A.A. baseball schedule in the spring and said that they could not afford to field a football team that fall. The O.I.A.A. wanted to give each team a balanced schedule, with two home games and two away games, but Buchtel's decision put a snag in the plan. With just three opponents available per team, the only way to balance the schedule was for each team to face one other team twice. Ohio State and Wooster were scheduled to play each other twice, as were Denison and Kenyon.[20]

Wooster was a daunting opponent. During the 1889 season they were the most dominant team in the state, playing two games, scoring 98 points and giving up none. On September 20 the Wooster student newspaper, the *Voice*, had written, "There is more real live interest in foot ball here in Wooster than in any other college in Ohio."[21] Kinley McMillan was no longer coaching the Wooster team. He had left that March to take the position of pastor at Baltimore's Central Presbyterian Church.[22] The football team that he left behind, however, remained the most knowledgeable and best trained in the state. The *Wooster Voice* wrote, "It means something to be on the foot ball team this year. It means a great deal. It means a regular old-fashioned plum pudding."[23]

Thanksgiving would be on November 27. Ohio State scheduled their Thanksgiving game against Kenyon. Denison had hoped to play Wooster on that day but Wooster had other plans. The Wooster representative said that he could not schedule a Thanksgiving game within the O.I.A.A. because they were negotiating a game with Washington & Jefferson College, a school in Pittsburgh.

Martin brought the O.I.A.A. schedule back from the meeting, and the *Lantern* published it with a warning that fans might need to curb their expectations: "It was found necessary for the O. S. U. to play two games with Wooster (which is by far the strongest team) and we may congratulate ourselves if we break even."[24]

*

As manager, Caesar Morrey had other issues to deal with before the start of the season. Paul Lincoln complained that team practices were useless without bodies to practice against. Students had been eager to try out for the varsity team but, like George Cole, most were uninterested in the less glamorous role of joining a practice squad. The team also needed money to cover the season's travel expenses. Morrey did not seem to look forward to begging for donations door to door.

Morrey arranged to address these needs with a plea in the *Lantern*. He stated, "Every student who is at all foot ball-wards inclined is urgently requested to come every evening to help the team practice."[25] Students who were not able to assist on the field were offered another way to support the team: "The team will need money to make its trips to Wooster and Denison."[26] The plea for support concluded with an appeal to school pride: "Football is an experiment at the

O. S. U., but with proper encouragement financially and otherwise, there is no reason why we should not have the best eleven in the state."[27]

Among the students who answered the call to help in practice were Herbert Scott and a sophomore named Fred Patterson. Scott was the son of the university president, and Patterson was the son of a former slave. President Scott had named his son after the Social Darwinist Herbert Spencer. Charles Patterson had named his son after the abolitionist Frederick Douglass.

Frederick Douglas Patterson was one of only three African Americans attending Ohio State that year. His father had run away from a Virginia plantation where he had been trained as a blacksmith. As a free man he started a carriage company that he built into the most successful business in the town of Greenfield, Ohio.[28] Fred Patterson left Greenfield and his father's buggy company to prove himself on his own. He took a job as a train porter, which took him to Columbus, and there he enrolled at the university in the fall of 1889.

Even with these new additions to the practice squad, Morrey remained a few players short of forming an eleven-man second team. The tennis player Horace Whitacre also showed up for the practices, as did students named Arthur Bronson, Pearl Griffith, and Raymond Krumm. Rounding out the practice squad were veterans from the spring team: Charles Foulk, Herbert Johnston, and Hiram Rutan.[29]

*

Starting in mid-October Al Lilley began stopping by the Ohio State practice field. He would be spotted some afternoons and evenings riding a pony the three miles to campus from his home downtown. On October 17 the *Lantern* announced, "An ex-quarter back from Princeton is coaching the foot-ball team."[30] The *State Journal* printed a similar notice a few days later.

Lilley tried to give the Ohio State players the benefit of his experience, but having a coach did not reduce the leadership role of a team's captain. A coach, by rule, could not provide direct leadership during games. All in-game decisions, including calling plays, were the responsibility of the captain. If a coach were to come to a game he might use discreet hand signals to make suggestions, but if a referee caught him it would mean a penalty.

Snake Ames happened to be in Columbus one day that fall and Lilley suggested that he come along to campus as his assistant. Ames tried to teach the Ohio State players proper kicking technique. "I can still hear the crack of his kick!"[31] wrote Cole years later. In 1891 Ames would become the football coach at Purdue University.[32]

Lilley's more frequent assistant at practices was his younger brother Mitchell Lilley, Jr. "Mit" Lilley had graduated from Lawrenceville the previous spring and had not yet begun his own college career. Al Lilley was 20 years old, younger than many of the Ohio State upperclassmen, and Mit was only 18. Some of the newer members of the team seemed to appreciate the Lilleys' coaching but the team veterans were less enthusiastic. Caesar Morrey was particularly unimpressed, later claiming that he did not even remember whether Al or Mit had been the coach that year.[33]

Lilley patterned his approach to coaching on Walter Camp. A few years earlier Camp had become the coach at Yale, where he occasionally watched the team practice. Afterward Camp would talk to his players informally, giving them a few pointers based on what he had seen.

Chapter Twelve

It is an honor to be a player in the Ohio State University foot ball team

The hopes of the Ohio State campus were high entering the school's first full football season, and it seemed especially appropriate that the first game of the season would be against Wooster after the seemingly unprovoked attack the previous spring by the *Wooster Collegian*. Wooster had a strong team but even in the face of such a test the excitement over Ohio State's own team felt earned. The game was scheduled for November 1, and fans had the date circled on the calendar. They wanted to see the "theologues" upset by the state's flagship school.

✻

Before the football season could start, the Ohio State baseball team played three fall games—two against Capital and one against Ohio Wesleyan. They swept all three. The Wesleyan game, on October 4, started late due to rain and by the end of the fifth inning the evening sky was turning dark. Wesleyan was winning 11 to 10 and their manager argued that the game should be called. The umpire disagreed, saying that they could play one more inning. After six innings Ohio State was winning 12 to 11. Wesleyan then wanted to play on. The umpire disagreed again and declared Ohio State the winner. Wesleyan protested the game.[1]

The football team at Wesleyan was also looking for a game, and their manager sent a message through the *Lantern* challenging Ohio State.[2] He made clear that his team had a continuing interest in scheduling a rematch. Caesar Morrey looked into the challenge but found no change in the policy of the Wesleyan faculty. Any game would still have to be played in Delaware.[3] Morrey rejected those terms.

Morrey did accept a challenge from an organization named the Dayton Athletic Club. He wanted the team to have a tune-up before the Wooster game on November 1. The Dayton A.C. was the team formerly known as the Stillwater Canoe and Athletic Club. They had members from Yale, Princeton, Dartmouth, Michigan, Stevens, and, most recently, Charles Bosler from Denison. The Stillwater club had not received many responses when they sent their open challenge to the *Columbus Daily Press*, so after the game on May 3 between Ohio State and Wesleyan, the renamed Dayton club challenged those two schools directly.

The Dayton club scheduled a game with Wesleyan that they played on October 11. Dayton dominated, scoring seven touchdowns, two goals-after-touchdown, and one safety. The final score was 38 to 6. After the game the Wesleyan students invited the Dayton players to dinner, and after dinner the guests began singing for their hosts. Some Wesleyan students joined in, but others thought that the Dayton songs were much too coarse and vulgar for their campus. The *Transcript* commented, "Instead of indulging in a legitimate serenade as was expected of them they sang songs by no means fit for the ears of ladies and in other ways acted in a manner ill becoming gentlemen."[4]

✻

Two weeks later, on October 25, was a game between Dayton and Ohio State. The Dayton club rented a playing field at their local fairgrounds. In advertisements they positioned their team as underdogs, the selling point being that a local Dayton team was taking on a celebrated opponent. The Dayton team was waiting at the station when the train carrying the Ohio State players arrived. They treated their guests to lunch and gave them a comfortable place to change into their uniforms. At two fifteen the teams travelled to the field. Two hundred paying spectators filled the fairgrounds grandstand.

The game began at three fifteen. Ohio State won the coin toss and took the ball, beginning their first drive at midfield. Halfback Hobart Beatty started the game with a rush attempt and was tackled as soon as he hit the line. Three more attempts failed to move a single yard and Ohio State turned the ball over on downs. Dayton carried the ball twenty yards on their first play. Then they picked up another ten yards, and then added fifteen more. The game was just starting and it already appeared to be getting out of hand.

The Dayton players were surprisingly large but Lincoln reminded his rattled men that they had beaten a larger opponent before. End Mike Kennedy and full-back Walter Landacre both began making plays. The inspired Ohio State defense stiffened and Dayton also turned the ball over on downs.

On their next drive Ohio State again failed to move the ball and this time they punted. The Dayton return man dropped the ball but immediately recovered his own fumble. Dayton's ensuing drive stalled at Ohio State's 25-yard line and their kicker attempted a field goal. He missed, but a missed field goal was a live ball and Dayton recovered it for a touchdown. The goal-after-touchdown was successful and Dayton led by a score of 6 to 0. Dayton was playing sloppily but they were too well trained to let Ohio State take advantage.

Dayton wore Ohio State down through the rest of the first half. The game soon became a rout. A Dayton field goal, worth five points, made the score 11 to 0. Then another field goal made it 16 to 0. Minutes later Dayton scored another touchdown and goal-after-touchdown to push the score to 22 to 0. Then Walter Landacre fumbled and Frank Rane recovered the ball behind the Ohio State goal line, giving Dayton a safety and a 24 to 0 lead. After another failed drive Landacre shanked a punt and Dayton recovered the ball for a fifth touchdown. The score at halftime stood at 28 to 0.

Manager Caesar Morrey, watching from the sidelines, wished that he was in the game. He got a chance early in the second half when Hobart Beatty took a blow to the hip and had to be helped off the field. Lincoln sent Morrey in to replace him.

The second half was little better for Ohio State. Dayton scored four more touchdowns and made three of the four goals-after-touchdown. Ohio State punted near the end of the game. A punt in those days was a live ball and tackle Dick Ellis fought for it, successfully recovering the ball on Dayton's ten-yard line. He then also had to be helped off the field. It was the only time in the game that Ohio State had possession of the ball in Dayton territory but they were still unable to punch it in. The final score was Dayton A.C. 50, Ohio State 0.

Coverage in the *Dayton Herald* followed the theme that the Dayton A.C. had established in advertisements before the game. The paper stated that Ohio State was "generally regarded as one of the best elevens in the State" and credited Dayton's success to "hard practice" and "faultless play."[5] Coverage in the *Dayton Journal* was more realistic. It praised the "plucky" Ohio State players, but noted that their inexperience hurt them.[6]

The Ohio State players chalked the loss up as a learning experience, consoling their pride by considering the superior training on the Dayton side. The *State Journal* observed, "The Dayton club is made up of college graduates from the Eastern colleges, and they literally wiped the ground with the Columbus men."[7] The *Lantern*'s coverage was brief. It read, in full:

> Our football team went over to play the Yale-Princeton-Ann Arbor etc. team of Dayton. Our boys were knocked down and tramped all over by their huge and experienced opponent, to the tune of 50–0. It is better for such a defeat to come early in the season, however, for then all is to gain and not much is to lose.[8]

With a brave front after the game some Ohio State players suggested a rematch but Caesar Morrey got his team out of town without seriously pursuing the idea.[9] The start of the O.I.A.A. season was just a week away.

*

Joe Firestone had been watching as the Dayton A.C. scheduled their games. The team that Firestone led with S.P. Bush, the Columbus Foot Ball Club, decided to follow the Dayton team's lead by sending challenges to both Ohio State and Ohio Wesleyan. They also sent a challenge to Dayton.

Similarly following the lead of the Dayton team, Firestone and S.P. Bush now called their team the "Columbus Athletic Club."

*

Paul Lincoln needed to make adjustments to his lineup before the game against Wooster, particularly in his backfield. Hobart Beatty was injured so Lincoln moved George Schaeffer from end to take over at halfback. In addition, Frank Rane had been disappointing in the Dayton game, especially given how much had been expected from him. Lincoln was beginning to realize that track speed did not necessarily translate onto the football field. Fullback Walter Landacre was excellent defensively but his failures in punting the ball were unacceptable. Lincoln switched Landacre to halfback and Rane to fullback. Rane did not complain publicly but he began to question his own interest in staying with the team.

Lincoln also wanted to make a change at quarterback. He decided that the team could no longer afford Ed Martin at the position. He gave the job to Charles Foulk. Foulk, a member of the practice squad, had been working hard to get back into the lineup, and Lincoln appreciated the effort that he had seen from Foulk in practices.

Finally, Lincoln rushed to make adjustments on the line. With George Schaeffer at halfback, Lincoln needed to put someone at end. He slid Jack Huggins down the line and then added Horace Whitacre, the tennis player, to fill the open spot at guard. At tackle, a substitute named Pearl Griffith had entered the Dayton game after the injury to Dick Ellis. Ellis was unable to return for the Wooster game and Lincoln decided to stick with Griffith.

*

Caesar Morrey also had preparations to make before the Wooster game. The most pressing item on his list was finding a place to play. The job of finding a suitable field belonged to the home team's manager. The North Dorm field that the team used for practice was considered inadequate for intercollegiate competition. It was a bit lower at one end, always giving one team the advantage of running downhill. It also did not have a grandstand and Morrey did not want to repeat Ohio Wesleyan's mistake of not charging for admission.

The solution that Morrey chose was to play the game at Recreation Park in downtown Columbus. This plan was risky. Ohio State sports had been set back for years when the baseball team rented Recreation Park in 1884. That baseball game had coincidentally also been against Wooster. Morrey had confidence in his plan because of the attendance at the games in Delaware and Dayton, not to mention the record attendance at recent games in the East. Football crowds seemed to be much larger than the crowds that typically turned out for college baseball games.

Under O.I.A.A. rules, the home team's manager also had the job of finding a referee for the game. Morrey would be forced to fill the position himself if no one else offered. Team managers regularly served as game officials. Everyone recognized the potential for a conflict of interest but, given their limited finances, teams often had no other choice.

Morrey was trying to avoid that responsibility because it would destroy his chance to appear in the game as a player. After the Dayton game the Dayton players had singled out his performance for praise. At Kenyon College the best football player was a chemistry professor named Charles Brusie. Professor Brusie served as a game official for the Kenyon College games but he also participated as a member of the Kenyon Military Academy football team. Morrey believed that he deserved to fill a similar role at Ohio State.

The team still needed bodies to practice against but a solution to that problem arrived with the return of Joe Firestone. When the Columbus Athletic

Club sent a challenge, Morrey declined because he did not want to see his players repeat their Dayton experience. Firestone then proposed a scrimmage between his team and Ohio State, arguing that it would satisfy a mutual need for practice. Morrey agreed, and the teams arranged to meet on the O.S.U. practice field.

The scrimmage also turned out to be valuable for social networking. Morrey recruited the services of the Columbus quarterback, Dick Jones, to referee the Wooster game. Firestone and Bush meanwhile recruited Mike Kennedy to referee the game that they had scheduled with Wesleyan. Firestone and Bush were also looking for new athletic talent and when they learned where Ohio State coach Al Lilley had played college football they invited him to join their team. Lilley then secured an invitation for his brother Mit.

*

The Columbus daily newspapers began promoting Ohio State's upcoming game. On the Wednesday of that week the *Dispatch* promised, "Our boys will use every endeavor to win, and a splendid contest may be expected."[10] On Friday the *Post* chimed in, "The contest will be an exciting one and those attending may promise themselves a good time."[11] On Saturday morning the *Daily Press* mentioned that a game would be played later that day and observed that football "seems to be the most popular sport among Ohio colleges this year."[12] None of these articles mentioned the opponent that Ohio State would be facing.

The *Wooster Voice* wrote that week, "The Foot Ball team will play their first Inter-Collegiate game this year with the O. S. U. at Columbus, November 1st. The practice of the past week proves that Wooster has a stronger team than she had a year ago."[13] The Wooster players were confidently awaiting the game.

The Ohio State players met their guests at the Columbus train station on October 31. The Wooster right tackle was surprisingly large but the other players on the team were not as big as those from the Dayton Athletic Club. The Wooster players bunked that night at the North Dorm. The campus was filled with excitement over the game the next day. It was Halloween night and loud holiday revelry kept the Wooster players awake.

The next morning the Ohio State players escorted their guests on the streetcar down to Recreation Park. Many other Ohio State students, still celebrating, also tagged along. Residents of the city showed up at the Park by the hundreds, curious to see students from the local university play the new sport. The price of admission was twenty-five cents, and with five hundred people in attendance the team easily recovered its investment.

Despite raw, cold weather, the atmosphere surrounding the game was festive. Three of the city's newspapers covered the game and two noted a surprising number of women in the grandstand.[14] Frank Rane took some ribbing from his teammates for waxing his moustache to make a good appearance for the crowd.[15] The Wooster players took the field wearing tasseled caps that the Ohio State players thought looked foppish.[16]

Wooster won the coin toss and chose to have the wind at their back. Ohio State took the ball and started the game with a wedge. They picked up 15 yards, but on the next play Frank Rane fumbled. The Wooster quarterback picked up the ball and ran it back for a touchdown. Most of the crowd was not quite sure what was going on but the score was already 4 to 0. Ohio State stalled on their next drive. Wooster took over and methodically moved the ball downfield for another score, 8–0. Wooster's foppish tasseled caps now seemed to be mocking Ohio State.

Wooster played the game with machine-like precision. By the end of the first half they had scored eight touchdowns and no points-after-touchdown. Their weakness was a poor kicking game but it did not matter. The score was 32 to 0. Wooster was on the Ohio State five-yard line when time in the half was called, but the Wooster players casually jogged off the field, seemingly unruffled by the missed opportunity. The Wooster players did not even seem winded while the Ohio State players were already exhausted.

The second half proved to be a mirror of the first, and the final score of the game was 64 to 0. Because of the rule of the time that allowed a team to maintain possession of the ball after a touchdown, the Wooster players held possession for most of the game. Ohio State had carried the ball into Wooster territory only three times in the entire game. Each time a cheer went up from the crowd, but each time Ohio State was shut down.

✻

Many in the crowd were shocked by the physicality of the game. Wooster's huge right tackle, named Joseph Tyndall, would wait until the umpire was not looking and put in an extra hit on his opponent at the end of a play. Tyndall kicked George Schaeffer in the ribs while Schaeffer was lying on the ground and the game had to be stopped as Schaeffer was carried off the field in a stretcher.

Tackle Pearl Griffith replaced George Schaeffer at halfback, and a substitute named Arthur Bronson replaced Griffith at tackle. Soon afterward Bronson was bleeding. James Hine also took a fierce hit and his teammates were impressed that he was able to remain on the field. After the game, Mike Kennedy, the "handsomest man on campus," was sporting a black eye.[17] The violence became so prevalent that Ohio State fans began accusing the umpire, a Wooster man, of intentionally looking the other way.

Tyndall was a full-blooded Native American. Dick Ellis was not in the game but he grew increasingly angry on the sideline. After Bronson was hit Ellis snarled, "Now I tell you, boys, I don't want to boast or anything like that, but I would like to play against that Indian for about ten minutes."[18]

✻

The Columbus newspapers were disappointed by the performance of the local team. The *Dispatch* wrote at length about the impressive crowd and the atmosphere that surrounded the game but about the team mentioned only "there was not the remotest possibility of their winning."[19] The game coverage in the *State Journal* was a bit more extensive but it was summed up by its opening sentence: "The football game at Recreation Park yesterday afternoon between the Wooster and State university teams was too one-sided to be interesting."[20] The article went on to discuss the superiority of the playing by Wooster, as well as the rash of injuries in the game. "The playing of an Indian on the Wooster team attracted considerable attention."[21]

In the *Lantern*, the latest editor-in-chief, Edward Sigerfoos (later a brigadier general in the U.S. army), wrote a front-page editorial that criticized the team as not properly prepared to play: "The most inexperienced person on the grounds last Saturday could see that the Wooster team knew more about the game, was better organized and had greater powers of endurance than our own."[22] Sigerfoos called on the team to raise their performance and consider the reputation of the school: "It is an honor to be a player in the Ohio State University foot ball team. It represents the greatest university in Ohio. Every man on the team should think of this, and should see that he makes every effort in his power to represent his university well."[23]

Another article in the same issue focused primarily on Joseph Tyndall. The article acknowledged that the Wooster players on the whole were "as gentlemanly a lot of fellows as one often meets. They played a fair, honest game and won only by their superior playing."[24] Yet the article went on to emphasize, with rising fury, that there was one exception:

> It was this—the right tackle of the Wooster team was a noble red man, fresh from his native wilds, who, when the game began to grow somewhat fierce imagined he heard the war-whoop of his tribe. The blood of his ancestors began to boil in his veins. He thirsted for gore and scalps.... In fact, throughout the game this Indian bully acted more like a wild beast than a man. It required the combined efforts of the other players to keep him from using his tomahawk and scalping knife right then and there.... If the Wooster players care for the reputation of their college or their foot ball team, they will take a little advice and send him back to the reservation where he belongs or at least not allow him to play in a game in which there is such an opportunity for the display of a brutish nature.[25]

The rest of the issue of was filled front-to-back with more discussion of the game. One writer pointed fingers at problems both on the offense—"What is wrong with Landacre's playing? Was Rane rattled?"—and defense—"Huggins, your tackling Saturday was not very good."[26] A notice in the gossip section picked up the savage-Indian theme: "Schaeffer was on the warpath Saturday night. The Indian will probably never know how near he came to going to the happy hunting grounds."[27] A feature writer tried to lighten the mood by developing a legend of "the curse of Ed Martin's trousers." First Martin and then Rane wore them before being injured in the spring, and now, he claimed, Mike Kennedy was injured wearing the exact same pants.[28] Why Kennedy would have been wearing those pants instead of his own was not explained.

Across the state there were disagreements over just how embarrassing the loss was for Ohio State. Partisan self-interest largely drove the differences of opinion. The *Lantern* downplayed the margin by arguing that such scores are not unusual in football. They noted that on the very same day Yale defeated Wesleyan of Connecticut 76 to 0 and Princeton defeated the University of Virginia 115 to 0. "So, you see, we are not so 'clear out of sight'."[29] The *Kenyon Collegian* had a different perspective. Kenyon lost to Denison 14 to 0 in a game played in Granville. It was Kenyon's first game ever and the *Collegian* commented, "One balm to our wounded feelings was that O.S.U. the same day had been defeated by Wooster 64 to 0."[30]

*

George Schaeffer was back on his feet by the evening after the game, but his injury had seemed serious enough during the game to throw a scare into the crowd. Because Schaeffer worked as a clerk in the office of President Scott, the injury became a topic of conversation at the highest levels of the administration. President Scott began floating a suggestion that the university should form an athletic department to give the faculty greater supervision over student athletics.[31]

The board of trustees considered the proposal at their next meeting but as a general policy the school had always given the students a degree of autonomy in the governance of their activities. In addition, it could be expensive to form an athletic department. The board tabled the idea for future consideration.[32]

Chapter Thirteen

Does anyone still persist in saying that we can play foot ball?

T he O.I.A.A. still planned to expand, and schools throughout northern and central Ohio were mailing in applications.[1] Those schools included Otterbein University, the Evangelical school in Westerville, and Wittenberg University, the Lutheran school in Springfield. Ohio Wesleyan had been applying ever since the O.I.A.A. was originally formed. Of all the applicants, the most attractive was Adelbert College.

Adelbert was the undergraduate college of Western Reserve University, in Cleveland. Most of the students at W.R.U. attended one of the school's many graduate or professional programs. Only seventy-five students there were undergraduates, and they attended Adelbert.[2] Those few students felt separate and distinct from the larger W.R.U. student body, and Adelbert traditionally formed varsity teams independent of the university as a whole.

The population of Cleveland was soaring. It was projected to surpass Cincinnati that year as the largest city in Ohio. Cincinnati had grown in the mid-nineteenth century on river trade, but at the end of the century the industrial factories in cities like Cleveland were becoming a more significant part of the nation's economy. People moved to the northern Midwest looking for jobs, both from the overcrowded communities of the East Coast and from eastern and southern Europe. The O.I.A.A. took into account the financial benefits of having a member in such a well-populated region.[3]

✻

The Ohio State team was idle on the following Saturday, November 8, but another game was played that day that grabbed the school's attention. In Delaware the Columbus Athletic Club played its game against Ohio Wesleyan. Several Ohio State students came up to watch, including some O.S.U. coeds. A writer for the Wesleyan *Transcript* noted enthusiastically, "Several young ladies from Columbus attended the foot ball game last Saturday."[4]

The lineup for the Columbus A.C. was full of familiar faces. They included Joe Firestone, S.P. Bush, Dick Jones, and the Lilley brothers. The most familiar faces, however, belonged to two Ohio State students: Hobart Beatty and George Schaeffer.[5] Beatty had injured a hip against Dayton, and Schaeffer had bruised a rib against Wooster, but both seemed to have recovered well enough to accept invitations to play for the Columbus team.

Columbus won 22 to 0, scoring four touchdowns, two goals after touchdown, and a safety. The score would have been even more one-sided if the teams had not agreed before the game that the halves would be only thirty minutes. A writer from Wesleyan's *Practical Student* griped that Mike Kennedy, an Ohio State student, had served as referee, although he conceded that it ultimately did not matter: "But we cannot cry over the matter. We were beaten."[6]

Hobart Beatty and Coach Lilley's brother Mit received the greatest praise after the game. In the local newspapers Beatty's performance in particular was highlighted.[7] If Paul Lincoln and Caesar Morrey had any misgivings about Beatty playing for another team, however, those concerns were fully realized. Neither he nor Schaeffer reported to practices for Ohio State's game the following Saturday, November 15, against Denison.

Just as frustrating were other new absences from practice. When Frank Rane had joined the team he anticipated mastering football as easily as he mastered most sports that he tried. He didn't. Never before had he played a sport so poorly, and never before had fans criticized his playing so harshly. After the Wooster embarrassment he decided to quit the team.

Meanwhile Mike Kennedy and Jack Huggins were both preparing to leave school altogether. Personal issues forced Kennedy to take a leave of absence. He told his friends that he needed to take an emergency trip to Chicago, and he left town immediately after refereeing the Columbus-O.W.U. game.[8] Huggins had few ties to campus remaining after his friend Kennedy left, and he decided to drop out of school as well.

Huggins had been losing interest in school since soon after the fall term began. Orphaned since he was a small boy, he had come to college mostly in search of adventure ("fantastic, frolicsome, and wild; with all the trinkets of a child"). In October he had gone downtown and auditioned for a role in a local production of *Ben Hur*.[9] It was a small part but he won it.[10] He decided then to pursue an acting career.

Ohio State's next two games—Denison that weekend and Kenyon on Thanksgiving—both seemed winnable. Winning those games would go a long way toward validating the team's efforts before facing a rematch with Wooster on December 6. With the football roster becoming so thin the team could not afford to lose another player.

Lincoln and Morrey had attitudes toward education much different than that of Huggins. Lincoln was the son of an immigrant and for him education was the key to achieving the American Dream.[11] Morrey came from a family of intellectuals and for him education was an end in itself.[12] The two tried to convince Huggins to remain enrolled, and he agreed to stay at least through the end of the term.

✳

Paul Lincoln began work before the Denison game to repair his backfield. Without Frank Rane, the team was missing a fullback. At halfback they still had Walter Landacre available on the right side but, without Beatty or Schaeffer, Lincoln was running out of options on the left.

Caesar Morrey was ready and willing to play but he was unavailable for other reasons. Ohio State would be the visiting team so Morrey, as manager, was responsible for recruiting an umpire. Recruiting a referee for the Wooster game in Columbus had turned out to not be difficult but finding someone to travel to Granville proved to be a bigger challenge. Morrey knew that if he took the position himself he would be unavailable as a player. The decision preoccupied him. While teaching Latin that week he distractedly referred to the grandeur of the "Roman Umpire."[13] Ultimately he accepted that he had to take the job.

Lincoln's choice at left halfback came down to the substitutes Herbert Johnston and Raymond Krumm. Johnston had been a lineman in May but he had friends at Denison and he hoped to show off. Krumm was a seventeen-year-old freshman from a wealthy family, and too hot-headed and undisciplined.[14] Lincoln decided to give Johnston a chance.

Finding a fullback required Lincoln to shuffle his lineup. He gave the position to a student named Arthur Bronson. In the Wooster game Bronson had played left tackle, the position originally filled by Dick Ellis. Ellis remained too injured to play so Lincoln moved Jack Huggins there. It was Huggins's third position change in three games. To replace Huggins at right end, Lincoln promoted substitute Herbert Scott, the son of the university president.

*

On November 8 most of the Ohio State students had been focused on the Columbus A.C. game with Wesleyan, but on that same day Denison had played a game against Wooster. Denison lost 58 to 0.[15] Denison and Ohio State would each be looking to balm their dignity after such embarrassing performances against Wooster.

The Denison manager invited the entire Ohio State team to stay overnight in Granville on the Friday before the game. Only Herbert Johnston accepted.[16] The rest of the team went up to Denison Saturday morning. The trip required an eight a.m. train to Newark, then a transfer, taking an electric rail the rest of the way. A large group of Ohio State students accompanied the football players. Caesar Morrey was pleased to see that the team still had the support of campus fans. The Denison manager was pleased to see such a large crowd of visitors coming to their campus that morning ready to buy tickets.[17]

The game started at three. Rain was falling—not enough to postpone the game but enough to make the ball slick and the field muddy. Denison looked strong on their opening drive, and two and a half minutes into the game they scored a touchdown. After a missed kick the score was 4 to 0. The game became a more even defensive struggle for the rest of the first half until Denison picked up another touchdown just before halftime. The score was 8 to 0. At the start of the second half the Denison players recovered their own punt to take possession of the ball downfield. Again they pushed the ball over the goal line. This time the goal-after-touchdown was successful, and the score was 14 to 0.

Early in the second half Herbert Johnston suffered a wrenched back and had to leave the game. For Caesar Morrey this opportunity to take over at halfback was exactly what he had feared missing. Dick Ellis was still not 100 percent healthy but he also was itching to get back onto the field. He lobbied to take Johnston's spot, and Lincoln agreed.

The second half was a more even contest and Ellis seemed to be the difference. Morrey remained as neutral as possible but he could not help feeling proud of his team. Ohio State was holding its own for the first time all season. As time in the game was running out, Ellis led a desperate last-minute drive. Ohio State was nearing the Denison goal line when Ellis ran wide and saw a hole open in front of him. He just needed quarterback Charles Foulk to pitch him the ball and he would have a touchdown. Foulk was indecisive though and the play fell apart. Ellis fumed. Ohio State had lost its best opportunity that season to score.

Both sides praised Morrey after the game for his evenhanded performance as umpire, but he quickly reverted back to his role as the Ohio State manager. The second half of the game had been the team's best performance of the season and Morrey believed that Ohio State would have a chance if the teams played a rematch in Columbus. He sought out his Denison counterpart and offered a challenge. The two arranged a game to be played the following week, on November 22.

In the next issue of the *Lantern* the tone of the game coverage was mixed. Some writers praised the Denison players—"a more gentlemanly game could not be wished. None of the underhanded dirty work was done as during the Wooster game here"[18]—and excused some of Ohio State's mistakes by noting that so many were playing out of position. "On the whole it was the best game O.S.U. has taken part in."[19] Others in the same issue noted that the early hopes for football were turning into frustration. The "Local and Personal" column stated bluntly, "Our foot ball team is not in it yet."[20] Meanwhile, a reference to the upcoming baseball season stated, "The base ball team has a good deal to redeem for the college, but we will not boast (in vain as it proved) as over the foot ball club."[21]

Caesar Morrey wanted the rematch with Denison to be played in Recreation Park. Joe Firestone and S.P. Bush had already scheduled a game at the park the same day—the Columbus Athletic Club would be playing the Dayton Athletic Club. Morrey suggested that the four teams could give the fans a double header. The rematch between Ohio State and Denison would be the opener, followed by the game between the two community Athletic Clubs.

Much of what hope remained for the football season became emotionally tied to the Denison rematch. "Everybody should attend the game to-morrow at Recreation park, as we intend to 'do or die'," wrote the *Lantern* on Friday.[22] The newspaper asked the students to be good hosts in recognition of the favor that the Denison team had offered them.[23] Later the Denison manager sent a telegram stating that they were not coming. They had changed their minds.[24] Denison had their revenge for Ohio State's no-show in baseball in the spring.

In the game on November 22 between the Columbus and Dayton Athletic Clubs, nine different colleges, including Ohio State, were represented on the rosters. Hobart Beatty again played halfback for Columbus. Arthur Bronson was the new fullback and Dick Ellis was listed as a substitute.[25] For Ohio State players who had been embarrassed by Dayton in October, the game offered a chance at redemption. Paul Lincoln might have been annoyed if he were not serving in the game himself as referee. The Dayton and Columbus teams turned out to be evenly matched, and the game ended in a 0–0 tie. Beatty was again singled out for praise.[26]

✻

Throughout the fall the Wooster students had been anticipating a Thanksgiving contest with Washington & Jefferson College in Pittsburgh. The Pittsburgh team was not considered elite but they were established well enough that their games were reported in Eastern newspapers. Wooster was already regarded as the best team in Ohio but a game against Washington & Jefferson would provide an opportunity to establish a reputation nationally.

When the Wooster faculty discovered the team's Thanksgiving plan, however, they refused to allow the game. Thanksgiving was a day for praise, they said, not for violent play. A Wooster literary society made a formal presentation titled "A Plea before the Faculty for a game of Foot Ball at Pittsburgh on Thanksgiving."[27] The faculty was not moved.

On November 15, as Ohio State was playing Denison, Wooster intended to take out their frustrations against Kenyon. Kenyon surprised everyone by giving Wooster its best game to date.[28] Kenyon claimed that the final score was 30 to 2 but Wooster refused to accept the legitimacy of a safety scored by Kenyon. Wooster claimed that the final score was 30 to 0. The game was called because of darkness with fifteen minutes left on the clock. The *Wooster Voice* insisted that the score could have been doubled if the teams had played those last fifteen minutes of the ninety-minute game.[29]

✻

Otterbein University was one of the schools that had recently submitted an application for O.I.A.A. membership, and their football manager, Bert Leas, hoped to increase their chances. His plan was to establish relationships with the O.I.A.A. members, and the quickest way to build a relationship, he thought, was to schedule a football game. He had no interest in facing Wooster but he did intend to send challenges to the other three schools.

The weekend before Thanksgiving, on November 22, Leas challenged Kenyon to play that day but Kenyon instead sent a team composed of students from their Military Academy. The K.M.A. team gave Kenyon its first football win, 48 to 6.[30] The highlight of the game was a trick play suggested by Professor Brusie.[31] Denison then agreed to play Otterbein as their Thanksgiving game.

Burt Leas planned to challenge Ohio State next.

*

On November 19, Professor Lazenby sent a letter to the board of trustees, making a new plea for development of the campus athletic grounds. He said that at "an institution of the size and scope of our University, suitable development for physical development and maintenance should be provided."[32] He added that "a full measure of health can only maintained by regular wholesome physical exercise."[33]

Lazenby then detailed what he saw as the as the students' specific needs. He requested "a base ball diamond, foot ball grounds, and a quarter mile cinder track, the whole thing enclosed by a light board fence of suitable height."[34] These grounds, he said, should be developed on the field by the North Dorm. He estimated that the total cost would come to $1,950.[35]

The trustees placed the letter into their official minutes without comment.

*

Among the students, hope for the football season now focused on that year's Thanksgiving game. It would be played in Columbus. Caesar Morrey again reserved Recreation Park. Kenyon's Professor Brusie served as umpire and Morrey agreed to serve as referee. Both teams had identical O.I.A.A. records of 0–2, both having lost games to Wooster and Denison.[36]

Paul Lincoln had to prepare another new lineup. The latest player to be replaced was halfback Walter Landacre. Landacre's mother had died unexpectedly and he had gone home for the funeral. Hobart Beatty again failed to report to practices but George Schaeffer returned at halfback. Herbert Johnston returned as halfback on the other side. Lincoln moved Dick Ellis to end. At the other end position Lincoln decided to replace Herbert Scott with Fred Patterson. Scott had played acceptably in the Denison game, and the team had reason to avoid offending Scott's father, but Lincoln thought that Patterson had earned a chance.

A Thanksgiving game remained an event whatever the disappointments of the season, and most of the city newspapers sent a writer to cover the game between Ohio State and Kenyon. Caesar Morrey had scheduled it to be played in the morning in order to accommodate a Thanksgiving feast at the North

Dorm that afternoon. The O.S.U. Athletic Association invited the Kenyon team to the feast as guests of honor.

Snow was falling as the two teams and their supporters arrived at the Park, and the teams took the field just before ten. Otterbein's game with Denison was scheduled for that afternoon but the Otterbein players joined the crowd at the park that morning. Bert Leas had mailed Caesar Morrey his challenge the day before and he wanted to scout Ohio State while the letter was in transit. The Otterbein team planned to watch the first half before leaving to make their trip to Granville.[37]

Ohio State began the game with their best football of the season. Kenyon opened with a wedge but they did not pick up much ground. After two more unsuccessful plays, they punted. On the next play fullback Arthur Bronson surprised Kenyon by punting on first down and Ohio State recovered the free ball. On the drive that followed, halfback Herbert Johnston took the ball and attracted the Kenyon defenders, and then lateraled to Schaeffer. Schaeffer ran the ball in for a touchdown—Ohio State's first score of the season. Lincoln attempted the goal-after-touchdown himself but missed. The score was 4 to 0.

About fifteen minutes into the game Bronson punted again, and when the Kenyon fullback caught the ball Jack Huggins slammed into him to jar it free. Fred Patterson picked up the loose ball and then crossed the goal line for a second Ohio State touchdown. Afterward a Kenyon player gave Patterson an angry shot to the shoulder. Patterson, the only African American playing football in the O.I.A.A. that year, did not respond to the provocation. Ham Richardson attempted the kick this time and sent the ball through the goal.

The teams sparred for the rest of the half, mostly on Kenyon's side of the field. Dick Ellis played like a man on a mission, downing every ball carrier that tried running in his direction. The *Lantern* wrote, "Ellis tackled way out of sight. He surprised everyone, including himself."[38] Halftime arrived with the score 10 to 0.

The Otterbein team left to catch their train, and when they arrived in Granville they reported that Ohio State was dominating Kenyon. The Denison team cheered the news because a Kenyon loss would assure Denison of sole possession of second place in the O.I.A.A. Only later did Otterbein and Denison learn what happened in Columbus in the second half.[39]

Eight minutes after halftime, Herbert Johnston was gang tackled, twisting his ankle and receiving a gash over his eye. He had to leave the game and Lincoln needed a replacement. Lincoln sent in the seventeen-year-old freshman Raymond

Krumm. At that point Kenyon began turning the game around. On the next play a Kenyon halfback made 40-yard touchdown run. The kick failed and the score was 10 to 4.

After another series of punts Kenyon recovered the ball at the Ohio State seven-yard line. The Kenyon halfback then scored again. Again the kick failed but Ohio State's lead had narrowed to 10 to 8. Dick Ellis' aggressive play, that had been so effective in the first half, began to draw penalties in the second. Two consecutive off-sides calls gave away five yards each. Kenyon scored again, and this time they made the goal. Kenyon led 14 to 10.

On their next drive Ohio State made a desperate push to score, at least tie the game, and possibly retake the lead. George Schaeffer began tearing off yards at a time. The *Kenyon Collegian* praised, "For O.S.U. Schaeffer played a splendid game. He has lots of dash and nerve and is quick. He is a good one."[40] Ohio State picked up a first down at Kenyon's four-yard line. Then they tried to pound the ball across the goal line.

Kenyon, however, rose to the challenge. Ohio State got six inches from the end zone before turning the ball over on downs. Kenyon then scored one more touchdown before the game ended. The final score was 18 to 10.

After the game the Kenyon team did not show up as expected to the Thanksgiving feast at the Dorm. The Kenyon players chose instead to have their dinner downtown at a Columbus restaurant. "The Dorm grub may be good," they later explained, "but we couldn't trust it on a feast day."[41] The Ohio State students were unwilling to forget the insult.[42]

✻

The *Lantern* and the city newspapers had a very different tone in their coverage of the game. The city papers emphasized the positive. The *Daily Press* said that "Both sides played brilliantly."[43] The *State Journal* said the game was the most interesting contest seen in Columbus all season.[44] The *Lantern*, however, focused on the Ohio State collapse. "O.S.U.'s lack of practice and training was very apparent. In the first half, while the men were fresh, Kenyon was not in it, but toward the last our boys began to weaken."[45] Another *Lantern* writer commented only, "Does anyone still persist in saying that we can play foot ball?"[46]

Chapter Fourteen

Everything that will add to the glory of the O. S. U.

A n issue of *Outing* magazine late in 1890 included an article on the topic "Athletics in Ohio Colleges."[1] The article brought attention to Ohio sports from across the nation. The *Harvard Crimson* wrote that, judging from the magazine's assessment of the state, "it is not unreasonable to hope for great progress in the future."[2]

The article concluded with a ranking of the athletic programs of seven schools—the five members of the O.I.A.A. plus Ohio Wesleyan and Oberlin. Wooster was ranked as best, with the writer taking particular note of Wooster's football team. Ohio State was ranked as worst.

The Ohio State students felt humiliated. Most of them disagreed vehemently with the ranking. A *Lantern* editorial in early December argued that *Outing* had weighed the sport of football too heavily in their evaluation:

> The idea of ranking us last in seven colleges in which the various sports are indulged in is certainly a false conception. The only thing in which Wooster has shown herself superior to O. S. U. is football. In base ball, tennis and on the State Field Day we can surely rank as high, if not higher.[3]

The article's author, E.W. Forgy, did not bother to disclose that he was a recent Wooster graduate.[4]

*

On November 28, the day after Thanksgiving, Caesar Morrey received the challenge from Otterbein. Otterbein manager Bert Leas offered not only to feed the Ohio State team and put them up in a hotel, but also to pay an additional

$10. The money alone would more than pay for the entire team's train fare to Westerville.[5] The only problem was the date that Otterbein offered: December 6. It was the same date as Ohio State's scheduled game at Wooster.

When the *State Journal* covered the Thanksgiving game, their writer ended his article by stating, "There is but one more chance for O.S.U., but as it is with Wooster, it is a slim one."[6] Morrey agreed with that assessment. He was not eager to see his team embarrassed again. He would prefer to see Ohio State play Otterbein, a team that had never won a game, than Wooster, a team that had never lost. Morrey delayed in responding to the challenge one way or the other.

A few days later Wooster announced that they had rescheduled the game in Pittsburgh to face Washington & Jefferson College. The exposure of the game would benefit not only Wooster but also the entire O.I.A.A. and Ohio football in general, but Morrey had a more immediate and personal reaction to the news. The announced date of the game was December 6. Morrey sent a telegram to Bert Leas accepting the Otterbein challenge.

The date by then was December 4 and Leas was annoyed. He responded:

We sent you a challenge on Nov 26 and expected an early reply. Just having one half a day to advertise the game it will be necessary to cancel the date. I have excused two of our men from town, thinking that you would not answer at such a late date. We will accept a later date if you notify us at once. Hoping this will not put you to any inconvenience and reply soon.[7]

Morrey and Leas ultimately arranged a game to be played during the 1891 season.

The game between Wooster and Washington & Jefferson turned out to be low scoring. Wooster won 6 to 4, with the margin of victory a successful kick-after-touchdown.[8] That outcome was surprising because kicking had been the weakest part of Wooster's game all season.

Elsewhere on December 6, Denison and Kenyon completed the O.I.A.A. schedule. Denison went into the game confident of victory but Kenyon upset them 22 to 8. The two teams finished tied in Association games, each with a record of two wins and two losses. If Denison had shown up for a rematch against Ohio State, that game would have served as a tiebreaker.

Jack Huggins dropped out of school as soon as it was clear that the O.S.U. football season had ended.[9] He joined a travelling theater troupe, fulfilling his goal of being an actor. After that he worked as a reporter, and he then organized a National Guard regiment. Soon afterward he left those positions to pursue another business opportunity. He then fought in the Spanish American War, caught malaria in Cuba, and died in 1901.[10]

✳

After the season the *Wooster Voice* ridiculed Ohio State, questioning why the Ohio State team had not shown up for their scheduled game. The *Voice* writer explained that Wooster's second team had stayed behind on December 6 and could have faced them. He added that Ohio State's failure to appear had spoiled the day because, with the Wooster backups playing, a game against Ohio State "might have had the semblance of interest for the spectators."[11]

This latest taunt was part of a war of words between the *Voice* and the *Lantern* that the two newspapers had been engaged in for most of the season. The hostilities had begun after the November 1 game when the *Lantern*'s coverage accused Wooster's Joseph Tyndall of being a dirty player. The *Voice* took offense at the characterization and claimed that Tyndall's rough play began only as response to illegal blocking by Ohio State: "It was only after the point when forbearance ceases to be a virtue had passed that Mr. Tyndall showed his determination to defend his own."[12]

The *Lantern* editor-in-chief Edward Sigerfoos was not willing to let that response go unchallenged. In a December editorial he said that if Tyndall was blocked illegally he should have turned to the umpire, a Wooster man, rather than taking the matter into his own hands by injuring his opponents. He closed the article by mocking the name of the Wooster newspaper, stating that if that school's newspaper is truly its *Voice* it is a voice of prevarication.[13]

The *Voice* answered with a similar tone, claiming that if the Ohio State newspaper is a *Lantern* it does not illuminate. Rather it "flickers with feeble ray."[14] The *Voice* offered the legalistic defense that, whatever Tyndall's actions, the *Lantern* could not refer to them as a violation because no penalty had been called. They then stated further that Tyndall's actions seemed both justified and appropriate to the Wooster people who were present:

> We admit that Mr. Tyndall did strike an O.S.U. player, during the game; we do not deny it, we do defend it. It was justifiable according to the testimony of both players in the game and witnesses among the spectators.[15]

In January Sigerfoos called this latest response "mere howling"[16] and added that if *Voice* would not address the points relevant to the discussion the *Lantern* had nothing further to say.

＊

On February 18 Wooster hosted the 1891 State Oratory Contest, and that setting made it particularly satisfying when an Ohio State student won.[17] Sophomore Katherine Morhart became the first woman ever to win the contest. She had in fact been the first woman to represent any college in the state. She would soon be the first woman to represent any state as she prepared to move on to the national level of the contest.[18]

In a year when Ohio State had not had much to celebrate in intercollegiate competition, Morhart returned from Wooster as a conquering hero and a campus celebrity[19]. A writer in the *Lantern* suggested that her success "will doubtless do much to dispel the unfavorable notions prevalent through the state, that O. S. U. is nothing more than a technical school and takes no interest in the classics, literature and oratory."[20] Edward Sigerfoos took the opportunity to brag that "the Ohio State University has always had the proud distinction of being an institution where discriminations on account of race, color or sex, have never been drawn."[21]

When Morhart set off for the national contest she was cheered as a warrior heading off to battle. The *Guernsey Times* of Cambridge, Ohio, wrote, "She will represent Ohio in the national contest to be held at Des Moines, Iowa, next May. Hurrah for the Buckeye girl, from the people's college!!" The *Lantern* reprinted that article in its entirety.[22]

A senior named Francis Stewart Kershaw, who would later be a curator at the Boston Museum of Fine Arts, celebrated Morhart in song:

We've an orator at last,
Hip, Hip, Hurrah!
All competitors she's passed,
Hip, Hip, Hurrah!
For to Wooster she has been
Where the judges crowned her queen,
Come then, help us swell the din —
Hip, Hip, Hurrah!
Justly proud, then, O. S. U.,
Hip, Hip, Hurrah!
Alma mater dear and true,
Hip, Hip, Hurrah!
Of your girls and boys so gay
May you be, as long as they,
Uphold the scarlet and the gray,
Hip, Hip, Hurrah![23]

The review of Morhart's performance in the *Wooster Voice* was noticeably colder. The writer declared "her enunciation good, though nothing more; her gestures were rather studied, but effective; her general manner more confident than earnest. The natural nervous strain of the occasion was apparent in the lady's delivery throughout."[24] He added that "no startling originality of thought was displayed."[25]

In the months after the contest, some O.S.U. students began to voice the opinion that too much attention was being given to campus sports. They argued that the students should focus on activities more appropriate to university life, such as oratory. "Does the man who makes a 'grand stand' play or strikes out a dozen men deserve more careful mention in the college paper than the declaimer who surprises his hearers with his ability, or the debater who shows mastery of thought and force in presentation?"[26]

The supporters of Ohio State sports meanwhile hoped to capitalize on the renewed sense of university pride:

> Success in base ball or in a field day contest will just as surely add to the reputation of a college as will success in oratory or any other college work. Let the student who calls himself a college man support both by word and deed everything, athletics included, that will add to the glory of the O. S. U.[27]

*

Following the pattern established the previous year, the winter meeting of the O.I.A.A. was held at the same location as the State Oratory Contest on the following day. Ed Martin was the Ohio State representative, just as he had been Ohio State's representative to the meeting in the fall. Martin had lost both the position of quarterback and the position of football manager but he still had this final responsibility to fulfill for the team.

A few days earlier Martin had gone down to the city with Charles Foulk. Both Foulk and Martin had been quarterbacks for Ohio State in 1890 and both had been criticized for their playing. As they returned to campus that evening they noticed a fire at the train station. They rushed, shouting, back to the dorm. It turned out that the fire had caused some panic earlier in the evening but by the time the two rushed in with the news it was already under control.[28] Their excitement after everyone else had calmed down made them easy targets to mock, and the incident remained a running joke for several days. The humor had a sharper edge than might have been expected if either man had still been considered a football hero.

On the day before the O.I.A.A. meeting Wooster's president, Sylvester Scovel, addressed his students. He said that he was withdrawing a commitment from the university to build a new gymnasium because the Wooster athletic association had not yet delivered on a $200 pledge to the project.[29] The news put the association members in a poor mood and in desperate need of cash.

Two items were on the meeting agenda. The first dealt with new applications for membership. Adelbert College, Ohio Wesleyan University, Otterbein University, and Wittenberg University had all applied to join the O.I.A.A. A proposal was on the table to admit three of the four schools and then divide the Association into northern and southern divisions.[30] Ohio State supported this proposal, considering it a useful means of reducing travel expenses.

The next agenda item responded to a complaint regarding game officials. Some people felt that the officiating in O.I.A.A. games had too often been biased, and a proposal was put forward to hire professional referees and umpires for upcoming games.[31] Since the O.I.A.A. had little money, this proposal would require further discussion.

Before the delegates could begin debate on either of these topics, the Wooster delegate, Aylette Fullerton, stood and asked to address the assembly. On behalf of the Wooster athletic association he wanted to discuss the problems that his school was having with Ohio State. He said that, because Ohio State had failed to appear for a scheduled game, that game should be counted in the O.I.A.A. record book as a Wooster victory. He added that Wooster had lost revenue that day and demanded that Ohio State pay Wooster a $50 penalty.[32]

Ed Martin was serving as O.I.A.A. secretary[33] and he seethed as he took the meeting minutes. He considered Fullerton's argument outrageous and he exploded with anger when it was finally his turn to speak. If any team was actually entitled to a forfeit it was Ohio State. Ohio State had graciously stepped aside so Wooster could play a more prominent game. Furthermore, Denison had earlier cancelled a game—the rematch on November 22—and Ohio State was not asking for a forfeit or financial penalty. If Wooster lost money on December 6, the fault lay with their athletic association for accepting the trip to Pittsburgh.

Martin and Fullerton continued to argue and the meeting ended with nothing decided. Fullerton was the business manager of the *Wooster Voice* and the *Voice* defended how he had taken over the meeting. They described his concerns as "of vital importance to the Association," and in fact "the most important business discussed," because if Ohio State got away with this behavior it would "in a short time prove fatal to athletic interests."[34] The *Voice* concluded by stating that "it is hoped that the other colleges will take Wooster's view of the matter."[35]

Informal polling in the weeks that followed showed that the O.I.A.A. was unlikely to support Wooster's demands. An editorial in the *Kenyon Collegian* made their position clear: "Wooster claims $50 dollar damages, but as this is no professional association and there was no contract it seems to us the claim is most unjust and unfair. This is *ex post facto* legislation and everyone knows that it is compatible neither with legality nor equity."[36] Without backing from the O.I.A.A., Wooster had no leverage against Ohio State.

Wooster then raised the stakes. They claimed to have outgrown the O.I.A.A. and Ohio sports in general, and threatened to secede. They said that they had been invited to join an association of Eastern colleges. After the *Outing* article, and the victory over Washington & Jefferson, the threat seemed credible. Losing Wooster would be disastrous for the O.I.A.A. because Wooster was by far the best team in the Association. They set a standard that other Ohio teams needed to meet if they wanted to compete against Eastern schools themselves. Wooster seemed to have the Association over a barrel.

Before the O.I.A.A. decided, however, the dispute took a new turn. For some time a rumor had been spreading that Wooster's victories during the 1890 season had not been entirely legitimate. The claim being whispered was that Joseph Tyndall had never registered as a student. He allegedly was a ringer, brought onto their campus merely to play football. That spring the rumor was confirmed.

This news changed everything. No national agency yet existed to deal with teams when they cheated, but college athletics were considered a gentlemen's activity. Schools were expected to police their own conduct. Washington & Jefferson demanded a forfeit and a chastened Wooster obliged. If an association of Eastern schools had really invited Wooster to join them, that invitation disappeared. The *Lantern* could not resist taking one more jab, jeering that Wooster would have to back down from "her $50 bluff" and that the Wooster team would have to continue to "play ball with ordinary mortals."[37]

*

At the start of spring Ohio State turned attention back to baseball. The "Kid battery" of Martin and Pearce returned to the field.[38] Charles Barnes, from the 1887 football team, was elected captain. A junior named Ernest "Bricky" Evans was elected manager.[39] Frank Rane hoped to hear some applause again after his football failures of the fall. On paper this team seemed to be the most talented that the school had ever fielded.[40]

They finished with a 3–6 record and last place in the O.I.A.A. The *Lantern* was mystified by the losses. After opening the season with two wins, the team lost six straight—a streak that corresponded with an extended slump by Rane. A low point for Rane was a ninth-inning strikeout with two outs and the bases loaded.[41]

Ohio State's campus field day was held on May 16. Because Rane had been injured the year before, this meet was the first chance to see direct competition between him and Hobart Beatty. Rane dominated their head-to-head races, winning at 50 yards, 100 yards, and 220 yards, as well as in the hurdles. Beatty's only victory was in the running broad jump. Other football players also had success at field day that year. Walter Landacre repeated as pole vault champion and Arthur Bronson won both the shot put and a football-kicking contest. Herbert Scott, the president's son, set a new campus record in the standing broad jump. Paul Lincoln won four events, including the hammer throw and quarter-mile run.[42]

A few weeks before the field day, the O.S.U. Athletic Association had voted for new officers. Dick Ellis was elected vice president and Paul Lincoln was elected treasurer.[43] As varsity football players, Lincoln and Ellis had faith that, with a little more effort, success in football was still within reach. Soon after his field day success, Lincoln told the football team to be ready for new practices in September.[44]

A junior from Xenia, Ohio, named Edwin Bloom had been elected Athletic Association president.[45] Bloom won two events at the campus field day that spring—the running long jump and the high kick. He also was the younger brother of George Bloom, who had been vice president of the Association under Harry Mitchell in 1889. Bloom did not believe that more practice would be enough to turn the team's fortunes around. Like C.C. Sharp before him, Bloom thought that Ohio State would be successful in football only when the O.S.U. Athletic Association held a tighter rein.

*

Three weeks after the campus field day was the 1891 O.I.A.A. State Field Day. It was held that year in Columbus, hosted by Ohio State. The *Lantern* emphasized the importance of making a good impression. "It will be a long time before we have another such chance as this."[46] The O.S.U. Athletic Association rented the State Fairgrounds, and they recruited Al Lilley, S.P. Bush, and Dick Jones of the Columbus Athletic Club to serve as judges. Ohio State won three events, including victories by Herbert Scott in the broad jump and Arthur Bronson in the shot put.[47] Frank Rane, Ohio State's expected best hope, won only the 50-yard dash.[48]

Rane graduated that spring. The following year he continued his studies at Cornell, and he became the first, and to date only, graduate student to hold the Cornell school record in the 100-yard dash.[49] Later he became the State Forester of Massachusetts and a nationally recognized advocate for parks conservation.[50] Soon afterward he married and had a daughter, and in 1922 that daughter married an actor named Osgood Perkins. Rane's grandson, Anthony, was born ten years later.[51] Anthony Perkins became a Hollywood legend due primarily to his quirky performance in the 1960 movie *Psycho*.[52]

✳

On the day after the State Field Day, the O.I.A.A. held a meeting in Columbus to resolve their outstanding issues, including their decisions on expansion. The plan to form two divisions had been set aside but the application from Adelbert was still on the table. The Adelbert students considered it a promising sign that the O.I.A.A. had invited them to participate in the State Field Day as Association guests.[53]

Denison, Buchtel, and Wooster all voted to accept but Ohio State and Kenyon voted against—blocking admission. Adelbert had previously been told that they had Ohio State's vote, but Ohio State supported Adelbert's admission only if it would create regional divisions. Travel between Columbus and Cleveland required an expensive three-hour train ride, and Ohio State had no interest in taking that trip regularly. Adelbert felt betrayed,[54] and the anger was palpable in the Adelbert student newspaper, even in their coverage of the State Field Day. They commented that "several features of the games went off in a way to remind us of hay-seed."[55]

The next item on the O.I.A.A. agenda was intended to prevent a scheduling crisis like Buchtel had created the previous fall. The representatives voted that every O.I.A.A. school must field both baseball and football teams if they intended to remain members. Buchtel agreed to form a football team and be ready to play when the new season arrived.

Finally the meeting explored the issues raised by the Tyndall incident. To prevent teams from using ringers in the future they formalized an eligibility rule. Any athletes competing in O.I.A.A. events were required to spend at least eight hours a week in the classroom. The O.I.A.A. rejected Wooster's demand that Ohio State forfeit the game that had been scheduled on December 6. They did offer an olive branch to Wooster's pride. They agreed that in future seasons any team that cancelled a game would have to pay a $25 dollar fine.[56]

*

The Ohio State students were farther from where they wanted to be than they had thought just one year earlier. A new issue of the *Makio* was published that June and within its pages a poet summed up the campus mood. He wrote an "Ode to Foot-Ball":

Lightly bounding, dully sounding,
    See the foot-ball roll
Never staying, ricocheting,
    To the hostile goal
Onward rushing, bearers crushing,
    Speed we o'er the plain
Heads are battered, shins are shattered,
    Curses rise in vain
Pain is laughter, if thereafter
    We get jolly tight
Drink we lager, till we stagger
    Out into the night[57]

Part Four

Our place is at the head of
Ohio's athletics, not at the foot

Chapter Fifteen

Well, why can't we play football?

ootball in Ohio had never been under greater scrutiny than in the fall of
1891. The incident involving Joseph Tyndall had left the University of
Wooster embarrassed, and the Wooster faculty decided that their football team threatened their school's reputation overall. Wooster's President Scovel
took a stand. All intercollegiate athletics there were suspended, effective immediately.

This news was a blow to the entire O.I.A.A. Whatever grudges existed,
Wooster fielded the association's best-known and most-respected team. The
O.I.A.A. leaders argued that the action of the Wooster president was unnecessary because the new O.I.A.A. eligibility rules were designed specifically to eliminate the risk of any team using ringers. The *Lantern* found itself in the awkward
position of defending Wooster students. Irvine Dungan, the new *Lantern* editor-
in-chief, wrote a front-page editorial:

> Wooster and O. S. U. have always wrangled. Wooster and other colleges have
> often had hard feelings and harder words, and it is possible that this fact has had
> an influence with the Wooster faculty in their action. It is a fact, however, that
> under all the exhibitions of ill-feeling between colleges, there is always a solid
> bottom of respect for each other....We sympathize with Wooster, and hope that
> the prohibition will be removed.[1]

The administrations of other schools also began to worry about the risks
associated with intercollegiate athletics, and the Ohio State faculty decided to
offer a demonstration of their authority. They set a rule that O.S.U. sports teams
could practice only one hour per day.[2] The O.S.U. football players thought that

this new rule was arbitrary and unfair, but after the action taken at Wooster they knew better than to complain too loudly.

Ed Bloom, the president of the O.S.U. Athletic Association, saw the new level of scrutiny as an opportunity. He wanted to increase his Association's authority over the school's football team and he quietly began negotiating with the faculty.

*

Paul Lincoln and Charles Foulk both hoped to improve their own football reputations. When the new term began Lincoln asked Foulk to be his new roommate at the Dorm. Foulk was smart and passionate about football, but as a quarterback most people saw him mediocre. Lincoln, as promised, called the team back together in September, and soon afterward the players called for the election of new leaders. They voted Lincoln out as captain, replacing him with Dick Ellis. Foulk must have suspected that Ellis was unlikely to keep him in the starting lineup. The rest of the players seemed to have the same suspicion because they elected Foulk to be their manager.

Dick Ellis brought new energy to the role of captain. He had always played football with a reckless spirit and unflagging enthusiasm. As a captain he now drove the team as hard as he drove himself. He said that they all became exhausted too quickly and that only improved conditioning would bring them victory.[3]

Ed Bloom supported Ellis's assessment that the team was out of shape. Bloom, in addition to being the president of the Athletic Association, was also a writer for the *Lantern*. He and a friend named William Morrison Ray had together taken charge of the newspaper's "Local Notes" column that fall. "'Wind' is what our team lacked last year," Bloom and Ray wrote, "and without which we shall have the same reverses this year."[4]

Charles Foulk began his work as manager by focusing on recruiting. He brought in two respected varsity baseball players, George "Kid" Pearce and Louis "Dutch" Ernst, and also Charles Powell, the treasurer of the Athletic Association. In addition, he brought in recruits that he hoped would be willing to put in time on the practice squad—students named Dunlap, Fullerton, Gillen, Haas, Lawrence, Nagel, Smith, and Withoft. Foulk brought so many new recruits to practices that Ellis was able to form a second team.

Some of those new recruits had previous experience with gridiron football. Mortimer Lawrence was a newly enrolled student but his high school in Cleveland had begun fielding a team the previous year. Frank Haas and Clarence Withoft were new students from Dayton,[5] and they had played football with a Y.M.C.A. team that was founded under the guidance of the Dayton Athletic Club.[6]

Ellis moved Paul Lincoln from center to his original position at guard. He put Mortimer Lawrence at center. Lincoln, despite his setbacks, continued to be a vocal supporter of his team. He again gave a speech in praise of football at a Horton Literary Society meeting of the fall.[7]

*

Caesar Morrey was no longer the team's manager but he was still on campus. The faculty had even given him a new teaching responsibility. Morrey had confirmed that he planned to become a professor of biology and the faculty let him try teaching introductory biology to the freshmen.[8] This work was in addition to his previous assignment of teaching Greek and Latin to the prep students. Morrey now held a status as grand old man of the football team despite the fact that he had even less free time to offer.

Morrey's older brother William was on campus that year as well. After he finished college in 1888, William Morrey worked as a school principal in his hometown of Chester Hill. In 1890 he came back to Columbus to take a high school teaching job. By 1891 he decided to further his education and he began taking post-graduate courses at Ohio State, studying physiology and Spanish.[9] The *Lantern* asked him to serve in an advisory position called "Alumni Editor."[10]

Like his brother, William Morrey intended to become a college professor and he assumed that, like his brother, he would need to start his career as an instructor in a preparatory program. During his time back at Ohio State he sent job applications to prep schools across the country, including the prep school at the Stevens Institute of Technology.[11]

*

Ohio State's varsity baseball team played a short fall season during the month of October. Bricky Evans continued as manager. Kid Pearce, the catcher, served as captain.[12] The pitcher, Edward C. Martin, was rarely called "Kid" anymore because it had become confusing that he and his catcher had the same nickname. People now called him "Eddie."[13] Behind Eddie Martin's pitching, the team finished the fall season with four wins, no losses, and one tie.[14]

The emotional highlight of the season was a game in Delaware on October 3 against Ohio Wesleyan. The Delaware fans were as raucous as ever but Ohio State won 6 to 2. In the bottom of the ninth inning Ed Pedlow made a clutch throw from the outfield to tag a runner out at third base, ending Wesleyan's final scoring opportunity. The win was Ohio State's first against Wesleyan in a nine-inning game since 1882. "Delaware is defeated," wrote Irv Dungan, "and our 'hoodoo' is broken."[15] Hope grew for the upcoming baseball season in the spring when the team would face their O.I.A.A. rivals.

After the game, Elisha Walden, the Wesleyan football manager, came over to Bricky Evans to say that he also challenged Ohio State. Evans replied that he would pass that message along to Charles Foulk, the O.S.U. football manager. Walden emphasized that the game should be played on October 24. Evans said that he would include that information. The next issue of the *Transcript* trumpeted, "The first foot ball game will be played two weeks from next Saturday. Manager Walden has secured a game with O. S. U. for that date."[16] The Wesleyan students did not realize that Evans actually had no intention of delivering Walden's message.

Evans, around this time, complained to the *State Journal* about Ohio State's continuing frustrations with O.W.U.: "The innocents from the rural regions who attend Ohio Wesleyan University are not allowed by a parental faculty to wander out of sight of their town clock."[17] The Wesleyan students did not appreciate his tone. The *Practical Student* investigated and discovered that Evans had been raised on a farm, and made the point that he should not call anyone else "rural."[18]

*

The O.S.U. football team headed to Westerville on October 17 to play the long-delayed game against Otterbein. A manager's job included negotiating a schedule but the Otterbein game was not arranged by Foulk. It was a leftover from 1890, scheduled by Caesar Morrey. Morrey served as the game's umpire.[19]

Otterbein was not a member of the O.I.A.A. so the outcome of the game would not affect the season standings. For that reason, despite the fact that Westerville was only fifteen miles away, only thirty Ohio State students chose to accompany the team. The *State Journal* attempted to promote the game but they sounded equally unenthused. An article published the day before the game stated that "the football team is going to Westerville to practice on the Otterbein boys."[20]

This line drew some attention because the town of Westerville was within the *Journal*'s circulation area. Otterbein had still never won a football game and was not considered much of a threat, but when the Otterbein students read the article they considered the word "practice" to be more disrespectful than they deserved. Since the previous season they had taken on a coach. That coach, Abraham Lincoln Artz was a member of the Dayton Athletic Club and a former football player from Dartmouth.[21] Through "Link" Artz, Otterbein learned an advanced offensive scheme and developed crisp and efficient teamwork.[22] They were chomping at the bit to face Ohio State even before they took the *Journal*'s word choice as a personal insult.

Ohio State meanwhile showed up in Westerville underprepared. They were confused by Otterbein's rapid lateral passing, pounded by Otterbein's solid wedge-work, and looked even sloppier and more out of rhythm than they had the year before. After one half the score was 22 to 0 in favor of the home team. Ohio State seemed to pull together for the opening drive at the start of the second half but they fumbled the ball into the arms of an Otterbein player just short of the goal line. Halfback Herbert Scott had a chance for a tackle but missed, and the Otterbein player returned the ball for a touchdown. Scott redeemed himself on the next possession by scoring Ohio State's first touchdown, worth four points, and Dick Ellis kicked the goal after touchdown for two more, but those were the only Ohio State points in the game. The final score was 42 to 6.[23]

Throughout the game the Ohio State students felt abused by the taunting of the locals. In the grandstand the Westerville fans outnumbered the visiting O.S.U. fans 17 to 1, and a *Lantern* writer complained of the "insulting remarks and ridicule."[24] He called the shouts from the seats "offensive and impertinent" and "wholly unworthy of college students."[25] Afterward the Ohio State players and fans were fuming.

None of the players was angrier than a freshman on the second team named Hugh Fullerton. Fullerton was the brother of Aylette Fullerton—the Wooster representative at the O.I.A.A. winter meeting in February who had demanded a $50 penalty from Ohio State. Hugh Fullerton was a proud Ohio State student, and he challenged a footrace to whoever Otterbein considered their best runner. Otterbein's left tackle, R.C. Kumler, accepted Fullerton's challenge. Kumler was an elite-level track athlete, and three years later he would set a world record in the broad jump.[26] The race in Westerville was 100 yards and Fullerton was left embarrassed.

Several of the local newspapers covered the game and they all praised Otterbein generously. The *Columbus Dispatch* wrote, "At the very beginning of the game it became apparent that the home team was superior in every way."[27] The *State Journal* wrote, "The superiority of Otterbein in passing, tackling, guarding and rushing showed that they have been well-coached and subject to considerable training."[28]

Some newspapers reminded their readers of the *Journal*'s "practice" line. The *Dispatch* and the *Daily Press* both sounded amused that their competitor's confidence had turned out to be unearned.[29] The *Daily Press* went on to adopt the Otterbein team. They conceded any claim on the Ohio State team, leaving it to any fans—or any newspaper—that might still want it, but took the Otterbein players as "our boys."[30] The Otterbein student newspaper also referenced the *Journal*'s word choice. They titled their game coverage "O. S. U. practices on O. U."[31]

*

Ed Bloom and Morrison Ray tried to remain supportive in their "Local Notes" column in the *Lantern*, but they also offered blunt criticism. They singled out several Ohio State players for individual praise. Herbert Scott and Hobart Beatty both played well at halfback. Mortimer Lawrence, at center, "filled his position with credit"[32] and freshman Renick Dunlap, at right end, "kept his opponent busily engaged."[33] The veterans Paul Lincoln, Ham Richardson, and Raymond Krumm all provided noteworthy performances on the line. Especially impressive was Dick Ellis's performance at fullback: "Capt. Ellis' 'punting,' 'tackling,' and general 'all around' hard work surprised the highest expectations of his friends."[34] Individual effort was not enough, however. "Phenomenal plays, brilliant spurts are good," they said, "but steady hard work is better and surer."[35] They particularly noted a lack of effective teamwork.

Bloom and Ray then challenged the student body as a whole to accept a share of responsibility for the failures of the team. "Some say we can't play foot ball," they wrote. "Well, why can't we play foot ball? Do we mean to say that the O. S. U. can't do what other colleges have done and are doing today?"[36] Bloom and Ray argued that the success or failure of the team reflected not just on the players but on the entire culture of the university:

> The fault lies not so much with the team as with the college. Give the foot ball boys your hearty support and O. S. U. will take her proper rank in that sport. If

we can orate, if we can play lawn tennis, if we can play base ball, we can play foot ball. If we can find material for the former, we can for the latter. And it is the duty of the college to aid in doing so.[37]

*

Charles Foulk sensed the campus losing patience and he wanted to bring everyone back on board. He decided to write an essay and arranged to have it published in the *Lantern* under his own byline. In his essay Foulk addressed the value of football and Ohio State's potential place in the sport. He insisted that the new season would have to turn out better than the year before. The team had solid veterans and talented new men, and Foulk promised "if we don't win at least a *few* games this fall it will be for some cause not apparent now."[38]

He acknowledged that the team faced challenges. The players were struggling because they had no "experienced men as coaches."[39] In addition, the team was allowed just one hour per day for practice "while some places have three or four hours."[40] Good training and teamwork were essential, Foulk argued, because in a football game "no one is ever idle. As soon as the ball is put in play every man has something to do quickly and well."[41] For success in football, "Trained limbs and a clear head count for more than any 'beef'."[42]

Foulk reminded his readers of an old sports cliché: "The Duke of Wellington well knew what he was talking about when he said that Waterloo had been won on the foot ball fields of Rugby. There it was that those men 'who didn't know when they were beaten' got their training."[43] Some on campus were beginning to criticize football as a violent sport. Foulk acknowledged that they were right. "Well, what of it?" he asked, "It does any fellow good to get a few hard bumps occasionally."[44]

A few days later students trashed the North Dorm room that Foulk shared with Paul Lincoln. Foulk and Lincoln had heard rumors that a raid could be coming. "Both stayed home to watch the room, but leaving it for about five minutes, returned to see nothing but wreck and disorder," the *Lantern* reported. "They found part of the bed clothing and furniture the next day, and some other articles 'will never come back'."[45]

*

The rule of the Ohio State faculty allowing only one hour of football practice a day was a handicap, but Dick Ellis used every minute of that hour to build the endurance of his men. Ellis's efforts were helped by the return to campus of Mike Kennedy. The charismatic Kennedy embraced Ellis's new discipline and he helped drive the others. Hugh Fullerton especially admired Kennedy and the ferocity of his playing. He gave Kennedy the nickname "Dirty Mike."[46] Soon the entire team was practicing with the same reckless spirit and unflagging enthusiasm as Dick Ellis himself.

After the Otterbein game Ellis decided that he would fill the day's allotted hour of practice with a short scrimmage. His original plan had been for the first team to practice against the second, but after the Otterbein embarrassment he decided to shuffle the players and re-test them all against teams of approximately equal strength.[47] Charlie Powell, from the second team, outperformed Mortimer Lawrence and took over at center. In the backfield, Frank Haas and Clarence Withoft, the players with experience with the Dayton Y.M.C.A., also played well enough in the scrimmage that Ellis added them to the first-team lineup—Haas at quarterback and Withoft at fullback. Ellis himself had played fullback against Otterbein but for the upcoming O.I.A.A. games he moved back to left end. Among all the players in the backfield, only Hobart Beatty held onto his position.

The fiercest battle of the day was for the halfback position opposite Beatty. Mike Kennedy had been a halfback eighteen months earlier, in the very first game against Ohio Wesleyan, and he wanted the position back. Kennedy's primary competition was Fred Patterson. Patterson, at this time, had been elected president of the junior class.[48] In the scrimmage Patterson was credited with "several fine runs"[49] but "Dirty Mike" Kennedy scored the game's only touchdown and grabbed the open spot.

*

The O.I.A.A.'s fall meeting was held on October 24 at Kenyon. Caesar Morrey agreed to serve as Ohio State's representative.[50] The O.I.A.A. needed a new member to replace Wooster and they turned again to Adelbert's application. Ohio State and Kenyon had by then both removed their objections, and an Adelbert representative was already on hand to formally accept the invitation and participate at the meeting.[51]

Wooster's 1890 games had been voided, and Denison and Kenyon were left by default as O.I.A.A. football co-champions. The meeting representatives voted that similar ties would be settled in the future with a one-game playoff. They made quick use of their new asset, the population of Adelbert's city, by agreeing

The 1891 football team. (Photo courtesy of The Ohio State University Archives)

to hold the potential playoff game in Cleveland with profits split evenly among all O.I.A.A. members. Morrey negotiated one concession to soothe Ohio State pride. If one of the playoff teams turned out to be Ohio State and the other was not Adelbert, then the playoff game would be held in Columbus.[52]

The meeting next turned to concerns about biased officiating that had been introduced in the spring. The proposed solution of paying professional umpires and referees was deemed too expensive, but the meeting representatives agreed on a different change. Team managers would no longer be allowed to serve as officials in their own teams' games.[53] Morrey might have preferred to have seen this rule adopted a year earlier, when he was still a manager.

Finally, the meeting turned to preparing a schedule for the season. For Morrey, the most important part of this task was the scheduling of that year's Thanksgiving game. The Ohio State football team considered it essential that they play their holiday game at home. Renting Recreation Park twice a year was expensive and if they hoped to turn a profit that year they needed the large crowd of ticket-buyers that were expected to attend a Thanksgiving game. Kenyon had been Ohio State's holiday opponent in 1890, but in 1891 Kenyon wanted to play their Thanksgiving game in Cleveland vs. Adelbert.[54] For Ohio State's Thanksgiving game, Morrey arranged to play Denison.[55]

Adelbert meanwhile had to arrange its O.I.A.A. schedule around two games that they had previously scheduled with Oberlin. Oberlin had continued to play gridiron football informally even after their faculty cancelled their varsity game with Wooster in 1889. They also continued lobbying their faculty for permission to have a varsity team. The Oberlin faculty finally relented, and Oberlin and Adelbert had each come to consider the other an important local rival.[56]

To accommodate all of these scheduling moves, Ohio State and Adelbert had to fit their game in on a Wednesday, beginning the O.I.A.A. season in Columbus on November 11. Three days later, on November 14, Ohio State would play at Kenyon. The Thanksgiving game, against Denison, would be at home on November 26. The season would end in Akron against Buchtel on December 5.[57]

*

On the same day as that O.I.A.A. meeting, the Ohio Wesleyan football players waited impatiently on their campus for the arrival of the Ohio State team. When it became clear that no one was coming, Elisha Walden sent a telegram to Charles Foulk demanding an explanation. Foulk expressed confusion but offered to play Wesleyan at any time in Columbus.[58]

The Wesleyan students were indignant, assuming that they had been the victims of a prank. The *Practical Student* wrote, "For want of a better reason we attributed their declination to fear.... They know very well that we are not allowed to go away to play and yet they decline to come up here, and give no reason for it, but try to smooth it over by inviting us to play on their grounds."[59]

Another writer in the same issue attributed the O.S.U. no-show to a character flaw of the entire university. They had recently heard from sources within Ohio State "that some of its faculty were unbelievers" and "some even do not attend chapel."[60] This report confirmed a suspicion that the Wesleyan students had long assumed.

*

When the Stevens Institute of Technology received William Morrey's job application they invited him for an interview. Morrey caught a train from Columbus to Hoboken in early November, and Stevens immediately offered him their open position as an instructor in their preparatory program. He would begin in the fall of 1892.[61]

Morrey was surprised to learn that the Stevens prep students did not share a campus with the Stevens college students. Stevens taught preparatory classes in a building across town, and the preps were never even mentioned in the Stevens yearbook or student newspaper. The two student bodies were kept separate in every way.

In the East a stigma was attached to any college that was too closely associated with its preparatory program. Such colleges were compared to remedial schools—such as the Carlisle Indian Industrial School in Pennsylvania—that served the underprivileged and undereducated. To most in the education community those schools were not thought of as colleges at all.

Morrey recognized the implications for a college like Ohio State that offered a nearly seamless transition between its preparatory and collegiate programs. He sent a letter of warning to the O.S.U. board of trustees. The board discussed Morrey's concerns at their next meeting and they agreed that his observation fit with their own. They told the faculty to begin the process of phasing out the preparatory program.[62]

Meanwhile, Caesar Morrey replaced his brother William as the *Lantern* Alumni Editor.[63]

*

Irv Dungan had recently stepped down as *Lantern* editor-in-chief, and Ed Bloom's friend Morrison Ray took over the position.[64] Bloom informed his friend that a major shake-up was coming to the Athletic Association. The next meeting would introduce a new organizational structure. That reorganization, Bloom guaranteed, would set Ohio State athletics right.

Ray published an editorial about athletics in the next issue. He began by reminding the readers of the importance of college sports. "Athletics should form a prominent feature in college work," he stated. "It is a fact that much of the fame of some of our eastern colleges is due mostly to their efforts in the field of Athletics."[65] He then addressed the recent campus criticisms of sports. He agreed that a problem exists when the "pitcher of the Varsity nine, or the daring half back of the foot ball team or the sprinter who can cover one hundred yards in 9½ seconds is more widely known and spoken of than the class day or University day orator."[66] He claimed that "We do not want to see Athletics have such a prominence, but rather its due share of prominence."[67] The proper goal, he

Caesar Morrey (back left) and Fred Patterson (back right) among the 1891–92 *Lantern* editorial staff. (Photo courtesy of The Ohio State University Archives)

claimed, was that "the O. S. U. will lead the state in athletics as well as in oratory and scientific research."[68]

At Ohio State, however, the progress of athletics had gone "terribly wrong."[69] Ray listed various possible explanations for the recent failures. Maybe the problem arose from not having a proper athletic field ("The Athletic grounds are but a castle in the air"[70]). Maybe a "technical and scientific school" simply cannot prosper in sports, and should not expect to.[71] Ultimately he pointed his finger at the Athletic Association. He did not point at its leadership, as had been done previously, but rather to what he said was the Association's inefficient organizational structure.[72]

He said that he had it on good authority that a solution to this problem was coming.

Chapter Sixteen

Victory at last

To the people in downtown Columbus, the biggest sports news in 1891 was happening in professional baseball. In 1890 a third major league had appeared to challenge the National League and the American Association. That new league, the Players League, upset a financial balance of power.[1] In many cities, including Columbus, the local teams began to struggle, and of the three leagues only the National League survived. The Columbus Buckeyes/Solons folded soon after the end of the 1891 season, just before the rest of the American Association.[2]

The city of Columbus found itself without a source for sports entertainment. The students at Ohio State dared to wonder whether their teams could fill that gap.[3] It was an ambition that, at the time, the rest of the city would have laughed at.

✳

At Ohio State in 1891, some students were starting to fear that the feel of campus life was changing. The university had grown to nearly six hundred students, and due to that quick expansion the culture of the university seemed at risk.[4] The prejudices of the outside world threatened to overwhelm the traditional expectation of broad-minded tolerance.[5]

Nowhere was this change more apparent than with the arrival of a student named Walter J. Sears. Sears had come to Ohio State as a sophomore in 1890 after transferring from Kansas State University. His family had strong ties to Sigma Nu, a fraternity originally founded by former Confederate soldiers at the Virginia Military Institute. As a freshman at Kansas State, Sears had composed the "Creed of Sigma Nu," which included an injunction "to exalt the fundamental virtues of the race."[6] His "Creed" would eventually be adopted by the fraternity nationally. In 1890 Sears's younger brother Lorin began attending Ohio State and Walter was worried that Lorin could be led astray by the local values. He followed his brother to Ohio State in order to establish a Sigma Nu chapter there.[7]

Walter Sears practiced oratory as a member of the Alcyone Literary Society, where some said that he was most notable for admiring the sound of his own voice. The *Makio* described him as "Intoxicated with the exuberance of his own verbosity."[8] The *Lantern* claimed that Sears possessed "a powerful, melodious voice such as is rarely Nature's gift to man," and that his speeches were "composed in good language, smooth and lyrical."[9] Their only flaw was that they lacked "a distinct line of thought and a foundation of argument."[10] Borrowing from the poet William Baldwin, the *Makio* observed, "The empty vessel makes the greatest sound."[11]

✻

The 1891 football season continued on Wednesday, November 11, as Ohio State and Adelbert opened the O.I.A.A. schedule. Charles Foulk rented Recreation Park, and the Ohio State faculty gave the students a half day off so that they could attend the midweek game.[12] The *Lantern* told the students to go downtown and "Show 'em who O. S. U. is."[13] The newspaper avoided making any predictions but they had reason to hope that a football team from a school with almost six hundred students could compete with a team from a school with only seventy-five.

Adelbert, however, was another team that had benefitted from coaching. When the Adelbert students first established their football team in 1890 they formed a relationship with the Cleveland Athletic Club. They used the Cleveland club's field to host their home games, and the Cleveland captain trained the Adelbert players every year.[14] In 1891 the Cleveland captain was Billy Rhodes, a former All American tackle from Yale.[15] Rhodes had received his coaching directly from Walter Camp.[16]

Two weeks before Ohio State played Adelbert, the Cleveland Athletic Club had travelled to Pittsburgh to face the Allegheny Athletic Association, a nationally recognized community team. With Rhodes as captain the Cleveland team shocked Allegheny, winning 22 to 4.[17] The upset victory was noticed by sports fans even in the East. The football team at Yale happened to be looking for a new coach and they offered the open position to Rhodes.[18] For Rhodes the offer was too good to turn down. Yale was his alma mater, their football team was the best in the country, and he would be directly succeeding Walter Camp. On Tuesday, November 10, while the Adelbert team was taking the train from Cleveland to Columbus, Rhodes caught the train from Cleveland to New Haven. On Wednesday morning the Yale team welcomed Rhodes as their new coach.[19]

On Wednesday afternoon Adelbert played Ohio State, and from the start it was obvious that an Ohio State football game would again be one-sided. Adelbert scored in each of their first five possessions and the score at halftime was 32 to 0. Near the end of the first half quarterback Frank Haas grew so frustrated that he threw a punch and was disqualified.[20]

Dick Ellis also was knocked out of the game. He suffered an injury early in the second half and had to leave the field. He turned out to have a season-ending broken collarbone.[21]

Despite the disparity in training, Ohio State played throughout the game as if they "didn't know when they were beaten." Their effort was tireless, and it was the Adelbert players who looked more winded by the end. The Ohio State fans cheered as they saw their team's grit and cheered even more loudly when the team's grit remained even after the game got out of hand. After the game the local newspapers praised Ohio State's endurance, with the *Columbus Post* crediting captain Dick Ellis by name for the team's new physical conditioning.[22]

Near the end of the game Ohio State forced an Adelbert fumble and began driving the ball back the other way. By this time Fred Patterson had replaced the disqualified Haas at quarterback. Forty yards from the goal line, Charlie Powell, at center, snapped the ball to Patterson, who then tossed it to Hobart Beatty. Beatty ran left, rounded the end, and sprinted on to a touchdown. Paul Lincoln made the kick, and the Ohio State students roared.[23] The *Dispatch* called that final scoring drive, in the face of a clearly superior opponent, "one of the grandest fights ever seen on a football field."[24]

The final score was 50 to 6. The *Dispatch* helped those who were new to the sport by explaining that the score was comparable to a 10-to-1 blowout in baseball.[25] It was becoming obvious that poor conditioning had never been Ohio State's only problem. At least as important were the team's tactical shortcomings. They needed a good coach to train them.

✻

Just hours after the end of the game, Ed Bloom called a meeting of the Athletic Association to propose an amendment to the Association charter. The amendment would create a new governing body called the "Athletic Board of Directors," with each graduating class selecting one director and a "director-at-large" selected from among the faculty. The director from the senior class would serve as chairman of the board. Bloom insisted that this new Athletic Board would be the key to solving the school's lingering sports problems.

The responsibilities of the Board listed in the amendment included:

(1) To select the players and managers of the base ball, foot ball and tennis clubs.
(2) To remove any players or managers whenever, in their judgment, it would be for the best interest of said clubs.

The Association had for years been trying to claim authority to select team managers and Bloom now explicitly proposed giving that power to the Board. According to his plan, the Board would begin selecting managers in February.

Bloom was aware of the campus history surrounding this issue. He knew that no O.S.U. sports team would submit to outside authority unless that authority took responsibility for the team's expenses. For that reason, Bloom's list of proposed responsibilities continued:

(3) To provide ways and means for the raising of funds for the promotion of general athletics.

Bloom's list concluded with an assurance that his amendment was not a personal power grab. It gave most of the authority previously held by the Athletic Association officers to the new Board:

(4) To have general supervision of all college athletics and to make such laws as are necessary for their proper regulation and execution.

The executive authority previously held by the Association president—that is, by Bloom himself—went to the chairman of the board.

The position of director-at-large offered the faculty a voice within student athletics and a practical means of monitoring student affairs. Bloom assured everyone that this seat would be filled by Professor Lazenby—someone trusted by both the students and faculty. In exchange, the faculty had agreed to be flexible about the limitation that they placed on practice time. The male students at Ohio State had always been required to participate one hour per day in military drill, but the faculty agreed that members of the sports teams could replace that hour with an hour of regimented practice in their sport.

The Association approved Bloom's plan and passed his amendment. Some of the veteran football players were unhappy but they no longer had any leverage to object. Bloom announced the news in his "Local Notes" column and claimed

that the concession from the faculty "has already proven the wisdom of the organization."[26]

*

The Kenyon game was scheduled for November 14, just three days after
Adelbert. The Ohio State team needed a new captain after Dick Ellis's broken
collarbone. A captain, by rule, had to be available to participate on the field. The
team was forced to name a replacement and little time to choose one.

They chose the freshman quarterback Frank Haas.[27] Despite his youth and
his immaturity during the Adelbert game, fans had begun seeing him as a future
leader of the team. The *State Journal* wrote, "He is undoubtedly the best player in
the university, has had more experience and understands the game better."[28] The
team decided that Haas's time to lead had come earlier than expected.

Kenyon was confident entering the game. They had been playing well all
season, building off their streak of success that had begun at the end on the 1890
season. A few weeks earlier they defeated Buchtel 42 to 0. The Kenyon students
were starting to think that their team might replace Wooster as the dominant
member of the O.I.A.A.[29]

The game official chosen by Kenyon was a Kenyon student named Robert
Watson. A few minutes into the game Watson flagged Raymond Krumm, the Ohio
State left end, for a late tackle. Krumm jumped up, shouting that the ball-carrier
had still been on his feet and moving forward when he was hit. Watson immediately tossed Krumm from the game. He said, "You can't come that on us. We are
not going to have our men hurt by you fellows."[30] The pronouns that Watson used
infuriated the Ohio State players, who expected a game official to at least give the
appearance of being impartial. Kid Pearce, Dutch Ernst, and Mortimer Lawrence
were all similarly threatened with expulsion during the game.

Late in the first half the fullback Clarence Withoft was injured and Haas
made a radical lineup change. He moved Paul Lincoln, the team's biggest man,
from guard to fullback. The replacement of Lincoln, paired with the ejection of
Krumm, disrupted the cohesiveness of the line and undermined the effectiveness
of the entire team. As the game progressed Ohio State played as poorly as ever
and Kenyon won 26 to 0.

Ohio State fans were quick to point fingers. Some blamed Frank Haas for
his ineffective lineup moves. The blame that fans offered with the greatest resentment and most intensity, however, was the bias that they saw in Kenyon's Robert

Watson. The *Lantern* sub-titled their game coverage "O. S. U. Lose to Superior Running and Unfair Umpire."[31] The article stated, "In every other particular than that of sprinting, the O. S. U. had the advantage over the Kenyon team, but *not Kenyon's umpire*."[32] It concluded that "there is no doubt that with a fair umpire O. S. U. would have shown up better in the score."[33]

The *Kenyon Collegian* accused the Ohio State students of deflecting blame. Their writer observed, "The Kenyon team was vastly superior to that of the Ohio State University in every respect."[34] He praised the individual efforts of Kid Pearce and Dutch Earnst for Ohio State, but stated that a successful football team has two necessary qualities: "superior training and a little skill…O. S. U. had neither."[35]

In Gambier, Charles Foulk ran into Kenyon's Professor Brusie. They arranged a game for the following week between Ohio State and the Kenyon Military Academy. Not everyone at Ohio State seemed pleased with that decision. Heavy rain was falling the following Saturday morning, and halfback Mike Kennedy assumed that the game would have to be postponed. Kennedy worked a weekend job at the local insane asylum and did not bother asking his employers for time off. Ohio State's other starting halfback, Hobart Beatty, also failed to catch the train to Gambier, as did the lineman Raymond Krumm.

Haas then made a decision that surprised everyone, opting not to start himself in the game. He would instead serve a role more like a coach during the first half, observing the team from the sidelines and playing only in the second. Kid Pearce, the baseball catcher, would start the game as quarterback. Haas was also forced to start two backups at halfback—Herbert Scott and Fred Patterson.

Ohio State lost 10 to 0, and the Ohio State fans again pointed fingers. Haas's strategy of trying to lead from the sidelines had proven to be a disaster. Others blamed Charles Foulk. They said that he was responsible as manager for keeping the players informed, and that he should have made sure that Kennedy, Beatty, and Krumm were on the train and ready to play. The *State Journal* commented afterward that football at Kenyon overall was "far ahead" of Ohio State.[36]

*

By this time each graduating class had elected a director to represent them on the new Athletic Board. The seniors elected Herbert Johnston, the former football player, as their director. As the representative of the senior class, Johnston served as Chairman of the Board.[37]

Johnston was earning a degree in engineering but he had a good head for business. Under his leadership the Board focused primarily on their responsibility to "provide ways and means for the raising of funds."[38] Many on the Board were convinced that to assure the financial well-being of the university's teams they would have to make better use of the campus athletic grounds. They argued that the football team could bring in good money if not for the expense of renting Recreation Park for every home game.

Developing the grounds for professional use would involve additional expenses, however, including hiring workers to build a grandstand big enough for the team's needs. Recreation Park seated five thousand but Ohio State could presumably get by with a tenth of that capacity. Others pointed out that the grounds would need to be enclosed behind a tall fence if they expected anyone to buy a ticket.

The Board also began talking about the need for a coach. The example of Wooster, Otterbein, and Adelbert had convinced them that Ohio State's football team would need better training to ever be successful. Some even suggested offering a salary to make sure that a new coach would be more accountable to the team than Al Lilley had been. The Williston Prep School in Massachusetts made national news in 1890 for giving their coach a salary. That coach, Amos Alonzo Stagg, was a former All American and teammate of Billy Rhodes at Yale. Ohio State could make a similar hire, but that plan also required funds that the Board did not have.

The Board asked the university's board of trustees for a loan of $1,900 to cover the proposed expenses. The trustees turned them down.[39]

✧

The Thanksgiving game was just twelve days away and Morrison Ray made a new plea in the *Lantern* for the students to take more responsibility for the success of the team:

> If there is any loyalty among us, if we take any pride in this University, now is the time to show it. It is the duty of every student who has the interest of the O. S. U. at heart to lend his hand in elevating the standard of our athletics. You may be unable to play the game yourself; if so then contribute to the support of those who can play and encourage the players and manager in whatever they may do.

Ray claimed that a university of more than five hundred students should be able to field a competitive team. He concluded, "Let us have a team that the O. S. U. can be proud of. Our place is at the head of Ohio's athletics, not at the foot." He asked the students to build on the accomplishments of the Athletic Association.

"The faculty has already met us half way and granted excuse from drill to the first and second elevens. It now rests with the students to do the rest." Students who wanted to help the team were told to give their name to either Charles Foulk or Herbert Johnston.[40]

The football team asked Kid Pearce, the baseball captain, to serve as their captain for the Thanksgiving game. Frank Haas had sprained his ankle in Gambier, which made it possible to replace him without any controversy. Pearce rebuilt the backfield. He kept Mike Kennedy at halfback but he replaced Hobart Beatty at the other halfback spot with a substitute named Pete Gillen.[41] Gillen had played semi-professional baseball before he enrolled at Ohio State, and he had by then earned Pearce's trust, playing shortstop on the baseball team during the short October season.[42] Pearce moved Paul Lincoln back to the line and made a prep student named Gus Smith the new fullback. Pearce left himself at quarterback.[43]

The *Lantern* described the campus mood as the team approached their second Thanksgiving game: "Denison confident of victory, and O. S. U. doubtful."[44] On Wednesday the *Dispatch* wrote, "O. S. U. will try to choke down her defeat last Saturday by winning the game with Denison to-morrow."[45] The *State Journal* sounded more supportive but no more optimistic. "Today Recreation Park will be the scene of an exciting contest. The Ohio State University eleven are going to try their hand at football again and with a vengeance." They cautioned, "The Denison team, however, is a strong one and will make a hard fight."[46]

As on Thanksgiving the year before, Ohio State arranged to play their football game in the morning in order to accommodate the feast that afternoon. Charles Foulk had rented Recreation Park and the holiday attendance was as large as the team had anticipated. The crowd that year even included some curious members of the faculty.[47]

The sky was clear but rain overnight had soaked the field. The bare areas that served as the baseball infield were two inches deep with mud. Ohio State won the coin toss and took possession of the ball. Denison decided to defend the muddy end of the field.

Pearce opened the game with a series of wedges, looking for weaknesses in the Denison line. He found one and continued to exploit it. Mike Kennedy, Pete Gillen, and Gus Smith took turns picking up several yards at a time until Smith scored an Ohio State touchdown. Ham Richardson missed the extra points try and the score was 4 to 0.

Ohio State vs. Denison, Thanksgiving 1891. (Photo courtesy of The Ohio State University Archives)

Momentum shifted back and forth throughout the first half, and Denison sustained a scoring drive just before halftime. Their touchdown tied the game. The Denison kicker also missed the goal and the score at the break was 4 to 4.

In the second half Ohio State showed the improved endurance that they had been working on all season. Ohio State's aggressive defense began to stifle a tiring Denison offense. The large crowd cheered wildly, their enthusiasm growing the longer the game went on. Ohio State's offense picked up another touchdown and the score was 8 to 4. Former captain Dick Ellis shouted encouragement from the sidelines, ruining a good pair of leather shoes running through the mud. Ohio State was again approaching the Denison goal line when the final whistle blew.

The Ohio State players began celebrating, jumping in the mud. The fans rushed down to the middle of the field to join the celebration. Charlie Powell had been hit in the head during the game and his ear was ringing, but he was also splashing in the muck. Charles Foulk had arranged for a photographer to be on hand for a team photo, and the team stopped celebrating just long enough to pose for the picture. A substitute named William Zurfluh rolled in the muddy field so that his clean uniform would not stand out.

Team photo following the 1891 Thanksgiving game. (Photo courtesy of The Ohio
State University Archives)

"Victory at Last!" read the headline in the next issue of the *Lantern*.[48] Walter
Sears held the position of toastmaster at the Thanksgiving feast that afternoon,
but he found that people wanted to talk primarily about the game. The highlight
of the afternoon was when Sears called Foulk up to deliver a toast to football.[49]

✻

Other games of local interest were played on that same Thanksgiving day.
In Cleveland, Kenyon's game against Adelbert determined the 1891 O.I.A.A.
championship. More than one thousand people watched from the Cleveland
grandstand as Adelbert won 42 to 6. The *Kenyon Collegian* wrote, "As the score
signifies, the Adelbert team was too strong for us.... *Consideratum omnem*, the team
of Adelbert College is one that merits its position at the head of Ohio colleges."[50]

The biggest football story of that Thanksgiving, however, was the latest
showdown between Yale and Princeton. The Columbus newspapers gave more
column space to that game than to any Ohio team.[51]

✻

The Buchtel game remained for Ohio State, but Charles Foulk had trouble finding anyone to serve as the umpire. As a team manager he was forbidden under O.I.A.A. rules from serving the position himself. With the date of the game growing closer, a notice appeared in the *Lantern*: "Manager Foulk of the Eleven has handed his resignation to the Board of Directors for reasons known only to himself. He resigns with the good will of everybody, leaving the team in better shape than it ever was before."[52] The team elected Dick Ellis to replace him. On December 5 the team headed to Akron, with Foulk serving as umpire.

Buchtel had not had a successful first season. They had won only one game and that had been against a new team composed of graduate students from Western Reserve University—that is, the W.R.U. students who did not attend Adelbert College. Facing the Case School of Applied Science, another new team, Buchtel had lost 42 to 0.[53]

Kid Pearce, Pete Gillen, and Gus Smith kept the same positions that they had held in the Thanksgiving game. Frank Haas now played halfback on the side opposite Gillen. Buchtel started the game with a series of rushes and soon turned the ball over on downs. On Ohio State's first play Pearce tossed the ball to Gillen. Gillen fumbled and a Buchtel man fell on it.

Buchtel drove the ball downfield but they turned the ball over just short of Ohio State's goal line. Ohio State then drove the ball the other way, ending with a 23-yard touchdown scramble by the tackle Ham Richardson. Haas attempted the kick but missed.

The second half of the game proved to be far less entertaining. Each team had taken a feel of the other and countered each other's moves as if they were reading from the same limited playbook. Neither team got close to the other's goal line. The game ended 4 to 0.[54] Both sides left the field content with the score.[55]

✳

All through the football season the Columbus Asylum for the Deaf had been challenging Ohio State to a game. For the Ohio State team this challenge had little appeal. The Asylum taught grades 9 through 12, so defeating them would not aid the university's reputation and a loss would be devastating, wiping out all the good feeling created by the last two games of the season. On the other hand, declining the challenge would look little better. Dick Ellis, as the new manager, found a solution by offering the Asylum students a scrimmage.

Ellis announced that he would send a practice team composed of the first-team line and the second-team backfield. In truth, the backfield had been in flux all season and by that point it was hard to differentiate the first-team from the second. The line, meanwhile, had developed into a veteran squad. Ohio State won the scrimmage 32 to 16.[56]

*

After the football season, Ed Bloom called another meeting of the Athletic Association to announce the final part of his reorganization plan. There he introduced a proposal that was even more radical than the one from the month before. He argued in favor of turning the Association into a publicly-owned for-profit joint-stock corporation.[57]

Bloom said that shareholders in an O.S.U. Athletic Company could expect regular healthy dividends. He estimated that expenses for all sports activities would not come to more than $250 in most years while receipts from those activities should come to a minimum of $500 per year. With a little luck downtown those numbers would get even better: "Should Columbus fail to have a professional team in either of the major associations we will draw a good attendance from down town and receipts will run far beyond present calculations."[58]

Bloom estimated that they would need at least $1,100 to build both the grandstand and the fence enclosure. Under the new plan, the Association would sell stock at a price of one dollar per share until the necessary funds had been raised. Shares could be sold to students, alumni, faculty, and any other "loyal friends of O. S. U."[59]

The Association approved the plan, and Bloom then used his "Local Notes" column in the *Lantern* to pressure everyone on campus to participate. "Remember this, that the more hearty your support the more respectable we can make the grounds. You will be called upon soon to take shares. Be prepared."[60]

Chapter Seventeen

Part of the proud and cherished history of O. S. U.

On February 11, 1892, Ed Bloom used his column to update everyone on the status of the Athletic Association. The Athletic Board of Directors had been in charge of day-to-day athletic operations for several months, and in that time, Bloom argued, the Board had been filling its responsibilities well. He did offer one small gripe, asking why the Board never called on the Association officers to "report its work and needs" and "ask for suggestions."

Bloom announced that the stock certificates had been sent to the printer and would soon be ready for purchase. He acknowledged that people worry about the security of any investment but he told his readers that an investment in the Athletic Company was not only safe but a personal duty: "No student should refuse to enter the market. It you think it a speculation it is at least a safe and righteous one and all should venture according to his needs."[1]

*

Some of Ohio State's most veteran football players were preparing to leave the team. Paul Lincoln and Ham Richardson would be graduating that spring. Charles Foulk, who had also helped found the team, decided that it was time for him to move on as well.

Among the candidates for the job of football manager was Walter Sears. Sears was known to be ambitious. He had previously sought leadership positions at both Alcyone and the *Lantern*. After the football team's victory on Thanksgiving, he began taking note of the enthusiasm that again was growing toward sports at Ohio State, and he turned to his ambitions there. *Makio* editors now quoted Edmund Burke: "Men who undertake considerable things, even in a regular way, ought to give us ground to presume ability."[2]

The elections of Athletic Association officers were held in mid-February. Kid Pearce was elected Association vice president and Eddie Martin, his battery partner, was elected president. Charlie Powell was reelected treasurer, a position that was growing in significance.[3] In the era of the Athletic Board the positions of president and vice president no longer came with the same authority that they had offered previously, but in the era of the joint-stock Athletic Company the position of treasurer promised even greater importance.

The Athletic Board selected team managers that same day. Bricky Evans had served for the past year as the baseball team's manager and the Board returned him to that role.[4] Walter Sears, aspiring to the position of football manager, needed a strategy to set his nomination above the others. He informed the Board that he could accept the position only if they met one condition. The Board would have to allow him access to Company funds for the purpose of hiring a football coach.[5] The Board apparently admired Sears's confidence and bravado because they selected him to manage the team.[6]

*

The winter meeting of the O.I.A.A. was scheduled for February 20, in Akron, following that year's State Oratory Contest. Herbert Johnston, the Chairman of the Athletic Board, happened to be Ohio State's orator at the contest, so the Board thought it a natural fit to ask him to serve as Ohio State's representative at the meeting.[7] Johnston agreed, but a few days later he decided that he was spreading his time in Akron too thin.[8] The primary purpose of the winter meeting was to prepare that year's baseball schedule so Johnston handed the responsibility to the respected baseball player Ed Pedlow.[9]

Johnston was preparing to graduate in June, and after his graduation he would take a position with Hobart Manufacturing. At Hobart he invented the electric mixer. He then patented his invention, founded the KitchenAid line of products, and made a fortune.[10] He eventually endowed a fellowship that still exists to assist Ohio State engineering students.[11]

Pedlow helped schedule the O.S.U. baseball season, but after the O.I.A.A. winter meeting it turned out that he was unable to play that year. He was forced to leave school for personal reasons before the spring.[12]

*

The Athletic Association began selling Athletic Company stock in mid-February but by early March they had sold only one hundred shares.[13] Edwin Bloom was no longer an Association officer, but in the "Local Notes" column he recommended lowering the investment target. Charlie Powell, as Association treasurer, asked Bloom to deliver a message defending the plan and endorsing its long-term prospects. Powell said, "I want it understood that those who subscribe stock in the Athletic Company are not making a free donation, but a bona fide investment."[14] Bloom added that the *Lantern* would reward loyalty to the project by printing the names of all investors at the end of the school year.

A student named Albert Sidney Johnston Eylar argued that the Athletic Board's fence plan was a waste of money. He told Bloom that there was no need to pay professional workers just to build the enclosure. For the cost of some wood planks the students could build one themselves. "Yes sir, a regular old fence-raising," he said. "Let all the students turn out, every one that can drive a nail or dig a post hole, and I warrant it that we can put up that fence in a single day."[15] Bloom forwarded the suggestion on to the Board.[16]

In early March Bloom insisted that he was still enthusiastic about the joint-stock project, but he conceded that investors would likely not be receiving any dividends that year.[17]

*

By this time the Ohio State University prep students had formed a football team of their own, and in late February they played a game against a Columbus high school. The preps won 8 to 0. The *Lantern* described the contest as "rather a pretty game."[18]

The newspaper editors seemed of two minds about the tone that the newspaper should take in reporting the news. Their writer conceded that the victory was probably "a small matter considering the inferiority of the team that was playing."[19] He went on to say, however, that every victory in the name of the university should be celebrated because "those who represent the University in any athletic sport should remember that O. S. U. expects them to represent her well—she expects them to *always win*."[20]

*

With the spring baseball season quickly approaching, it was clear that the Athletic Company would not have enough money before opening day to build both the fence around the field and the grandstand. They decided that having an enclosure was of more immediate importance than offering seats. Professional workers arrived to build the fence in mid-April. The first planks that they brought were too short for the job and they had to be sent back for the correct ones.[21] Some people on campus began to wonder why no one had listened to Albert Eylar's fence-raising plan.

By the end of April the fence was complete but the Athletic Board found itself in a new financial crisis. The final bill came to $750, which was more money than the Board was expecting, and more than the Company had yet raised. Professor Lazenby warned the Board that they needed to begin managing their funds more wisely.[22] Charlie Powell found some relief to the crisis when he discovered that local merchants were more willing than the university's board of trustees to extend the Company a line of credit.

Soon afterward Bricky Evans, the manager of the baseball team, approached the Athletic Board hat in hand and asked for $117 to purchase new uniforms. The Board agreed that it would be embarrassing to see the baseball team face O.I.A.A. opponents in their raggedy old suits. They approved the expenditure.[23]

*

The baseball team reassembled in April. Kid Pearce was captain, as he had been in the fall, and the spring season started well.[24] The team began O.I.A.A. competition with a game on April 23 against Denison in Granville. Denison was the preseason favorite to win the pennant but Ohio State won the opener 6 to 5.[25]

The team then came home to face Kenyon. Admission was set at twenty-five cents—the first paid attendance for any game on the Ohio State campus. There were no seats but three hundred people bought tickets, bringing seventy-five more dollars to the Association coffers. Ohio State won the game 10 to 2,[26] and the Athletic Board ordered work begun on the grandstand.

On April 30 the team played two non-O.I.A.A. games downtown, the first against a community team and the second against Capital University. After their strong start the team came to those games overconfident. They lost to Capital 9 to 6 and to the downtown "Town Streeters" 21 to 17. The *Lantern* questioned the character of the team, but Captain Pearce used the ugly losses to motivate and refocus his players.[27]

Three weeks later, on May 21, the team played two more games. In the morning they played Adelbert on the O.S.U. campus, winning 6 to 4, and their record in O.I.A.A. games rose to 3–0.[28] That afternoon they went to Delaware to face Ohio Wesleyan again. Ed Pedlow had remained in Columbus after he left school and he agreed to umpire the O.W.U. game. The Wesleyan team remembered Pedlow from his success against them in October.

Ohio State led 2 to 1 late in the game. Wesleyan's center fielder E.H. Barnes had earlier scored his team's only run, and in the bottom of the ninth inning he came to bat again. The pitch arrived and Barnes batted the ball downward, bouncing it off home plate, and then kicked it as he ran to first base. Pedlow called him out, ending the game. The Wesleyan team and their fans were furious. "Then it was that we were greeted with that Christian courtesy for which O. W. U. is becoming so well known," the *Lantern* reported. "The spectators joined the players in a wild and disgraceful attack upon the umpire."[29]

The Wesleyan students acknowledged the trouble but denied any responsibility. The *Transcript* wrote, "The slight exhibition of rowdyism over the contested ball game Saturday is regretted by all thoughtful persons. We are glad to say that those in authority deprecated the rude display and were in no way responsible for the occurrence."[30] They put most of the blame for the incident on Ed Pedlow: "The talk of the past week has demonstrated the fact that Umpire Pedlow has not gained a very warm place in the hearts of base-ball people nor would such work as his be tolerated again on the home diamond."[31]

The Ohio State Athletic Board passed a resolution forbidding their manager from scheduling any more games with Wesleyan. The resolution stated that "any future contests in athletics between O. S. U. and O. W. U. cannot but arouse unwarranted ill-feeling between these universities."[32] The resolution was understood to be directed toward the football manager as well.

Ohio State played three more games the following week. The first was against Otterbein on Saturday, May 28, which Evans had scheduled mostly due to new taunting from Otterbein students. O.S.U. won 18 to 3, and the *Lantern* bragged, "We gave her such a drubbing that they will not soon forget."[33] The next game, on Monday, was a rematch against Denison. The Ohio State second baseman Puggy Shaw hit a game-winning RBI single in the twelfth inning. Twenty-five years later, when Shaw was a probate judge, he was still regularly asked to talk about the game.[34] After a victory over Buchtel on Friday, June 3, the team had a 5–0 record in the O.I.A.A.

The team ended the season with a road trip in early June. They faced Kenyon, Buchtel, and Adelbert in consecutive days. Back in Columbus, students waited for news at the telegraph office. A few minutes after the Adelbert game the team sent a message: They had swept all three games. Fred Patterson and Charlie Powell left the telegraph office, grabbed a pair of drums, and began marching across campus spreading the news. The Athletic Association flew a flag off University Hall and they prepared an impromptu celebratory feast.[35]

The *Lantern* wrote:

> The pennant is ours. It is easily ours. It was gloriously won. Eight straight victories attest our undisputed right to it, and we are all delighted. Who can fully express the pride and admiration we feel for O. S. U. and her matchless baseball team? The record they have made has never been equaled and can never be surpassed. It will become part of the proud and cherished history of O. S. U.…. Their deeds shall never be forgotten, but the future shall claim them as the heroes of O. S. U. as we do today.[36]

✻

Earlier that spring new leadership had come to the *Lantern*. The April 28 issue had announced that Morrison Ray was stepping down as editor-in-chief and a student named Edwin Moody would be taking Ray's position. Walter Sears took over Moody's previous position as managing editor.[37] Sears and Moody were friends, and together they tried to take advantage of the turnover, developing a plan to modernize the newspaper.

Sears and Moody were acquainted with the business manager at the *Columbus Daily Press*, a man named Charles Harper, and Harper told them that the *Lantern*'s approach to journalism was too quaint for the era of Hearst and Pulitzer. The *Lantern* had always been as much a literary journal as a newspaper, with each issue featuring at least one extended academic essay—a remnant of the fact that the newspaper had been founded by literary societies. Harper also argued that the name "*Lantern*" was pretentious. Sears and Moody soaked up their mentor's insights.[38]

They said that they wanted to revise the student newspaper as a modern broadsheet and to give it the name "*Wahoo.*" They argued that a name based on the school yell would show a connection to the school's athletic traditions and be more fun for the readers. Then they convinced the rest of the staff of their plan.

The *Lantern* announced the coming change in the June 16 issue, stating that, "Next to a victorious ball team, the best advertisement for a college is a hustling,

COLLEGE CHAMPIONS OF OHIO.

J. T. DANIELS.   L. C. ERNST.   C. W. WITHOFT.   ROY YODER.   P. M. GRIFFITH.
        A. P. GILLEN.   E. C. MARTIN.   E. EVANS, MANAGER.   T. T. SHAW.
                                              E. A. WAGSTAFF.   G. D. PEARCE, CAPTAIN.

Ohio State University Base Ball Team 1892.

Ohio State's O.I.A.A champion 1892 baseball team, promised never to be forgotten.
(Photo courtesy of The Ohio State University Archives)

wide-awake newspaper."[39] Most of the readers thought that the name *"Wahoo"*
was ridiculous. They called it undignified and an embarrassment to the university. The *Makio* again criticized Sears, this time quoting Shakespeare's "Cymbe-
line": "Not Hercules could have knocked out his brains, for he had none."[40]

✳

As the school year came to a close, Charlie Powell released the Athletic Company's financial statement. The Company had raised $971.95. Of that, $465 came
from stock sales—$255 from students, $183 from faculty, and the rest from alumni.
Only eighty-nine students had invested, and of the money from the faculty $50
had come from Professor Lazenby alone. The Company raised the additional

$506.95 through other means. Baseball receipts brought in $460.20, the campus field day brought in $31.25, and tennis added $3.50. Twelve dollars came from the sale of various surplus assets. The Company was left approximately $300 in debt.[41]

Despite the Company's financial state, Powell maintained a positive outlook on the larger goals of the project. "The splendid success of our ball team resulted from the financial backing of the Stock Company and the strong support of the Board of Directors," he wrote. "If our good luck continues our foot ball team will win the pennant in the fall."[42]

✳

The following fall Walter Sears grew upset when he discovered that some more of the football veterans were turning down invitations to return to the team. Those included Hobart Beatty and Raymond Krumm. The "Local Notes" column reported, "Hob. Beatty will not play football this fall and Manager Sears is mad."[43]

Beatty, in fact, soon left school altogether. He had not been any more successful as a student than his older brother William had been. Two years later Beatty committed suicide after falling in love, the *Lantern* said, "with a woman incapable of fidelity, whose love even if won and constant, would have been of no credit to him."[44] Beatty was still not yet twenty years old.

After college Krumm pursued a business opportunity in Korea, but his short temper followed him even there. In Korea he fell in love with the local culture, and he also fell in love with the niece of an American diplomat. Krumm proposed, his proposal was rejected, and he nearly created an international incident. He accused the diplomat of defrauding the Korean people. The case went to court, where the judge warned Krumm to curb his hot-headedness.[45] In his will Krumm donated funds to establish a scholarship for Ohio State students from Korea.[46]

Hugh Fullerton left school in the spring of 1892, never getting a chance to play in an Ohio State football game. He later became a well-known sports reporter, noted for his rich use of language and credited with introducing slang and human-interest elements to sports writing. Ring Lardner and Grantland Rice were among his protégés. In later years he occasionally returned to Ohio State to reminisce about his time there, often joking that he had been forced to leave because as a student he had "batted .126 in math."[47]

In 1920 Fullerton found his most honored place in sports history when he uncovered the events that would come to be known as the Chicago "Black Sox" baseball scandal.[48] In 1963 Major League Baseball posthumously awarded him the Spink Award, the so-called "writer's wing" of the Hall of Fame.[49]

*

The Ohio State bicycle club that F.L.O. Wadsworth had founded in the mid-1880s had long since folded, but the bicycle races that his club had started had since been absorbed into the Ohio State campus field day. In the spring of 1892 a prep student named Arthur French competed in that year's bicycle race. He had only recently begun riding but he won the race. He continued racing throughout the summer.[50]

He came back to campus as a freshman in the fall with three races still on his schedule. The first was in his hometown of Cincinnati, the second was in Louisville, Kentucky, and the third was in Chicago.[51] He told the Athletic Board that he wanted to represent his university in those races by wearing scarlet and gray. The Board endorsed French's plan and declared him an at-large varsity athlete.[52]

Joseph Nelson Bradford was an O.S.U. faculty member, and he had recently purchased ten shares of Athletic Company stock.[53] Ten years earlier he had been the O.S.U. cadet who had organized the Ohio State marching band. The university hired him in 1886 to teach technical drawing, and soon afterward he established departments in the fine arts and photography. He would go on to establish the university's school of architecture in 1899.[54] In 1892 he wanted to help Arthur French in his efforts to represent the university, and he designed the first Ohio State University logo to put on the racing outfit.[55]

Chapter Eighteen
The sake of truth and conscience

K ate Morhart became the first editor-in-chief of the *Wahoo* in the fall of
1892, and in the very first issue she addressed the controversy that
already surrounded the change in name. She stated that school yells and
other athletic rituals were a legitimate part of the student experience, and, if only
for that reason, they were as worthy of recognition as any other. She pointed out
that the weekly humor magazine at Princeton University, the *Princeton Tiger*, was
given its name in reference to their athletic traditions. She promised that in the
weeks ahead she and the other editors would listen to all criticism. "But in the
meantime, as editors, we will endeavor to make *Wahoo*, in spite of its abused name,
a first class paper."[1]

Walter Sears was still the newspaper's managing editor, and he promised
that an increase in advertising sales would prove the value of all his changes.[2]

*

No new prep students were admitted to Ohio State that fall. That decision
was the university's first step in the process of shutting down the preparatory
program completely. President Scott described the change in his annual report
as an opportunity to take "an important step toward raising the work of the
University to its true level."[3]

Some people outside the university saw an opportunity of a different sort.
If Ohio State would no longer be preparing young students for college work,
then the city of Columbus would need new prep schools to fill the gap. One of
those new schools was named the Columbus Latin School, founded by a man
named Frank Cole.[4]

Cole gave a teaching position at his school to Frederick Bushnell Ryder,[5] who had previously been a student at Oberlin College. Ryder then came to the attention of students at Ohio State when they discovered that he had experience with college football. Most recently he had played for Williams College in Massachusetts.[6] Walter Sears had not yet fulfilled his pledge to hire a football coach, so when he learned of Ryder's history he went downtown for a talk.

It was football that had pushed Ryder out of Oberlin. He had been trained in gridiron football as a prep student in Andover, Massachusetts, and he used that training to form the Oberlin varsity team. In 1889, he scheduled a Thanksgiving game against Wooster, but the Oberlin faculty ordered it cancelled. Ryder decided that if Oberlin would not let him play football he would go back to Massachusetts.[7]

He enrolled at Williams College and joined the varsity football team there. During this time he played the sport at its highest level, competing against Harvard, Yale, and other top teams. Frank Cole was a Williams College alumnus, and when Ryder graduated from Williams two years later Cole brought him to the Columbus Latin School.

Walter Sears was impressed with Ryder's story and he asked Ryder to coach Ohio State's team. He added that he was authorized to offer a salary of $15 a week. Ryder jumped at the offer.[8]

✻

In September Emma Scott came back to Columbus to visit her parents. She had been studying at the Cincinnati Medical College and would soon have a degree to practice medicine.[9] Of all of President Scott's children, Emma most seemed to share his passion for spreading the Gospel, but President Scott could now see that her interest in missionary work had an additional purpose. In that era, a desperately poor and underdeveloped country might be more accepting of a female doctor than would most parts of the United States.[10]

President Scott may also have begun thinking about other students that he had known during his nine years serving the university. They had always offered him as much to think about as he had ever taught them. Those students were likely to have a strong reaction to his upcoming retirement announcement.

✻

By the fall of 1892 the Columbus Athletic Club was on the verge of falling apart. Joe Firestone's career at Columbus Buggy was advancing and he had grown too busy for football. Al Lilley had moved away, accepting a job opportunity in San Francisco. S.P. Bush put a notice in the September 12 issue of the *State Journal* announcing open tryouts.[11]

The Ohio State team was also having problems holding together. Dick Ellis did not understand the attitude of veteran players who were abandoning football. He believed that the team was on the verge of a breakthrough and he was eager to begin the new season. He was not concerned about organizational changes within the Athletic Association or about who was allowed to choose the football manager. He had lost the position of captain at the start of the 1891 season due to an injury and he expected another chance.[12]

Ellis rallied seven players from 1891 back to the team—Dutch Ernst, Pete Gillen, Frank Haas, William Nagel, Charlie Powell, Clarence Withoft, and William Zurfluh.[13] Those seven players were joined by two freshmen: William Genheimer and William Reed.[14] These players reelected Ellis as captain.[15] The team, however, still remained short of an eleven.

Another student who was not returning to the football team that fall was Mortimer Lawrence. Lawrence had lost his taste for college sports. In the spring he had invested $25 in the Athletic Company[16]—the equivalent of over $600 today. After seeing how the Company was handling its funds he had no reason to believe that he would ever see his investment again.

A writer for the *Wahoo* regularly followed the team, and after one frustrating practice Dick Ellis approached that writer to vent. He complained that "if fifteen or twenty men don't come out occasionally…all our training is going to be in vain."[17] He added, "I just wish you would say to these people who are anxious for our success to come out on the grounds and express their sentiments in a practical way."[18]

Charlie Powell had returned to the team despite the fact that he had injured his ear the previous year and dreaded putting it at further risk.[19] Mike Kennedy had been away from campus at the beginning of the year,[20] but he had recently returned to campus and returned to the team. Kennedy had an idea to help Powell protect his ear. He designed a covering made of heavy felt and helped Powell construct it.[21]

Manager Walter Sears decided to see what he could do to help save the season. The year before, in a similar situation, Charles Foulk had made his case in the *Lantern*. Sears now wrote an essay of his own and had it published in the *Wahoo*. He opened his essay with two questions: "What are our prospects for foot ball this fall, and how shall we win?"[22]

These are the questions we constantly hear on every side. They are being asked by every loyal student and university man—by everyone who feels some pride in the athletic glory of O. S. U. The matchless record made by the base ball club last spring has raised the standard here of what can be justly expected in athletics and the query now is, can the foot ball team keep up the pace so proudly set.[23]

The primary need of the team, he said, was for bodies. "At present we have not enough men for one strong eleven. We ought to have big surplus over enough for two."[24] Between the efforts of Ellis and Sears, they eventually brought twenty-two players to the team.

Sears also arranged for the Athletic Board to make a new rule, stating that Ohio State's baseball team must stop scheduling games in the fall. The idea was to avoid conflicts over player recruitment between the baseball and football teams. Kate Morhart agreed with this decision and supported it in a *Wahoo* editorial. She said, "It is the 1000 per cent mark of the base ball nine in the Intercollegiate games that must be equaled by our foot ball team this fall."[25]

The baseball team had by then already arranged a fall game with Capital University but the Board refused to sanction it. If the baseball players wanted to face Capital they would have to do so only as a "picked team" and not as official representatives of Ohio State. Although the Board did not sanction the game, they did intend to charge for any game played on their athletic field. Admission would be ten cents. As a bonus for the paying fans after the baseball game, the Board hoped to offer a football scrimmage between the first and second teams.[26]

Earlier that term, S.P. Bush had come to the O.S.U. campus looking for help to hold his team together.[27] He asked Walter Sears for a game, or at least a scrimmage, to be held in late September.[28] Before the two could arrange a game, however, the Columbus Athletic Club had folded.[29]

✻

That fall Charlie Powell was elected to represent the senior class on the Athletic Board, making him the Chairman of the Board.[30] He also still remained the Athletic Association treasurer. In late September he released a statement listing the expected assets and liabilities of the Athletic Company as they attempted to pay for the new football season. The season was projected to put the Company further in the red unless more investors appeared. In an interview in the *Wahoo* Powell made a new plea: "Why, if every man who hasn't already subscribed would give one dollar—buy one share of stock—we would have more than we need; why yes, just one dollar from each of these men would put us away up in the G."[31]

The *Wahoo* reprinted the Company's list of investors that the *Lantern* had published in the spring, and this time the editors used the opportunity to directly criticize the students who had chosen not to invest. "This list, in our judgment, is not as complimentary to the athletic pride of the student body as it might be."[32] Those who did not invest were called free riders who "simply lacked the proper college spirit, the proper amount of pride in all that concerns the success and glory of O. S. U."[33]

In early October Powell announced a new financial strategy in pursuit of additional investment. He offered all stock-holders a preferred-rate stock redemption plan. After all debts were paid off, and the Company was in the black, the Company would be liquidated and all stock certificates would be fully redeemed, with interest. "Thus, as may plainly be seen, the money put into the affair is considered merely as a loan and nothing else."[34] Powell estimated that the stock redemption would begin just after baseball season.

*

Fred Ryder arrived to begin his job at Ohio State on September 15, 1892.[35] In the early part of the twentieth century, he would become a nationally known sports-writer for the *Cincinnati Enquirer*, primarily covering the Cincinnati Reds. Upon his death in 1936 the commissioner of Major League Baseball, Kenesaw Mountain Landis, would release an official statement of condolence.[36] As a sportswriter Ryder adopted the pen name "Jack Ryder," but during his time at Ohio State he was known as Fred. In 1892 Sears introduced Ryder to the O.S.U. campus as "a thor-oughly able and competent man" and "a gentleman of many fine parts."[37]

Ryder wanted to train the team but he said that it was equally important to train the entire student body. He sought out the *Wahoo* writer who followed the team to say that he encouraged the entire campus "to come out strong to our practice games" to learn the "fine points" of game strategy and how to best follow the action on the field.[38]

> Now I believe that applause and good, hard cheering at the right time in the game goes a great way to make up the chances of victory. So I should think that it would be a good idea if your men should come out to our practice game every evening and learn all they can of the true ways of playing them. It would not only encourage the men who are now doing such faithful work on the elevens,

but it would be providing for the future—when we will want the united cheer of the whole student body, to help us on to victory.[39]

Ryder taught the football players all that he knew about the strategies of East Coast football. His favorite play used a formation known in the East as the "Williams Wedge," in which the traditional wedge protected a smaller wedge inside, and that smaller wedge protected the ball carrier. In Ohio this play would be known as the "Ryder Wedge."[40]

Although the Columbus Athletic Club had disbanded, S.P. Bush still made an effort to stay close to football. He was among those who began coming out to the grounds to watch the Ohio State practices. On a Saturday in early October he even brought a young woman with him on a date to watch a scrimmage.[41] Bush was impressed with Ryder's work and he volunteered to help as Ryder's assistant.[42]

Dick Ellis had heard about teams in the East using "training tables" to guide the diet of their players and he wanted the same for his men. Organizing such things was the responsibility of the manager, and Walter Sears sought advice from their coach. Ryder introduced a high-protein diet that was followed at Williams College. Breakfast was oatmeal, eggs, and toast. Lunch was meat, potatoes, and cabbage. Supper was more meat, more eggs, more potatoes, more bread, and cold stewed fruit for dessert. A single cup of coffee was allowed with breakfast, and tea was allowed with dinner, but tobacco was forbidden.[43] Ryder said that this diet originally came from the training regimen of the boxer John L. Sullivan.[44]

The Denison athletic association decided that they also wanted a football coach and they made an attempt to hire Amos Alonzo Stagg. They were outbid for Stagg's services by the students at the University of Chicago. The *Wahoo* commented, "O. S. U. is not so ambitious as that" but stated proudly that they have "a first class man in that position anyway."[45]

✻

On October 1 Walter Sears went to Kenyon for the fall O.I.A.A. meeting. The representatives agreed that, because football games played after Thanksgiving always felt anticlimactic, the teams would no longer schedule games to be played in December. Ohio State's O.I.A.A. season would open at home against Buchtel on October 22. The team would then travel to Granville to play Denison on November 5 and to Cleveland to play Adelbert on November 19. The Thanksgiving game would be at home, this year again with Kenyon.[46]

Sears also negotiated four games outside the O.I.A.A. He scheduled a game with Marietta College and another with the team from the Dayton Y.M.C.A. Both games were to be played on the Ohio State campus.[47] He scheduled two games against Fred Ryder's old team at Oberlin College, the first at Oberlin and the second at Ohio State.[48]

Oberlin had begun playing intercollegiate football in 1891 following the gridiron rules that Ryder taught them. In 1890, the year after the game that Ryder had scheduled against Wooster, the Oberlin students scheduled a game against Adelbert, but a blizzard forced the cancellation of that game. The Oberlin team then played four games in 1891. They defeated the team from the Case School, they lost a game to Michigan, and they split their pair of games against Adelbert. The first of Oberlin's two games against Ohio State in 1892 was to be the season opener for both schools.[49]

The O.S.U. Athletic Board put season tickets on sale but not many fans chose to buy them. The price of the package was greater than the per-game rate. The Board argued that the season tickets were another opportunity for students to show their loyalty: "It is to be hoped that the student body will look at the matter in the right light and not be prevented from buying them for the simple reason that by paying separate admissions to each game they may be able to save a quarter in the whole transaction."[50]

*

A chapel service was held on campus on a Monday morning in early October. The mood was light until President Scott rose to speak. His expression was so serious that the atmosphere inside the room suddenly turned grim. President Scott said that he had recently taken an action that would affect everyone at the university, so he owed it to everyone to make a public statement of explanation.[51]

He said that he had always believed that "All men were the children of God."[52] Thus it followed that "God and the human soul are of the same nature."[53] He said that as we each strive to be "completely at one with God" we must each find our own "close sympathy and fellowship with Him." Following from his belief that all people have a duty "to love God as their father with all their hearts, and to love their fellow men as themselves," he had concluded that each human soul must be free to seek their sympathy and fellowship with God independently, and without judgment, "according to the strength and clearness of their spiritual vision."[54]

He acknowledged that his new beliefs were not in accord with the teachings of the church in which he ministered. For that reason, and "for the sake of truth and conscience," he had submitted to his church a letter of resignation. He said that he would now "enter a freer and, as I humbly believe, a larger religious life."[55]

President Scott's announcement that he was leaving his church brought attention to the university throughout the state.[56] The Columbus newspapers looked for the reaction on campus but the faculty avoided making any public statements. The students followed the faculty's lead. The *Wahoo* did not even write its own coverage of the news, choosing instead to reprint an article about President Scott's announcement that had earlier appeared in the *State Journal.*[57]

To the students and faculty who still saw freedom of conscience as the university's core value, the president's action felt like a validation. Some remembered the campus battle over the chapel policy and the associated demerit punishment. During those years the *Lantern* had offered the students a voice in the fight. In the weeks after President Scott's announcement, the opinion began to be argued more loudly that the *Wahoo* must return to its original name.[58]

Since the start of the school year Kate Morhart, in addition to being the *Wahoo* editor-in-chief, had been elected the president of the senior class.[59] She agreed with those who wanted to return to the original name, and she was willing to fight for that change. She convinced most of the newspaper staff. Walter Sears still disagreed and argued that he had already sold advertising based on the new name. Morhart said that they would work around that problem.[60]

In late October Morhart wrote an editorial to declare, "We must have a paper that is worthy of representing this institution."[61] A change could not be made immediately, she said, due to business concerns, but unless a groundswell of opinion arose in support of the *Wahoo* name, the *Lantern* would be revived before the start of the winter term.

Chapter Nineteen

What does it mean?

On Friday, October 14, the Ohio State football players took a train north to play their game in Oberlin the next morning. They were expecting a challenge. Oberlin had matched up well with Adelbert the year before while Adelbert had easily swept through its schedule of O.I.A.A. games. Walter Sears worked to downplay expectations. In the days before the game the *Wahoo* reported, "Manager Sears does not hope to win, nor is that the purpose of the game. It is rather as a test of the strength of the present eleven."[1]

Coach Fred Ryder accompanied the O.S.U. players to Oberlin. He looked forward to seeing old friends on the campus but he was more focused on assessing the progress of his team. He had confidence in their training but he also had concerns that they were breaking in a new lineup. Dick Ellis returned at left end and Charlie Powell still played at center, but the rest of the line was filled with new recruits and former back-ups. In the backfield, Frank Haas, Pete Gillen, and Clarence Withoft had all returned, but Mike Kennedy was not considered ready. Kennedy had not yet had much practice so Dutch Ernst filled the other halfback slot.[2]

The team played as well as Ryder had hoped but the game itself turned out worse than he had feared.[3] The Ohio State players executed their plays with discipline and precision, and their bucking the line was particularly crisp, but Oberlin responded with plays that even Ryder had never seen. They easily defeated the Ryder Wedge, dismissing it as "a trick" that he had "imported from the Berkshire hills."[4] Powell at center and Haas at quarterback were harassed all afternoon.

Ryder discovered the secret behind Oberlin's tactical advantage when he noticed that Oberlin's captain was not calling their plays. Looking closer, he recognized the halfback who was actually in charge. It was John Heisman, a

Fred Patterson, third from the right on the balcony, among his dormmates in 1892.
(Photo courtesy of The Ohio State University Archives)

former standout from the University of Pennsylvania.[5] The final score of the
game was 40 to 0, and the Ohio State players were left disheartened. Ryder reas-
sured them on the train ride home that they had done well. They would not be
seeing a similar team that season.[6]

✣

Fred Patterson did not accompany the team to Oberlin. He had other issues
on his mind that fall. So far in 1892 the United States had been experiencing the
worst racial violence since the Civil War, with the lynching of African-American
men in the South becoming common practice. It was an election year and the
violence was intended in part as a means to maintain the older social order.[7] Patterson wanted to find a way to help.

Patterson had been feeling that he was living in a cocoon at Ohio State.[8] He
had just finished a year as the president of his class. He was confident that not

even the most racially intolerant student on campus wanted to hang him from a tree. The struggles in the South that Patterson was reading about seemed to be similar to the struggles that his father had faced as a slave. If he ever were to deserve to follow in his father's footsteps, he decided that he would need to find a way to make a stand.

✷

The Ohio State football players were anxious to see the tone of the game coverage in the Oberlin city newspapers. They were pleased to see their attitude and sportsmanship praised in *Oberlin News*. The newspaper added that "they may be assured of an equally warm welcome whenever they appear."[9] Kate Morhart was also pleased: "O. S. U. men, wherever they go, know how to conduct themselves in such a way as to leave an enviable impression behind. This should become one of the traditional characteristics among all O. S. U. men. College men first above all should be men."[10]

✷

The football team's home opener was scheduled against Buchtel on October 22. It was to be the first intercollegiate football game ever played on the Ohio State campus. The grandstand was completed and awaiting fans. Paul Lincoln had returned to campus to watch the game, and the team greeted his return by asking him to serve as their referee.[11]

Buchtel played a game with Kenyon the day before coming to Ohio State. They lost 52 to 0. Their athletic association had considered it financially prudent to schedule both games as a single road trip, but the Buchtel players were exhausted to be playing one game so soon after the other. As they got to Columbus they hoped to negotiate a shortened game.

A large crowd was in the Ohio State grandstand, including the Kenyon captain and manager, who both had accompanied the Buchtel players to Columbus to scout the game. Buchtel's captain, Carlos Webster, approached Dick Ellis to ask if they could play halves of thirty minutes instead of forty-five minutes. Ellis dismissed the idea and told Webster to start the game. Webster was stopped short by Ellis's brusqueness and said that he was going to take his team home. Ellis looked to the seats and imagined the reaction of the Athletic Board if the game was not played and hundreds of paying spectators demanded their money back. He offered a compromise. He agreed to a thirty-minute first half if Buchtel would play a full forty-five-minute second half.

Buchtel won the coin toss and took the ball. Ellis took the east goal. Going west would allow his team to run a slightly downward slope. Early in their first drive Buchtel turned the ball over on downs, and after two plays Mike Kennedy, back at halfback, scored an Ohio State touchdown. Ellis made the kick and the score was 6 to 0. Just a few minutes later, Kennedy had another touchdown and the score was 10 to 0.

Dick Ellis and the other Ohio State players were amazed by how well they were playing. Every play that Oberlin had easily shut down the week before was working to perfection against Buchtel. Even considering that Buchtel had never defeated an O.I.A.A. team, that Kenyon had routed Buchtel the day before, and even conceding Buchtel's claim to be exhausted, Ohio State's football team had never looked stronger.

On Buchtel's next drive, Carlos Webster complained that Paul Lincoln had ignored a foul and demanded that he be replaced. Ellis refused and Webster again threatened to pull his team off the field. Ellis wanted desperately to finish this game so he agreed to the change. Lincoln was replaced with William H. Foley, the captain of the Kenyon team.

Ohio State ultimately won 62 to 0. They scored twelve touchdowns. Kennedy alone scored five, and seven others were divided among five other players on the team. The *State Journal* opened their coverage with, "Wahoo! Wahoo! Zip! Bazoo! Buchtel done up by O. S. U."[12] The *Columbus Press-Post* (the result of a recent merger of the *Columbus Daily Press* and the *Columbus Post*) said that the game "was so one sided that details would be monotonous."[13]

The Buchtel coverage emphasized their need to find a coach. The student newspaper, the *Buchtelite*, wrote, "Systematic training is essential to success in football, and a competent trainer is essential to systematic training."[14] The *Akron Daily Beacon* was more blunt: "The Buchtel team needs coaching and needs it badly."[15]

Bricky Evans, the former baseball manager, had graduated the previous spring but he sent a congratulatory letter to the football team. He said that he and Kid Pearce would be coming back to campus to attend that year's Thanksgiving game.[16]

*

The *Wahoo* had asked Caesar Morrey, as Alumni Editor, to provide expert analysis of the game.[17] He agreed. With each passing year Morrey seemed less like a student and more like a member of the faculty. During the previous spring he had pitched for the faculty in a faculty-versus-seniors baseball game. That fall the faculty freed him of the responsibility of teaching Greek and Latin to the prep students and allowed him to focus on teaching biology. The football team, however, remained one of his priorities.

In the *Wahoo*, Morrey assessed the team's current running backs. He said that Mike Kennedy had been the team's most effective ball carrier because he used his blockers well, whereas Pete Gillen had seemed anxious and often outran his protection. When Kennedy did not have the ball, on the other hand, he had shown poor work as a blocker.[18]

Morrey also had other observations. He said that although Dick Ellis is "admirably suited" to his position at left end, he had hurt the flow of the offense as captain with inefficient communication with his quarterback. Billy Reed, the new left guard, took the worst of Morrey's criticism: "Reed is pretty weak and lacks nerve. He will have to brace up or lose his position."[19] Morrey concluded, "The boys played a good game in many respects, but they had a weak team against them," and said that, "Because of their first easy victory the players must not get the 'big head'."[20]

In an editorial in early November, Kate Morhart bragged about what the team's success could mean for the university. She noted, "Athletics are at last recognized as a worthy factor in the O. S. U." And because of the success of the team, the school was set to receive "increased interest by the outside world."[21]

✳

Ohio State's next O.I.A.A. game was to be against Denison on November 5 but scheduled before then was a game against Marietta College. In the years after they first challenged Ohio State to a game in 1887 Marietta had continued to play their local version of football—a version that was closer to soccer. In 1892 Marietta joined a new intercollegiate association named the Athletic League of Ohio Colleges, and a requirement of membership in this association—which included Ohio University, Otterbein College, and Wittenberg University—was to form a gridiron football team. Marietta's first gridiron football game was on the Ohio State campus on October 29.

Ohio State performed in the game beyond anyone's expectations. The final score was 80 to 0. Six Ohio State players scored touchdowns, led by four from Pete Gillen, who seemed to have taken Caesar Morrey's criticism to heart. The *State Journal*

The faculty versus seniors baseball game of 1892. (Photo courtesy of The Ohio State University Archives)

wrote, "Marietta was completely outclassed and outplayed. It was clever united team work on the part of Ohio State University that won against disunited, uneffective individual work on the part of Marietta."[22] The Marietta student newspaper, the *Olio*, wrote, "The interference of O. S. U. was excellent, while we had none whatever."[23] (What we call "blocking" today, they called "interference" then.) The *Columbus Press-Post* again complained that the game was too one-sided to be entertaining.[24]

While Ohio State was playing Marietta, other teams in the O.I.A.A. were playing games within the association. Adelbert defeated Buchtel 52 to 0 and Kenyon defeated Denison 10 to 0. The *Press-Post* writer began looking ahead to Ohio State's Thanksgiving game against Kenyon, "as it will probably be the hardest contest of the championship series."[25]

✳

Ohio State went to Granville to play Denison on November 5. The Ohio State students were developing a reputation for accompanying their team to away games and a railroad offered a discount rate for a group purchase of fifty tickets or more. The *Wahoo* advised interested students to give their name and money to Charlie Powell.[26] Ultimately seventy-five Ohio State students joined the group taking the train.[27]

Denison was considered the team's first significant test of the season, but Ohio State controlled the game from the start. As against Buchtel and Marietta, every play seemed to work. The *Wahoo* said, "In all its plays the team moved like one man, and with wonderful precision and effect."[28] As a result they were able to "tear through Denison's line like a cyclone."[29] The score at halftime was 23 to 0.

The game was coming so easy that the O.S.U. backs began fighting among each other for the opportunity to score a touchdown. Every time they approached the Denison goal line they were heard lobbying quarterback Frank Haas loudly for the ball. Caesar Morrey was unhappy hearing such a "vain and foolish" display.[30] Such "selfish desire"[31] was never seen on the team when he played the game.

Near the end of the second half Denison carried the ball within three feet of scoring, and the Ohio State players needed another goal-line stand if they hoped to preserve a shutout. The Ohio State fans had been trying to give the feel of a home game by shouting their school yell from the Denison grandstand, and they became even louder during this series of plays. The *Wahoo* later wrote, "The O. S. U. delegation was a splendid one. Their constant giving of the yell was a mighty slogan for our men."[32] The final score was 32 to 0.

The *Wahoo* gave the greatest credit to the coaching of Fred Ryder. They stated that "no more faithful work was ever done than has been and is being done by Mr. Ryder. He not only has the regard and respect and loyalty of every player, but he has already won the admiration of every loyal O. S. U. man."[33] The *Denison Exponent* also identified coaching as the difference in the game: "One thing is certain, and is acknowledged by all, we have not been properly trained."[34]

The game left the Ohio State students on campus wondering how good their team actually was. The *Wahoo* titled their game coverage "What Does It Mean?" In the following issue Kate Morhart wrote an editorial pondering when Ohio State would be mentioned in the same breath as Yale, Harvard and Princeton.

> When will our team be fit for a comparison with those of the east? If the advance be made as rapidly in the future as in the past year, scarcely a decade will be necessary to make the O. S. U. team a worthy competitor in first-class championship games.[35]

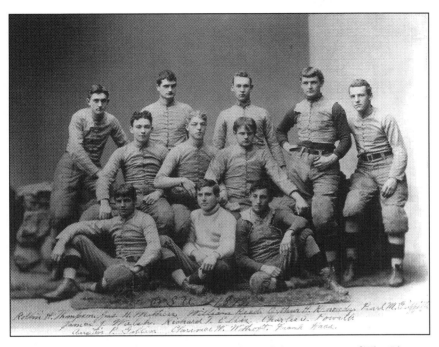

The 1892 football team, a.k.a. the Egotistical Eleven. (Photo courtesy of The Ohio State University Archives)

The football players were growing in confidence and on campus some people began to call them the "Egotistical Eleven."[36]

While Ohio State had been playing Denison, Kenyon defeated Adelbert 20 to 12.[37] The upcoming Thanksgiving game against Kenyon was looming on the schedule.

✻

On Monday, just two days after the Denison game, Ohio State played Oberlin again. Since the first meeting four weeks earlier the Ohio State players had developed a local reputation as an effective team, but during those same weeks Oberlin had developed a national reputation. After opening against Ohio State they defeated Adelbert 38 to 3, Kenyon 38 to 0, and Ohio Wesleyan 56 to 0. Everyone seemed to agree that Oberlin had succeeded Wooster as the elite team in the state. But if Ohio State were to win this game, the popular sentiment could possibly be thrown into doubt.

John Heisman meanwhile was building a reputation of his own. As the attention given to his team grew, Heisman could no longer hide anonymously, and with questionable legality, on the field. He began to take a coach's more typical position on the sideline. When other schools learned that Oberlin was not paying him a salary, they began to make offers for his services.[38]

Ohio State's rematch with Oberlin would be played on the O.S.U. campus. The *Wahoo* had been promoting it for several days: "Oberlin, the great giant team of the North, is to play foot-ball with O. S. U., on our own grounds, Monday afternoon at 2:30 o'clock. This is the opportunity of the season to see a first class game. Everybody come and bring friends."[39] The *Press-Post* wrote, "The game with Oberlin Monday afternoon on the O. S. U. grounds will be a highly interesting one."

The campus looked forward to seeing the Ohio State players attempt their revenge, but the team would not be playing at full strength. Dick Ellis was unavailable at left end, replaced with William Nagel. Pete Gillen was unavailable at halfback, replaced with Dutch Ernst. Mike Kennedy was healthy but he said that he needed rest. He started the game but soon went to the bench. Ellis then gave his spot to Caesar Morrey.

Oberlin won 50 to 0. The *Wahoo* said, "It was unfortunate that we were compelled to play so strong a team under so unfavorable circumstances."[40] Despite the score the *Oberlin Review* tried to be gracious, "Oberlin found O. S. U. a much stronger team, though full of substitutes, than last time. Our playing was good but O. S. U., having learned by experience, broke our interference badly."

The next day Grover Cleveland defeated Benjamin Harrison in the 1892 Presidential election. The election was of local interest because Harrison was born and raised in Ohio. The *Wahoo* wrote, "Each individual player must determine for himself whether he considers the results of the present Presidential campaign or of the yesterday's foot ball game of the most importance.[41]"

Oberlin finished that year undefeated, at least according to their own records. Two weeks after the game at Ohio State, Oberlin played the University of Michigan. The Oberlin captain announced when they arrived in Ann Arbor that they would need to leave in time to catch the last train back to Cleveland. The Oberlin players later insisted that Michigan had agreed to those terms but the Michigan players claimed that they had never made an explicit commitment.

When the Oberlin players left the campus they were winning 24 to 22. After waving goodbye the Michigan players lined up again and continued playing unopposed. Both schools still claim the victory in their official record.

John Heisman would explore his options after that season. He fielded a number of offers, but the most attractive offer came from Buchtel College. It was not from their students but from the administration. They offered him a faculty position if he would coach their football team.[42] It turned out to be the best coaching hire in the history of that school, even including the years after they came to be known as the University of Akron.[43]

*

Five days after playing Oberlin, Ohio State welcomed the team from the Dayton Y.M.C.A. No one knew what to expect but there was little enthusiasm on campus for the game. The Y.M.C.A. players had been trained by the Dayton Athletic Club, and Frank Haas and Clarence Withoft, two of Ohio State's best players, had both originally been trained there. Haas and Withoft were excited about the game, but the other students on campus saw it as little more than a fundraiser for the Athletic Association.

Heavy snow was falling on that Saturday, and very few students chose to attend the game. The two sides agreed to shorten the game time to sixty minutes. The score at the end of the first half was 26 to 0 in favor of Ohio State, but the *Wahoo* commented on the team's play: "The guarding was poor, the action was slow and the team put up the weakest game it has this season."[44]

Nearing the end of the game Ohio State was winning 42 to 0 and a Dayton back ran around the right end for 35 yards and was tackled near the Ohio State goal. The Ohio State players again needed a goal-line stand if they hoped to preserve a shutout. Dayton pushed the ball forward and across the goal line a few plays later. The few Ohio State fans watching from the stands believed that disinterested Ohio State players had simply conceded the touchdown. The final score of the game was 42 to 4. The *Dayton Daily Times* and the city's Y.M.C.A. newsletter both bragged that the Ohio State players had not previously been scored against all season except by the mighty Oberlin team.[45]

Chapter Twenty

Are we not quite as godly as they?

Charlie Powell was worried about the poor attendance at the Dayton Y.M.C.A. game. He could not see any way for the Athletic Association to break even. The Athletic Board accused the student body as a whole of disloyalty.[1]

Kate Morhart tried to come to the rescue. The Browning Literary Society had recently bought a piano and originally planned to pay for it with a fundraising reception at the home of President Scott. They managed to pay for the piano before the event, however, and Morhart suggested that the funds from the reception should instead be donated to the Association.

＊

On November 19 the team went to Adelbert. Kenyon had defeated Adelbert that year but Abelbert was the reigning O.I.A.A. champion and the Ohio State team knew better than to underestimate them. The trip to Cleveland was the longest and most expensive that any Ohio State team had ever made. Only six students, including Walter Sears, traveled with the team. Fred Ryder also accompanied the team, and he arranged for a former teammate from Williams, who lived in Cleveland, to serve as a game official.

The first half of the game was an even match. Ohio State threw at Adelbert every play in their playbook while Adelbert offered a steady diet of runs up the middle. The score at halftime was 20 to 18 in favor of Adelbert. In the second half Adelbert changed their offensive attack and began running around end. Ohio State was caught flat-footed and the final score was 40 to 18. The *Wahoo* titled the game report, "Our Waterloo."[2]

At dinner after the game the Ohio State players asked the Adelbert team how they had lost to Kenyon. The Adelbert players responded that the Kenyon players stole the game by playing dirty.[3]

✳

Ed Moody had heard that the Ohio State student newspaper was expected to reestablish the name *"Lantern"* and he was not happy. The change to the name *"Wahoo"* had been his work even more than Walter Sears's. He wrote a letter to the editor stating, "I may be too late, and it may be none of my business, but for my own satisfaction, and with little hope, I wish to enter a protest."[4] He argued that the name *"Lantern"* had always seemed "dusty and dry" whereas the *"Wahoo"* has a "far cheerier sound" because it "suggests the ball field and the 'high time'."[5]

An alumnus named Ferdinand Howald had been the first editor-in-chief of the *Lantern* in 1881 and when he read Moody's letter he was inspired to weigh in on the topic. He said that the name *"Wahoo"* was "barbaric" and that it "has a sound, but no essence."[6] The *"Lantern,"* in contrast, was "inclusive and dignified" and "the result of a careful research and selection."[7] He disputed that it was "dusty and dry," saying that it was not, as was often assumed, named for the lantern that Diogenes used in his hopeless search for an honest man. It was actually named after *"La Lanterne"*—a Parisian revolutionary satirical magazine that spoke truth to power and helped bring down Second French Empire. Ohio State's *Lantern* "has grown up with the institution, has become a part of it, is connected with its traditions."[8]

The *State Journal* commented, "The discussion concerning the proposed change of the name of the college paper from the *Wahoo* back to the *Lantern* still goes merrily on."[9]

✳

Kenyon had defeated Adelbert, and Adelbert had defeated Ohio State. If Kenyon were to defeat Ohio State on Thanksgiving, they would be the unde-feated champion of the O.I.A.A. If Ohio State were to defeat Kenyon, however, then Kenyon, Adelbert, and Ohio State would finish the year in a three-way tie. The *State Journal* reported, "The students are tiptoe on expectancy for the football contest Thanksgiving day, when the great game with Kenyon will come off at the university athletic field ending the season and deciding the championship."[10]

The game promised to be the most prominent athletic event ever held on the Ohio State campus. The lineup of the Ohio State team would be identical to the lineup for the home opener two months earlier against Buchtel. Aside from a few bumps along the way, the O.S.U. players had managed to stay healthy all year. S.P. Bush offered to fill the position of referee.

Consistent with Thanksgiving tradition that had developed over the previous two years, the game was scheduled for ten in the morning. The Athletic Association put up flyers throughout the city to advertise the game. The Athletic Board was nervous but Walter Sears assured them that the Kenyon team had confirmed the game time. On Wednesday, the day before the game, Charlie Powell decided to send a telegram to Gambier to make sure that the Kenyon team knew the schedule. The Kenyon manager sent back a response that his team would be on the Ohio State campus by Thursday afternoon.

Powell was stunned. He quickly gathered together as many members of the Board as he could find. They did not know who to blame. They did not know if Sears had made a terrible mistake or if the Kenyon team was intentionally trying to spoil their Thanksgiving event. They tracked down Sears and put him on a train to Gambier with a message to not return without the Kenyon team.

In Gambier the Kenyon players told Sears that they definitely would not be returning with him that night. Kenyon was holding a Thanksgiving social and they intended to attend it. Moreover, the other Kenyon students that would be attending the social would all be out late and would not be able to attend the game if it began at ten. Sears send a despondent telegram to the Board.

Powell and the others sat up late in a dorm room discussing what to do. They decided that they would get up early the next morning and put new flyers up over the old ones. Meanwhile they would ask to borrow the cart from the campus dairyman to ride through the streets announcing the news. Powell finally decided that he needed to get to bed to be ready to play in the game the next day.

Despite the efforts of the Board, residents of the city began arriving on campus on Thursday morning. By ten, five hundred people had arrived, which represented as many spectators as they had been expecting in total. The Board asked members of the university band to try to entertain the growing crowd. Earlier that year the *Wahoo* had written "while we cannot hope to rival the Fourteenth Regiment, perhaps, there is no reason why the State University of Ohio should not have a band of which she might be proud."[31] Some spectators grumbled but almost no one left. As the morning wore on the crowd continued to grow.

At noon a message arrived from downtown that the Kenyon players had arrived in Columbus and were having lunch in a hotel downtown. After lunch

The future "Best Damn Band in the Land" as they appeared in the early 1890s. (Photo courtesy of The Ohio State University Archives)

they gathered in the street to shout their school yell before taking the street car to the Ohio State campus. The *Columbus Press-Post* said that their yell had "a lusty note that forecast a plucky fight."[12] A little after one the Kenyon players, their fans, and Walter Sears all arrived on campus.

The Kenyon players had a reputation for rough play and the Ohio State players girded themselves for the worst. Charlie Powell abandoned his ear guard. He had learned over the course of the season that it was not wise to advertise a sore spot to a physical opponent.

The game began at two, and by kickoff twelve hundred spectators had arrived. Kenyon won the coin toss and took possession of the ball. Ohio State took home advantage of the slope of the field. From the start of the game the Ohio State students in the grandstand began shouting their school yell.

Kenyon threw a number of different plays at Ohio State. Kenyon bucked the line well but their runs around end were weak. Ohio State followed the strategy that they had learned from Adelbert and offered a steady diet of runs up the middle throughout the first half. Ohio State scored a touchdown fifteen minutes into the game. The Kenyon team had heard that the Ohio State team had improved that year but they had not really believed it. The *Kenyon Collegian* later wrote that "our opponents played with more skill than we had supposed them capable of doing and our sudden awakening to this fact seemed to rattle our men."[13]

The score at halftime was 10 to 4. At the start of the break the Ohio State students again began shouting their school yell. The Kenyon students then shouted their own yell in response. The Ohio State students began again, and this time they were joined by the Columbus residents. It would not be the last time that Ohio State football fans would adopt the rituals of the students. The *Columbus Daily Press-Post* reported, "The two college yells and innumerable tin horns made a din that put political demonstrations in the shade."[14]

Ohio State had possession of the ball to start the second half, and Dick Ellis set loose the Ryder Wedge. The team quickly scored a touchdown. The Kenyon team then attempted their own trick play, known as the Harvard Checkerboard. Fred Ryder had prepared his players for it and they easily shut it down. Ohio State dominated the second half and the final score was 26 to 10.[15]

The *Dispatch*,[16] the *Press-Post*, and the *State Journal* all agreed that the game was the best and most entertaining exhibition of football that had ever been seen in the city. The *Wahoo* reported:

> It was a glorious struggle and a glorious victory. Kenyon with all her boasting and all her prestige was laid low in direful defeat, while O. S. U. rose conquerer, bearing triumphantly the cherished scarlet and gray. The shame of the fall at Cleveland was wiped away and a redemption for every man and for the whole team, full and complete, was won.[17]

The *Wahoo* added that the victory "was not only a triumph over a rival college; it was a victory for careful, conscientious training extending over weeks and for unselfish, devoted team work. In short, it was a victory for Mr. Ryder and his training rules."[18]

After the game the Ohio State students belatedly began their Thanksgiving feast. Dick Ellis gave his team permission to "break training." During the Thanksgiving toasts Charlie Powell made sure to thank Kate Morhart for her generous fundraising, although after the haul from the Thanksgiving game it had turned out to be unnecessary. The guest of honor at the feast was Fred Ryder.[19]

*

Fred Patterson left school earlier that year. He traveled to Kentucky and took a job in Elizabethtown, near Louisville, teaching African American children. It was the best way that he could think of to enhance the living conditions of his people. He wanted to let his friends back at Ohio State know where he had gone and what he was doing, so he decided to send a letter.

After giving it some thought he decided to mail that letter to Walter Sears. He sent his regards from "down here in this land of 'good whiskey, fast horses and fair women'."[20] He said that the work that he was doing was very satisfying for him: "My eyes are being opened and I am getting a glimpse of the field which I will have to tread in a year or two."[21] He added that he wished that he could still be at Ohio State to graduate with his class, "but you can appreciate the fact that the O. S. U. is not the world and that my battles must be fought upon ground different from that occupied by you fellows."[22] He ended his note by asking Sears to pass along his regards to Kate Morhart.

In December, Sears had the note printed in the *Wahoo*. He added his own observation that Patterson is a "genial fellow that everybody knew and liked."[23]

*

In April 1893, central Ohio was shocked by news coming from Wittenberg University and Ohio Wesleyan University. At Wittenberg, students had ambushed an elderly janitor in the dark and severely beat him. At Wesleyan, rivalry between the classes took an ugly turn when a group of sophomores held down five juniors and painted their faces with silver nitrate. The victims were left in racking pain and two were said to be disfigured for life.

Morhart printed an editorial in the *Lantern*, addressing the two scandals in light of the criticisms that her school had received over the years. She wrote, "State University men and women are forever being told that they are attending Godless, immoral institutions; and by doing so they are told that they are endangering their souls and receiving into their lives an influence which will always make for evil. The religious college, these critics say, is the ideal place, free from all these vices, and surrounded by a Christian spirit of manly and womanly conduct."

She continued:

The truth is that these defamers of State universities are basing their attacks upon a hypothesis which does not hold in every case. There is such a thing as carrying the doctrines of religion until they are only pretenses, behind which the heart is really wrong. There is such a thing as too much discipline, too many rules of conduct, too much dependence upon outward keeping of forms. This is especially true with young men and women. It is only where their government is broad and independent in spirit, free from all trivial restraints, and dependent solely upon their individual honor and honesty that they develop into proper self-control and up-right living.

She concluded, "Without pretending, without boasting, are we not quite as Godly as they?"[24]

Part Five

*We want to get a great football team
and we shall then be a great University*

Chapter Twenty-One

Our athletic clubs have spread abroad our good name

H arwood Pool had been an editor of the *Lantern* in the spring of 1881.[1] That spring term was three years after Pool had served on the colors committee alongside Curtis Howard and Alice Townshend. In March 1881 he wrote the editorial that originally suggested the campus Athletic Association, and on March 17 some students held the first meeting for that purpose.[2]

These students asked a zoology professor named Albert Tuttle to call the meeting to order, assuming that the involvement of a faculty member would give their new Association the sanction and seal of the university. At the meeting Tuttle "gave some very good suggestions and advice as to the manner of going to work" but then left the charter in the hands of Harwood Pool.[3] One month later the Association had enough members to call another meeting and at that meeting, on April 18, they approved a constitution and bylaws. They also elected officers and committee heads. A student named Willis Jones called that second meeting to order.[4] Professor Tuttle's contribution to the first meeting, on March 17, 1881, was the last direct involvement in Association affairs by any member of the faculty until Professor Lazenby joined the Athletic Board as the at-large member in 1891.

As the 1890s continued, however, the Ohio State faculty and administration took a growing interest in the governance of student athletics.

✳

In late January 1893, Rutherford B. Hayes died. Ohio State began an official period of mourning for the former United States President and long-time champion of the university.[5] A portrait of Hayes had recently been commissioned, intended to adorn Hayes Hall, a new campus building, and both the unveiling of the portrait and the dedication of the building were more somber occasions than had originally been expected.[6] Kate Morhart wrote, "There will never come a time when the loyal sons and daughters of O. S. U. will not feel pride in the glory which the devotion of Rutherford B. Hayes shed over our young but sturdy University."[7]

In early February the period of mourning was abruptly cut short, at least among the students, when the faculty instituted a new rule regulating athletic eligibility. The faculty announced that students could compete in intercollegiate sports only if they held an academic record that was "above the average." The determination of being "above the average" was left in the hands of the university president.[8]

Kate Morhart was conflicted. Her personal reaction to the new rule was mostly favorable, declaring in a *Lantern* editorial "that the welfare of the college will be better preserved under the new rule, that the standard of the students both in athletics and studies will be raised," and that "the new rule would not have been made without mature deliberation."[9] But she also acknowledged, and wanted to represent, the majority of students who saw the new rule as a "death blow"[10] to Ohio State sports. The best argument that she could develop in support of their position was that it is difficult to be above average both as an athlete and as a student. Those who work to be the best students, she suggested, often choose not to "take from their studies the time required to become expert athletes."[11] The faculty did not find this argument compelling.

Three days later Morhart found a better means to express the majority point of view. She quoted a "prominent college man," letting him explain why he believed that the new rule was "perplexing and deplorable in the extreme." His first argument was simply that the timing of the decision was unfair: "You see it comes when we are least prepared for it. Had the Faculty given us something like six months notice of their intended legislation, we then could have arranged our plans accordingly." His second, and more fundamental, argument was that the new rule was sure to harm the reputation of the school:

> Do you not believe that our athletic clubs have generally represented the University with great credit to themselves and the University? Do you not believe they have spread abroad our good name and won friends for us all through the State? I tell you, in this day athletics are becoming just as much a part of a great University as Greek or mathematics, and they cannot be done away with except at a great cost to the college and the student body."

He suggested that the faculty consider the fate of the University of Wooster: "What has been the effect upon her of anti-athletic legislation? Her membership has fallen off one-half, and those that remain, I am told, are a set of weak and voiceless 'grinders' who will never make much of a stir in the world."[12]

Over the next few days the students began to take more formal action. On February 17 the Alcyone Literary Society drafted a "resolution of disapproval" in support of the athletes: "Resolved. That it is the opinion of this Society that to impose extra conditions on a student or body of students who may wish to take part in any regular college organization, is wrong, in principle, and as such ought to be condemned."[13] A few days later the students held an open meeting to form a "Committee on Arbitration" that would draft a list of grievances to present to the faculty.[14] Their list closely resembled the concerns of the "prominent college man."

In early March the faculty met again and discussed the students' concerns. They offered the students a new regulation, superseding the previous one. They changed their requirement of athletic eligibility from being "above the average" to simply not failing any subject recently, and they gave the students more time to prepare for the implementation of the rule:

> Resolved. That no student or preparatory pupil of the Ohio State University be allowed to take part in inter-collegiate athletic games, who within the two pre-ceding terms, has incurred a failure in any subject or has incurred conditions in more than five-hours work. This regulation shall go into effect at the opening of the University year—1893–94.[15]

Most students declared this new version of the rule much more fair and tolerable.

Kate Morhart's own thinking on the issue, however, had by then evolved. She had begun to question why the university should interfere with any student activity outside of academic work. Ohio State students had long believed that the state's sectarian schools treated their students like children, but now the Ohio State faculty seemed to be seeking jurisdiction "co-extensive with that of sectarian schools."[16] Morhart suggested that students learn best from being treated like adults: "Will not a young man or woman become more independent and better prepared to battle with the world by being thus thrown upon their individual responsibility?"[17]

✻

That fall the university administration instituted new policies toward the *Lantern*. The trustees agreed to assist the newspaper in meeting financial expenses, and the faculty announced that the English department would give college credit to the newspaper's editors. Walter Sears was the *Lantern*'s new editor-in-chief, and in the first issue of the new school year he commented, "To know that the University authorities are not only wishing it well but lending it generous support will inspire the editorial board to more careful and zealous work."[18]

These new policies began the process of turning the *Lantern* into a product of the university's School of Journalism.[19]

✻

Expectations for Ohio State football were at an all-time high that fall. "The outlook for foot ball this year is better than ever before,"[20] a writer from the *Lantern* claimed. The *Columbus Dispatch* wrote:

> O. S. U. has a team to be proud of. For the first time in the history of the university, she has a football eleven that can bid defiance to any other team in Ohio. They have been playing the game like a house afire, and have won games by scores seldom heard.[21]

The O.S.U. goal for the coming season, as a step toward their school's eventual domination of the state, was to beat both Adelbert and Oberlin.

The source of the confidence and optimism was the return of Fred Ryder as coach. "The practice, under the able direction of Mr. Ryder, is becoming systematic and thorough and the men are getting into good shape."[22] Mit Lilley, Al Lilley's younger brother, briefly served as Ryder's assistant. In the years since Mit's previous visits to campus he had become the starting quarterback for Yale. "M.C. Lilley, Jr.... did some very effective coaching. Many points of the game were given and the center and back were shown several new and effective plays and tricks. He returned to Yale Saturday night, and the team is grateful that he was secured, even for two nights' coaching."[23]

Pete Gillen was selected as the team's new captain, and Frank Haas was selected as Gillen's assistant. "Capt. Gillen and Sub. Capt. Haas seem to have excellent control of the men. They certainly deserve every respect from the men."[24]

✻

After Gillen and Haas were chosen, the *Lantern* took a moment for remembrance, looking back once more on the year before and the work of Dick Ellis:

> But while the new captain is being welcomed in, let us not forget the old one. For two years Capt. Ellis has had charge of the 'Varsity team, and the results

The 1893 football team, posing with Coach Fred Ryder. (Photo courtesy of The Ohio State University Archives)

which he has attained against the greatest odds, speak more praise for him than we can say. Above all he has been faithful, enthusiastic, able and just, and when these qualities are found in a foot ball captain they mean success for him. We should never cease to thank Capt. Ellis for the part he has played in bringing our foot ball interests to their present creditable position.[25]

Ellis later fought in the Spanish-American War, where he won the Silver Star for gallantry in battle.[26]

✻

The position of team manager returned to Caesar Morrey. In addition to his off-field management responsibilities, Morrey also came to team practices in uniform and ready to play. "Manager Morrey was out in a suit and he showed that he had not forgotten the game."[27] One new player asked Morrey for advice on how much protection his head would need for the sport. "Say Morrey," he said, "is my hair long enough to play foot ball?"[28]

On September 30, Morrey went to Gambier to the fall meeting of the O.I.A.A., and he found the organization in crisis.[29] A dispute arose at the State Field Day in May that had led to Adelbert and Buchtel each demanding the expulsion of the other. At the June meeting the other members had sided with Adelbert. Now, at the September meeting, the representatives from neither Adelbert nor Denison arrived. Adelbert had decided to withdraw from the association. Denison meanwhile sent word that they had suspended their football program. As a consequence of these actions, the O.I.A.A. was disbanded.

Morrey still wanted to schedule a season comparable in scope to the one in 1892, and he offered the *Lantern* the names of the schools that he was negotiating with, both within Ohio and in neighboring states: Oberlin, Otterbein, Marietta, Cincinnati, the Case School, as well as Purdue, DePauw, and Wabash in Indiana, and Western University and Washington & Jefferson in Pennsylvania. Morrey ultimately scheduled Adelbert, Buchtel, and Kenyon—the former members of the O.I.A.A.—plus Cincinnati, Marietta, Oberlin, Otterbein, and Wittenberg.

Morrey wanted Kenyon to remain Ohio State's Thanksgiving opponent, and he also wanted the Thanksgiving game to remain at Ohio State. Kenyon agreed, on the condition that Ohio State play another game earlier in the season in Gambier. Morrey agreed, and the schedule was set.[30]

✻

"Twenty-five men answered to Capt. Gillen's call on Friday last for places on the foot ball team," the *Lantern* reported in mid-September. "The prospects for a splendid team are very promising."[31] A seventeen-year-old freshman named Homer Howard was among those answering the call. Howard had always known that he would attend Ohio State. Most of his family had attended Ohio State.[32] His uncle, Curtis, had even helped choose the school colors fifteen years earlier. Homer Howard was selected to the second team.

The season opener, on September 30, was scheduled against Otterbein, but in the days leading up to the game the students received bad news. The faculty released the list of ineligible players and it was more extensive than had been anticipated. Four of the most experienced players had incomplete marks, making them ineligible, including team leaders Pete Gillen and Frank Haas.[33] Walter Sears especially mourned the loss of Haas, declaring him "the finest quarterback in the State."[34]

The team quickly prepared a new lineup, and over half of the students named had never played before, including Homer Howard, who became the new starting fullback. Howard played well against Otterbein, scoring two touchdowns and making two successful kicks for goals-after-touchdowns, but Ohio State lost 22 to 16. The *Lantern* was sympathetic, commenting, "It was the opinion of Mr. Ryder, as it was of all, that he never saw better playing by six new men."[35] The writer added that the faculty's ruling would, however, likely "destroy all possibilities of placing a winning foot ball team on the field this fall."[36]

The *Lantern* directed additional scorn toward the man serving as Otterbein's new player-coach: "The respectability of the game was marred by the playing of but one man—that of Semple, formerly of Kenyon, but now Otterbein's coach. He was brutal in the extreme, attempting, as he blatantly said, to get even for the thrashing O. S. U. gave him with Kenyon last Thanksgiving. Such a man should be drummed out of the game forever."[37]

Caesar Morrey concluded that the season was largely in the hands of the team's newest players, so he arranged to give those players more experience. He organized a freshman team and scheduled a game for them against a local high school. These freshmen included players named Edward French, Frank Nichols, and Frank Potter. They defeated the high school students 22 to 0, with Homer Howard successfully completing three of his four attempted kicks.[38]

Meanwhile the O.S.U. students reestablished their Committee on Arbitration and made a new petition to the faculty. The argument presented in the new petition was that if a football player is a successful student in the fall, but then struggles in class work after the football season, it is illogical to blame football for his failings. The Committee proposed that football eligibility be based entirely on an athlete's performance as a student the previous fall and baseball eligibility be based entirely on his performance as a student the previous spring.[39]

The *Lantern* expressed the student view regarding the stakes at hand: "If the rule is enforced we cannot hope to place a winning team in the field this fall, as by its action four of the best men on the eleven are disqualified. If the rule is modified or repealed, foot ball will be in the ascendant, and too much cannot be expected of the 'Varsity eleven this season."[40] After the Committee made its case, the members waited outside nervously as the faculty conferred.

The faculty accepted the terms of the new student petition, with one addition: "Those who play both foot ball and base ball must make a satisfactory record in both fall and spring terms.'[41] The Committee happily accepted this qualification and ran off to spread the good news.

One student commented on the outcome, set to the tune of "Yankee Doodle":

> Foot ball 'leven is my name,
> The O. S. U. my station.
> My greatest hope for this term is
> To pass the examinations.[42]

*

On the following Saturday, October 14, the team played a game against Wittenberg. The original lineup returned, with two changes that had been introduced in the Otterbein game. Homer Howard remained at fullback and William Nagel, who was now a junior, remained at right end. Ohio State won by a score of 36 to 10. The *Columbus Press-Post* celebrated the win: "The game was a one-sided one, our boys defeating the visitors."[43]

The team, however, did not feel as much like celebrating. Otterbein had defeated Wittenberg the week before by a score of 28 to 4, and the Ohio State students were expecting to celebrate a victory margin reminiscent of the 1892 season. "It was an easy victory for the Ohio State University team, but by it many faults and weaknesses in our team and individual work were brought to light,"[44] the *Lantern* claimed. The writer insisted that "good work should have resulted in a shut out."[45]

A game with Oberlin, played one week later, now carried added significance. A strong showing would signify that Ohio State's football aspirations were still on track. The team wanted a large crowd for the game and, following the lesson learned the previous Thanksgiving, Caesar Morrey put the university band to work. He asked the musicians to play throughout the streets of Columbus, drawing visitors to campus like pied pipers. Eight hundred spectators ultimately attended.[46]

Oberlin scored first to take a 4 to 0 lead, but Ohio State answered to go ahead 6 to 4. Oberlin scored twice more—16 to 6—before Ohio State scored again—16 to 10. From that point Oberlin dominated the game. The *Oberlin Review* gauged the mood of the crowd by the performance of the band in the grandstand: "A full band greeted the teams at the grounds. It was evidently out to blow the University boys to a victory. When they made their touch downs early in the game a dozen instruments tore the welkin into shreds. Then as the O. S. U. did not keep piling up the score, the instruments began dropping out one by one like cats returning from a night serenade, until at last only the bass drum was left to bay at the moon."[47] The final score was 38 to 10.

That score was a near-reverse of the score vs. Wittenberg, but the mood of the team also seemed a near-reverse of the week before. Simply to have scored twice on the powerful Oberlin team represented progress. The *Dispatch* and *Press-Post* both called the game "exciting."[48] The *Lantern* claimed that the "the good showing which our team made against Oberlin" gave credence to the belief "that from this time forward foot ball and college spirit will have taken their proper place in the curriculum of the Ohio State University."[49]

Quarterback Frank Haas was injured in the game, and some of the spectators thought that the Oberlin players had been too physical. The *State Journal* claimed, "Every dirty trick known to evil-minded players was resorted to by the visitors."[50] Walter Sears disputed that charge. He wrote, "As to their foot ball playing, the worst that can be said of them is that they play so terrifically, so desperately—so splendidly, in short—that often, perhaps, they play a little rougher than the average team of less skill and fame. Their manner of playing, in fact, is the kind which Mr. Ryder is trying to instill into our men and which is having its good effect."[51]

The first game against Kenyon, in Gambier, was one week later. A large crowd accompanied the team. The *Kenyon Collegian* wrote, "It was a great day for foot ball, though the weather was uncomfortably cold for the spectators, whose hopes were evenly divided, for quite a crowd of students from the University accompanied the visiting club."[52]

The students who remained back at Ohio State waited anxiously for the result of the game. At six thirty a telegram arrived stating that Ohio State had won 22 to 16. "Everybody went wild," reported the *Lantern*. "Horns and guns were produced and used vigorously and the dorm was a scene of indescribable confusion, attendant on the news of such a glorious victory."[53] The students headed downtown to the train station to cheer the returning heroes.

As the team exited the train, however, it became clear from the pained and disgusted expressions that that telegram had been a prank.[54] The game had actually been a 42-to-6 Kenyon victory, a retaliation for what Kenyon called their "defeat and humiliation" of the year before.[55] The *Kenyon Collegian* bragged that their advantage in the game was that they, like Oberlin, had learned to defend the Ryder Wedge.[56] The Ohio State players claimed that Kenyon won through intercollegiate espionage. When they arrived at the Kenyon field they recognized one of the Kenyon players as one of the twenty-five men who had come to the O.S.U. practices in September. Charles Wood, the Ohio State right halfback, complained, "They had all our signals down pat!"[57]

Walter Sears pointed fingers in the *Lantern*. He said that the team should have been trained in more than one code of signals, and also that the team's back-up quarterback, replacing the injured Frank Haas, had not been properly prepared. He placed the fault on Coach Ryder who, he said, with Ohio State's money and reputation on the line, should "use a little more care and judgment."[58] Sears also suggested that Caesar Morrey should focus more of his attention on managing the team and should give up his quixotic dreams of returning to the football field.[59]

Another *Lantern* writer joked that if the team hoped to win another game that season they should consider scheduling the high school team that the freshmen had beaten earlier that year.[60]

✳

A week later was the game against Adelbert. Haas was still out and Adelbert won 30 to 16.[61] Some pointed out that, like the Oberlin game, the score represented progress. "The Adelbert game was another experiment for us, as have been all the games played so far. But it was by all odds the most satisfactory experiment of them all."[62] Others were no longer in a mood to enjoy moral victories. Pete Gillen broke his leg in the game and, without Gillen or Haas available, the team found itself essentially in the same position that it was in when the faculty announced the ineligible list in September.[63] Doctors told the team that Gillen was out for the season and the best they could hope for Haas was that he would be back in time for the Thanksgiving game.[64]

Walter Sears continued to be critical of Caesar Morrey's work as manager. He said that Morrey was not working hard enough to bring twenty-two men to every practice. "Instead he has spent his time, from all accounts, in a foolish and unpardonable attempt to assume the duties of both Captain and Coach."[65] Sears said that for anyone to "interfere with the plans and wishes of Mr. Ryder or Mr. Gillen is a matter for sincere regret, for the team alone is sure to suffer for it."[66]

The following week was the game with Buchtel. No one knew what to expect. Buchtel had never had a strong football team but this year they were being trained by John Heisman. Ohio State won 32 to 8 and the *Lantern* declared that the "crisis has been passed."[67] This game, they proclaimed, would be "the turning point in the history of athletics for this season."[68]

The campus now dared to look ahead to the rematch with Kenyon. The *Lantern* noted that their Thanksgiving game would "be of as much importance to Ohioans as are the great Thanksgiving games of the East to the people of the Eastern States. It is expected that there will be an enormous crowd in attendance on Thanksgiving morning."[69] One rumor stated that even Governor William McKinley was expected to show up on the campus for the game.

Throughout the losing stretch one highlight for Ohio State had been the playing of seventeen-year-old Homer Howard. After the Adelbert game the *Lantern* had written, "Howard played his usually brilliant defensive game,"[70] and after the Buchtel game the *Lantern* commented, "Howard at full back played his usual brilliant game and both gained ground well and tackled hard and sure."[71] Walter Sears summed up Howard's playing so far that season: "Howard as a young player has already won a reputation for phenomenal work. For his years he has shown great pluck and daring and in time he is sure to develop into a player of wonderful powers. He should not let these words turn his head, however, he has much to learn yet and will not reach his best form only after years of devotion to the game."[72]

✳

On the following Saturday, November 18, the team from the University of Cincinnati arrived on campus. Ten years earlier, when Vernon Emery defended Ohio State in the *Lantern* from the attacks of Cincinnati's *Academica*, a competition between the two schools would have been promoted as the centerpiece of the season. Ohio State beat Cincinnati 38 to 0 and the victory was seen as little more than a satisfying warm up to the Thanksgiving game. The *Lantern* complained of a "rather small crowd" that showed little enthusiasm or energy.[73]

Meanwhile the *Press-Post* wrote, "The prospects for the success of the home team in the Thanksgiving game are brightening."[74] The final warm up before Thanksgiving was a game against Marietta on November 25. Ohio State won 40 to 8. The *Lantern* wrote, "O. S. U. easily out-classed and out-played Marietta, who, however, showed a great improvement over their work of last season."[75] Homer Howard scored three touchdowns in the game and successfully kicked four goals-after-touchdown.

*

On Thanksgiving morning the university band again took to the streets downtown intent on drawing a crowd. The *State Journal* reported that during the game the "O. S. U. band of thirty pieces filled the air with stirring music."[76] After the season the Athletic Association would give the band a gift of ten dollars in thanks for their service to the team.

By the start of the game 2,800 spectators arrived. The *Dispatch* was amazed that a sport few in Columbus had even heard of four years earlier now seemed to dominate the attention of the city. The Athletic Association started the day $600 in debt but after the game they reported a balance of over $400. The business plan in support of the football team was now built around the Thanksgiving game.

Far more spectators arrived than seats were available and the Association put up rope fences to try to keep the crowd off the playing field. "The throng of spectators was the largest that ever gathered in the Field," bragged the *Lantern*, "nor was there ever before such enthusiasm."[77] There were "colors and flags and horns and lusty throats everywhere."[78]

The Kenyon students found the behavior of their Ohio State hosts ungracious. By the end of the game the *Kenyon Collegian* was seething:

> The State University, as usual, disgraced her name by exhibiting a large crowd of 'muckers' wearing the red and gray. She evidently searched the byways and hedges of her agricultural farm to bring out this assortment of freaks of the 'ha! ha! ha!' and fish-horn variety. It would be well if her authorities added a course instructing these barbarians how to act on the foot ball field....These pitiable objects displayed their jealousy and sore heads by hissing and endeavoring to drown out every Kenyon cheer.[79]

Frank Haas was able to return for the game and again took over at quarterback. He also took the role of kicker back from Homer Howard. In the first half Ohio State scored a touchdown when left halfback Frank Nichols carried the ball in from one yard out. Haas missed the goal-after-touchdown and the score at halftime was 4 to 0. Kenyon answered with a touchdown on their first drive of the second half. Their kicker also missed and the game was tied 4 to 4. A few minutes later Kenyon scored again. This time their kicker made the goal and the score was 10 to 4. From there the defenses of both teams dominated the game until, just before time was called, right end William Nagel broke free for a

75-yard dash and a last-minute Ohio State touchdown. Frank Haas could have tied the game with a successful kick. He missed, and the final score was 10 to 8.

Despite the loss the *Lantern* called the game "the greatest athletic contest that the University ever witnessed."[80] The *Kenyon Collegian* generously offered some compliments to their opponents: "The features of the game were the line playing of Nagle [*sic*] and the tackling of Howard for O. S. U."[81]

*

At the start of the winter term, Paul Lincoln wrote a letter to the *Lantern*. He said that he felt compelled to speak up on a topic that had been bothering him since the fall. He reminded everyone that as a student he had sometimes carried twenty-five hours of coursework per week and usually passed with merit, all while being an active figure on campus. He said that unless the educational requirements had increased greatly since his time at Ohio State, the students should stop complaining about athletic eligibility and focus on playing football.[82]

At the campus field day in the spring of 1894, freshman Eddie French had the most successful field-day performance in the history of the school. He won seven of the eight events that he entered, and finished in second place in the eighth.[83] The campus hoped to see a similar athletic explosion from him on the football field.

Chapter Twenty-Two

We are to enter upon a period of real Thanksgiving

I n January 1894, the faculty received a letter from the Assistant Secretary of the State Board of Agriculture. The Board of Agriculture ran the Ohio State Fair, and every year they tried to bring in fresh new entertainment. For 1894 they decided to offer the fair-goers a football tournament, gridiron rules, "open to college teams only."[1] The faculty forwarded the letter to the Athletic Association.

The proposal was for six teams to play a total of three games over three consecutive days, the winning team in each game to be awarded new leather uniforms for all its members. As a grand prize, the team showing the best performance in the tournament would also receive ten new balls. The estimated prize value for the team winning the tournament was impressive. "It is needless to say that every effort will be made to win in this tournament and to secure the prizes which will be offered,"[2] the *Lantern* commented.

The Board of Agriculture stated that it would accept the first six teams that applied. Those applications came from Buchtel, Denison, Miami, Ohio State, Otterbein, and Wittenberg. Denison reestablished a football team in hope of winning the prizes. A few weeks later Otterbein rescinded their application and Ohio State, as the most local team, was asked to participate in two of the three games.

The fair began on September 3. Each football player was given free admission for himself and a date. On September 5, Ohio State and Buchtel played the opening game of the tournament. Frank Haas, the Ohio State quarterback, had become his team's new captain. John Heisman, the Buchtel coach, entered himself into his lineup as quarterback. Haas conceded that, as a Buchtel employee, Heisman may have been technically eligible to play, but he questioned the inclusion of three other men, all extremely large, who had never before been affiliated with the school. Tournament games were shortened to sixty minutes and Buchtel won 12 to 6.[3] "This year our highest ambition has been realized and O. S. U. has gone down before us," proclaimed the *Buchtelite*.[4]

Ohio State's second game was two days later. The opponent was Wittenberg. Haas claimed that the Wittenberg team was also filled with ringers. He recognized one of the players as Albert Tyler, a well-known Ohio athlete. Tyler played football for Princeton and in 1896 he would be a pole-vaulter for the United States at the first modern Olympic Games in Athens, Greece. Mit Lilley was one of the officials chosen for the game, but Lilley had no authority over player eligibility. At the end of sixty minutes neither team had scored but tournament rules did not allow a tie game. The teams played for two hours until Wittenberg finally won 6 to 0.

Buchtel took first place in the tournament and won the prize balls. Ohio State submitted an official protest with the Board of Agriculture, but the protest was dismissed. The team hoped to put the State Fair behind them. The *Lantern* suggested that the games offered a lesson in what can go wrong when money gets involved in college sports.[5]

*

By the fall of 1894 the Ohio State students had concluded that football would be their key to building a national reputation. The university, they said, would achieve football success, bringing it attention from across the nation, and only then would people discover and acknowledge its academic merits. C.A. Radcliffe, a lawyer in training and the latest *Lantern* editor-in-chief, made the case:

> Why is Yale, Harvard or Princeton greater than O. S. U.? Because they have a better football team. What we want to do is to get a great football team and we shall then be a great University. Let us be 'faithful over a few things' that we may be 'ruler over many things'.[6]

As the 1894 season progressed, the response of the campus to every game seemed to take on a ritualistic pattern. The students celebrated every victory as a demonstration that the school had taken an exalted place in the football establishment, and they were driven to despair following every loss as they doubted that belief. It was a pattern that would continue more or less unchanged for at least the next twelve decades.

In 1894, however, football in the state of Ohio was actually very competitive. After the disappointments of the 1893 season, the Ohio State Athletic Association began to question whether Fred Ryder was still worth the salary that they were paying him, and they began to make inquiries regarding the availability of Mit Lilley to coach the team.[7] Ryder had provided a tactical advantage in 1892, but by 1894 the other schools in the state seemed to have caught up. Soon afterward the Association announced Lilley as the team's new coach.[8]

One of the first changes that Lilley made was to change the team's approach to practices. Ryder had favored open practices, advertised to fans, to build the bonds between the team and the rest of the student body. Lilley instituted closed practices, letting the team train in private. Under Lilley's system, the only outsiders who could attend were the press and the administration.[9]

Frank Haas was no longer captain, nor was he even a member of the team. The faculty announced that Haas was ineligible due to his academic record in the 1893 fall term.[10] The students had no room to protest. William Nagel was selected to be the team's new captain, and one of Nagel's greatest challenges that season was to find a quarterback to replace Haas.[11]

Nagel, or Lilley, put a premium on size when building their lineup. They found a new big man named W.A. Snedecker to play center and an even bigger man named Edward Crecelius to play left guard.[12] Meanwhile Homer Howard was removed at fullback. Howard had scored the team's only touchdown in the State Fair games, but he was 5'7" and had not filled out as much as had been hoped between his freshman and sophomore years. Throughout the coming season the fullback position would alternate between Frank Potter and a student named Ord Myers.

A student named William Rudge was chosen to be the team's new manager. Rudge had played in one game in 1893 but had since found himself stuck on the second team. As manager he worked to build a schedule, talking to the usual opponents.[13]

Kenyon agreed to return to the Ohio State campus for that year's Thanksgiving game. The Kenyon students, like the Ohio State students, enjoyed the growing rivalry between the schools, and they conceded that their games attracted more attention when played in Columbus. The two schools agreed to remain regular Thanksgiving rivals.

The 1894 Ohio State football team. (Photo courtesy of The Ohio State University Archives)

At Ohio State, football had become so popular that some were suggesting that there was no room for any other sport on the campus. The *Lantern* disagreed, insisting that the baseball team was not destined to remain forever in the shadow of the football team: "The impression that baseball cannot be...as successful as football is not supported by the facts."[14]

These football discussions in the *Lantern*, early in the fall of 1894, under the watch of C.A. Radcliffe, were the first times that the newspaper contracted the name of the sport into a single word—"football," not "foot ball."

※

Mike Kennedy was no longer a student and had not been a student since the spring of 1893. He did not graduate with his class in the spring of 1894. But Kennedy appeared on campus that fall and asked if there was any role for him to help the football team. William Rudge asked Kennedy to serve as Ohio State's regular game official that season.[15]

The season began against Antioch College, a school founded by advocates of a religious separatist movement called the Christian Connexion. Ohio State's quarterback was a student named Edgar Denman and Ohio State won 32 to 0. The *Press-Post* raved, "From the indications at the present time the O.S.U. seems to have the best team in its history. The playing this year is far in advance of that last year at the same time."[16] Others pointed out that the Antioch team had not seemed properly trained and had not been much of a test.[17]

The following week the team travelled to Springfield for a rematch with Wittenberg. Ohio State lost 18 to 6, and the team leaders continued to accuse Wittenberg of using ineligible players. The *State Journal* reported, "The feature of the game was the dirty work put up by the home team…Wittenberg played her usual 'ringers'."[18] C.A. Radcliffe turned the *Lantern's* game coverage into an extended essay on the importance of athletic integrity.[19]

Marietta had been scheduled to play Ohio State on September 20, but the Marietta manager sent a note requesting a postponement, claiming that a few of his players were injured. William Rudge quickly scheduled a game with Ohio State's old baseball opponent from the Columbus military barracks. Nagel benched Edgar Denman and made a student named Friedrich Richt the quarterback. Ohio State won 30 to 0, but everyone conceded that the soldiers had also not been properly trained.[20]

The following week Ohio State lost to Adelbert, 24 to 4, and the *Lantern* and the *State Journal* both began to question the quality of Ohio State's training.21 The Marietta team finally arrived the week after that, and Ohio State won by a score of only 10 to 4. The *Lantern* headline was "From Bad to Worse." The accompanying article stated that "the 'Varsity eleven barely achieved a victory over Marietta, and those who saw the game heaved a sigh of relief when time was called and were glad the torture was over."[22] It concluded:

> It was a miserable exhibition of football and the victory means almost nothing.…Something must be done, and that soon, or O. S. U. will be distanced in the race, and above all, will lose the great Thanksgiving game. The outlook for winning that game is now unfavorable and the prospect gloomy.[23]

The Marietta team claimed that the only reason that they lost the game was due to questionable calls made by the Ohio State referee Mike Kennedy.[24]

※

A game in Cleveland with the Case School of Applied Science was next. Like Adelbert and Oberlin, Case had developed seemingly out of nowhere into one of the strongest teams in the state. William Nagel decided to try Homer Howard at quarterback. Howard played better than Denman or Richt but the change did not help, and Ohio State lost by a score of 38 to 0. The *Lantern* said of the team's performance, "They were outplayed and outclassed at every point, and what with the spirit with which they entered the game and what with the inexcusably poor playing on the part of several players, defeat was inevitable."[25] The game coverage was sub-headlined "Case School Scored Almost at Will."

Vernon Emery, the former *Lantern* editor, had taken a faculty position at Adelbert that year, and he had attended the game at Case. He felt compelled afterward to write a letter to the *Lantern*. He commented that it is "a rather painful thing to the alumni to see O. S. U.'s representatives give so poor an account of themselves."[26] Emery put the blame on the team's coaching, saying, "If the team has had good coaching it has certainly failed to profit by it, for the most conspicuous thing in the game last Saturday was the total absence of team work."[27] He continued, "Now the great superiority of football in the eyes of many over other games consists in the fact that it is not the place for individual brilliancy, but requires discipline, team-work and head work. Without these three things you don't have football."[28] Emery begged the Athletic Association: "Can't you do something to bring about a better situation at O. S. U. another year?"[29]

Some of the players had been blaming William Nagel for their failures that year, but after the Emery letter opinion consolidated that the fault was in Mit Lilley. Nagel submitted to a new election and he held onto his position, getting all but four of the team's twenty-two votes. William Rudge then asked for Lilley's resignation and rehired Fred Ryder for the last three games of the season.[30]

Fans in downtown Columbus weighed in on the firing of the Ohio State coach. The *State Journal* stated that the quality of the team's playing "has been going from bad to worst until the contests put up by the home team were disgraces," but concluded that the "crisis" was "passed yesterday by the securing of Mr. Ryder as coacher."[31] The *Press-Post* disagreed: "It cannot be seriously questioned that Mr. Lilley, who has been coaching the team this year, knows more about foot ball than any other man in Columbus."[32]

✳

Ohio State's next game, on November 17, was at Cincinnati. William Nagel and Fred Ryder kept Homer Howard at quarterback. Ohio State won the game 6 to 4 and, despite the closeness of the score, the *Lantern* claimed that the game represented a turning point in the season. The Thanksgiving game again became a symbol of hope:

> It would seem from present indications that the season of our discontent is now over, and from being made glorious summer we are to enter upon a period of real Thanksgiving. The hazy atmosphere of uncertainty which has enveloped everything related to football, and which had made us from the dimness to fear evils we knew not of, is at last being slowly but surely cleared away, and the cheer of the winter sun now envelopes everything with a radiancy of hope. The revolution in football, marred as it was by the action of a spirit not the best, has nevertheless worked a change for the better, for which all are truly thankful.[33]

A return visit by the Dayton Y.M.C.A. was scheduled for the following Saturday, but just before the game the Y.M.C.A. team cancelled. William Rudge quickly scheduled another game with the barracks soldiers, which Ohio State won 46 to 4.[34] After that game, Rudge secured the services of the soldiers to keep fans off the field during the Thanksgiving game.[35]

*

On Wednesday, November 28, the *Lantern* wrote, "By 2:30 o'clock tomorrow afternoon the O. S. U. athletic park will be one living, breathing, howling, seething mass of humanity such as has never been seen before in the history of football at our University."[36] The article went on, "The two teams that appear on the field will be those who have spent the last two months in assiduous preparation for this great struggle, and each will do or die."[37]

The dominant conversation on campus that week was assessing the team's chances in the game. Mike Kennedy had taken it on himself to scout that year's Kenyon team, and he claimed that Ohio State would not only win but that the score would not be close. Frank Haas claimed that the Ohio State backs would be successful if they showed confidence in their line.[38]

The university band added new songs to their repertoire for the Thanksgiving game. The relationship between the football team and the band had become interdependent. The team counted on the band to help draw a crowd, and the band was becoming more popular due to its relationship with the team. Over the previous two years the size of the band had nearly doubled, becoming the largest in the city, and the *Lantern* stated that the quality of the band had similarly advanced "from a few hornblowers" in 1892 to "a musical organization of established reputation and ability."[39] Even the *Kenyon Collegian* complimented the Ohio State band's entertaining contribution to the day.[40]

Despite the disappointments of the season, 2,500 spectators arrived for the Thanksgiving game. Ohio State won 20 to 4 and the *Lantern* wrote, "Kenyon was outplayed, outyelled and put out at every point and at every stage of the game."[41] With a win in the rivalry game, all the pains of the season seemed to disappear.

C.A. Radcliffe noted that the relationship between the football team and the entire campus had also become interdependent. It was football that gave the campus a sense of community. Ohio State had nearly one thousand students, and Radcliffe claimed that the diversity of those students and variety of their coursework threatened to tear them apart. He said that football keeps college spirit alive, and that college spirit would continue to buoy the success of the team.[42]

A student named Dessa High was the secretary of the junior class. She also was a member of the Browning literary society. In March of 1895 she wrote:

> What a triumphant success our O. S. U. ball-team gained over Kenyon! How many loyal throats were smarting from shouts and cheers sent up for our brave boys! How enthusiastic everybody was! Why cannot we be as enthusiastic over a literary contest as over a football contest?[43]

Chapter Twenty-Three

Football can do more than all the catalogues you can publish

Early in 1895 William Henry Scott stepped down as president of the university. The *Lantern* offered a tribute: "Doctor Scott's own exalted personal character has been reflected back upon the institution over which he presides, and the prejudice against State Universities as places devoid of moral and Christian influences has given way and sentiments of genuine respect, admiration and love have developed in their stead."[1]

The trustees replaced President Scott with a man named James Hulme Canfield. President Canfield had previously been the chancellor of the University of Nebraska. His daughter, Dorothy, was a talented writer and musician, and she enrolled at the university that fall.

In September the *Lantern* claimed, "President Canfield is a great enthusiast of athletics and believes in having a representative college team."[2] President Canfield addressed the students directly on the topic of sports. He said, "It will be a bad day for O. S. U. when athletic sports are allowed to flag. The time has come when we should intelligently view the whole athletic question. All forms of outdoor sports should be encouraged."[3] The *Lantern* seemed pleased and offered this prediction: "The rules governing participation in athletics will in the future be far less rigid than they have been in the past."[4]

The Athletic Association, at President Canfield's suggestion, approved a new constitution giving the faculty an opportunity to help the campus teams.[5] The new constitution included an Advisory Board, and on that board were President Canfield, William Rane Lazenby, and two other professors.[6]

*

Renick Dunlap was serving that year as both captain and manager, so in addition to training the men on the field he also was responsible for building a schedule.[7] He intended to finally find the team an opponent from outside the borders of the state. He scheduled a trip to Kentucky to play two schools there, and he scheduled a game at home against Purdue University, from Indiana. The first game in Kentucky was with Kentucky State University–Lexington (later renamed the University of Kentucky) and the second was with Centre College in Danville.[8]

Dunlap also scheduled a game with Ohio Wesleyan University. The Ohio State team had always promised to schedule Wesleyan again if they could ever come to Columbus. That year the students at Wesleyan had finally convinced their faculty to let them play games away from their campus. Dunlap fulfilled Ohio State's pledge.[9]

Dunlap soon announced the complete schedule. The season would start with games against Buchtel, Otterbein, Oberlin, Denison, and Cincinnati. Then would come the O.W.U. game, the two games in Kentucky, and the one with Purdue. The season would end with the game at Marietta and the traditional finale with Kenyon.

The *Lantern* then did its part to promote the coming season: "Among the old men back this year are Calkins, Crecelius, French, Johnson, Miller, Dunlap, Howard, Nichols and Potter. With all the good material there is among the new men and these nine old men, we should certainly have a good team to represent the University this fall."[10]

☆

Caesar Morrey did not come to the practices that fall. Since 1993 he had been taking classes from Starling Medical College, a medical school downtown, and he was preparing to graduate with his medical degree in the spring.[11] At Starling Morrey met a medical student named Sid Farrar. Farrar was a former football player from Princeton. Morrey convinced Farrar that a medical college could play football just like any other school and together they formed a Starling team.

Starling scheduled a game against Ohio State to be played on Wednesday, November 13.[12] That fall was the first time in six years that he had no involvement with the Ohio State football team.

☆

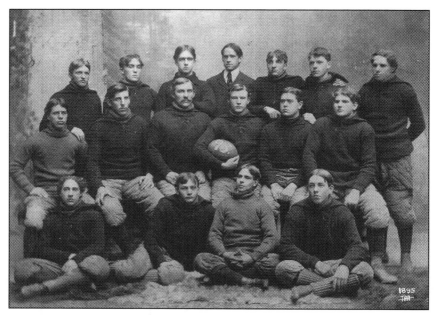

The 1895 team. (Photo courtesy of The Ohio State University Archives)

During that year a perception that football was too violent had been growing throughout the country. Political pressure against the sport was growing correspondingly. At that year's football convention in the East, a new rule was instituted requiring seven men on the line of scrimmage at the start of each play. The rule also stated that only one back could be in motion before the snap. This new rule was intended to ban the controversial wedge plays.[13]

Fred Ryder returned to coach the Ohio State team, and he reinstituted open practices. With the Ryder Wedge outlawed, the practices in September were largely devoted to learning a new set of plays, and while practicing these new plays the players suffered a series of injuries. The most serious injury was a severely sprained foot suffered by Homer Howard, and the campus suspected that Howard might miss the season.[14] About a week later, Eddie French and a player named Fred Butcher were also injured and their season left in doubt.[15] French seemed to have a propensity for injury and he had never finished a complete football season.

＊

The Ohio State team welcomed Buchtel on October 5. Frank Nichols took over at quarterback. Ohio State won the game 14 to 6 and the *Lantern* commented that the State Fair game in 1894 had been avenged. Five hundred spectators attended but the *Lantern* complained that they were not as enthusiastic as expected. The newspaper fretted that the fans were giving President Canfield a poor first impression.[16]

A week later the team had a setback in Westerville. They lost a game at Otterbein, also by a score of 14 to 6. A consolation for the Ohio State visitors was that the fans in that Columbus suburb seemed divided in their loyalties. They noted that "to a stranger it would have been difficult to tell whether it was an O. S. U. or an Otterbein town."[17]

The Oberlin team came to campus the following Saturday. The *Lantern* reported, "A large and enthusiastic crowd was out to see the game and they were well repaid."[18] Seven hundred spectators arrived. The game was tied late in the second half and the crowd grew louder. Oberlin finally scored for a 12 to 6 victory, but the game convinced the community that the team could play with anyone in the state. The *State Journal* called it "one of the finest exhibitions of the great game ever seen in this city" and predicted a strong end to the season.[19]

The *Columbus Dispatch*, on the other hand, noted that the loss demonstrated that the university needed a gymnasium in order to defeat the best teams in the state:

> Every one knows what a great benefit a gymnasium is…to an athlete and to the members of the football and baseball teams. O. S. U. will never have champion teams until gymnastic work forms a regular part of her curriculum. O. S. U. will never be the greatest in the state until she can furnish her students the gymnasium exercise necessary for their good health, and no one regrets this and feels this loss more than the 900 students now in attendance.[20]

A trip to Granville to face Denison was scheduled for the following week, but Renick Dunlap decided that the team first needed a tune-up. He scheduled a midweek game against the Columbus barracks, and the team defeated the soldiers by a score of 10 to 4.[21] Four days later the team played their game with Denison and that game ended tied 4 to 4.[22]

The Wesleyan game was next. On Wednesday the *Lantern* wrote, "Next Saturday our boys will meet their old time rivals—Ohio Wesleyan—for the first time in several years."[23] The newspaper later stated, "The appearance of the O. W. U. team on the home grounds has been looked forward to with eagerness by the students here all year."[24] Two thousand spectators arrived, by far the largest attendance on the Ohio State campus for a non-Thanksgiving game. Eddie French was declared fit to return to the team. Ohio State was leading 8 to 6 late in the second half, but an Ohio State fumble led to a safety, and the team suffered its second tie game in as many weeks.[25]

The game at Cincinnati was on November 9. Twenty years later, as Jack Ryder of the *Cincinnati Enquirer*, Fred Ryder would give the Cincinnati team their nickname. He regularly called them "Bearcats" and the name stuck.[26] In 1895, however, Ryder did not yet have any ties to the city of Cincinnati. Before the game on November 9, Homer Howard and Frank Potter were both declared healthy enough to return—Potter at fullback, Howard at quarterback. Ohio State won 4 to 0.[27] Afterward the team and their fans together sang Ohio State songs as they walked back to their hotel. One observer watching the students on the streets of Cincinnati that night later commented that "a good, enthusiastic football team can do more by way of advertising your university than all the catalogues you can publish."[28]

On Wednesday, November 13, the Starling Medical College football team sent a message to Ohio State cancelling the game scheduled that day. The *Dispatch* attributed Starling's failure to show up to lingering embarrassment from an earlier defeat to the Columbus Asylum for the Deaf.[29] The Ohio State players thought that it was just as well, because they were focused on their upcoming trip to Kentucky.

On Thursday, November 14, the team took the same train that they had taken to Cincinnati, but this time they continued further south. On Friday Ohio State defeated Kentucky State–Lexington by a score of 8 to 6. At one point some local fans charged the field to protest a ruling and the Kentucky players formed a barrier to shield the umpire and referee. The referee was Roy Wasson, an Ohio State backup player. When the game ended, the fans turned their attention to the other Ohio State players.

The players sprinted from the field, down a dirt lane to the local streetcar, with the fans in hot pursuit and throwing anything they could get their hands on. The last to make it safely onto to streetcar was Roy Wasson, who threw an uppercut at a bearded man who was grabbing him.[30] The *Evening Bulletin* of Maysville, Kentucky later wrote, "The State College boys were greatly humiliated at the action of the crowd."[31]

The Ohio State players were exhausted after the game but they quickly caught another train to head even deeper into Kentucky. They played Centre College the next day, and were defeated 18 to 0.[32] On the following Monday, Renick Dunlap received a telegram from Purdue cancelling their game that Friday. Everyone agreed that it was for the best: "Since our boys are to play Marietta Saturday it is well the Purdue game was canceled, for two games in succession do not work well."[33]

On Saturday was the game at Marietta. The Marietta players claimed that they had not heard about a change in rules that year. They said that they had been using the wedge all season and they refused to change their playbook at this late point. The Ohio State team agreed to play under the 1894 rules and lost the game 24 to 0. They later said that the lesson learned was that a new intercollegiate organization was needed to regulate these games.[34]

✻

On the same day as the game at Marietta, Starling Medical College played their only game of the season. Sid Farrar had challenged Ohio Medical University, another Columbus school, who formed a team in response. The two medical schools played their game the weekend before Thanksgiving because they knew better than to challenge Ohio State for a football audience in Columbus on Thanksgiving Day, and because they needed to borrow the Ohio State field for the game.[35]

Caesar Morrey played quarterback for Starling. Starling won the game, dominated by a performance by Farrar.[36] Morrey broke his nose in the game,[37] but with the victory he seemed to scratch an itch and was finally able to set his football dreams aside.

✻

On Thanksgiving, five days later, Kenyon returned to Columbus. The *Lantern* later noted, "It was an ideal day for football. The sun shone brightly and the air was just crisp and cool enough to be exhilarating."[38] Attendance at the game set a new city record—four thousand people—and the atmosphere was described as "pandemonium."[39] Columbus police officers assisted the barracks soldiers in keeping the fans off the field.

The Ohio State players seemed overexcited during the first half, losing fumbles and being called several times for holding. Near the end of the half Carl

Giessen, a new Ohio State left halfback, lost a fumble into the arms of the Kenyon left end, who ran in for a touchdown. The score at halftime was 6 to 0 and during the break President Canfield came down to give his students a pep talk. Near the start of the second half Frank Potter attempted a punt but his kick was blocked and Kenyon scored again—10 to 0.

Renick Dunlap benched Potter, replacing him at fullback with a sophomore named Harry Hawkins. Throughout the rest of the half, Hawkins seemed to dominate the game. He ran repeatedly through the line and Kenyon seemed powerless to stop him. He scored twice and the Kenyon lead was cut to 10 to 8.

Ohio State was approaching the Kenyon goal line again near the end of the game when another penalty gave the ball back to Kenyon. Kenyon needed only to run out the clock, but on the next play the Kenyon quarterback tossed the ball to his right halfback, who felt the ball slip through his fingers. Homer Howard saw the ball hit the turf, grabbed it, and charged for the goal line. Ohio State won the game 12 to 10.

The fans broke through the ropes and carried the Ohio State players off the field on their shoulders. President Canfield announced a plan to throw a reception for the team.[40]

*

After the 1895 season the board of trustees announced that, to accommodate the crowds that turn out every Thanksgiving, they would finance a new football field. The trustees also announced a plan to build a campus gymnasium. The proposed site of the gymnasium was just off of High Street, to the east of Hayes Hall.[41]

The students were grateful but they worried that the trustees were about to make a mistake. The Athletic Association petitioned that the new football field not be built at the site of the current field, at the corner of 12th and Neil Avenues, but instead be built in useful proximity both to the new gymnasium and to the streetcar stop from downtown.[42] The trustees accepted this suggestion and arranged to place the new field at High Street and 18th Avenue.

Chapter Twenty-Four
Not only marvelous but without an equal

W hen students returned to campus for the winter term in January 1896, they discovered that President Canfield had attended a meeting over Christmas break with other Ohio college presidents. The topic was intercollegiate athletics, with particular focus on keeping football free from corruption, professionalism, and fraud. The presidents proposed a set of rules to regulate athletic eligibility, including high academic standards, a ban on freshmen varsity athletes, and a rule that, when an umpire disqualified a player from a game for any reason, that player will remain disqualified until the presidents collectively clear him to play again. The penalties leading to a disqualification would include the use of any profanity or obscenity. These rules were declared to go into effect after five schools approved them.[1]

The students were horrified by the proposal and felt betrayed by President Canfield. The students at other schools were horrified as well, and the students from the University of Cincinnati called for a meeting of Ohio college students. Eddie French served as Ohio State's representative. Their meeting endorsed the presidents' goal of "eradication of professionalism and other evils creeping into our intercollegiate athletics" but proposed a different solution: a new intercollegiate organization, in the hands of the students, with strict, but flexible, rules of athletic eligibility.

The new organization was named the Intercollegiate Athletic Association of Ohio. It was not intended to oversee the scheduling of football or baseball games but it did schedule a new State Field Day. That year, for the first time, the O.S.U. athletes participating in the State Field Day called themselves the Ohio

State track & field team. Other Association members included Cincinnati, Denison, Kenyon, Oberlin, Ohio Wesleyan, Otterbein, and Wittenberg.[2]

This new organization achieved its primary purpose: distracting people from the presidents' plan before five schools could approve it.

*

In September the football players returned to the practice field in preparation for the new season. Eddie French was elected captain. The *Lantern* wrote, "Captain French, of course, will be at right end, and it goes without saying that ere the season has closed, many a long gain will have been made while our Captain had the ball."[3] The writer added a caveat: "French heretofore has been unfortunate in getting hurt during the season, and we hope he will have better luck this year."[4] Another reason for enthusiasm mentioned in the article was that "mighty Crecelius is back again stronger than ever and will again play left guard."[5] At halfback were Frank Nichols and Friedrich Richt: "Behind the line Nichols, our star half-back, who is thought by many to have no superior in the state, will play his fourth season."[6] At fullback was a student named James Westwater. Homer Howard returned at quarterback: "Howard, who played quarter the most of last season, is again in training, and will in all probability fill the same place this year."[7]

The manager that year was a student named Arthur W. Madden. Madden decided that the time again had come for the team to try a new direction at coach. Fred Ryder accepted the latest firing without complaint, and even offered to serve as a game official if needed. Frank Haas agreed to serve as coach until a permanent solution appeared. Madden eventually secured the services of Sid Farrar of Staring Medical. "Coach Sid Farrar played guard on the victorious Princeton team two years ago, and will undoubtedly make an excellent coach. It is a certainty that if hard work will accomplish anything Mr. Farrar will turn out a first class team this year."[8]

Madden received a challenge from the team at Ohio Medical University. O.M.U. wanted to play a real season that fall and challenged every team in the region. Madden agreed to open the season against them and play a follow-up game in mid-November. In the opener Nichols, Richt, and Westwater all scored touchdowns—Richt scored two—but the *State Journal* offered its highest praise to quarterback Homer Howard: "Howard played a perfect game at quarter, handling the ball quickly and accurately every time it was put in play and tackling

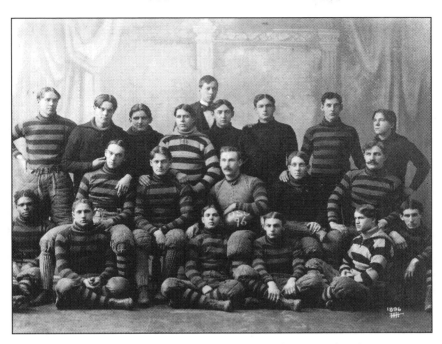

The 1896 team. (Photo courtesy of The Ohio State University Archives)

low and hard every time he made the attempt to down a runner."⁹ Howard also served as the team's kicker and successfully kicked the goal-after-touchdowns on all four tries. Ohio State won the game 24 to 0.

Some on the team grumbled after the game that Sid Farrar's understanding of the sport had seemed surprisingly out of date. Madden quietly dismissed him. With that decision, the Ohio State football team's reputation as a "graveyard of coaches" had begun. Madden next discussed the position with a man named Edwin Sweetland, formerly of Union College in New York, but Sweetland soon fell ill, ending the discussions. (Sweetwater would eventually become the Ohio State coach in 1904.)

Madden then hired a former captain from Williams, who had graduated just that year, named Charles Hickey. "Mr. Hickey has several good offers but has at last concluded to come to the O. S. U.," reported the *Lantern*.¹⁰ The *Lantern* added, "Mr. Hickey certainly means business by the way he took hold of the club Monday evening."¹¹ He introduced a complex and challenging new offensive system. The next game was at Cincinnati, which Ohio State lost 8 to 6. Fred Richt scored the team's only touchdown, with Homer Howard kicking the goal. The *Lantern* explained the loss: "Coach Hickey and his new system, of which so much had been expected, did not succeed because the men need a great deal more coaching before they can play Mr. Hickey's system successfully. The O. S. U. team apparently was much the stronger team, but so many fumbles at opportune times gave Cincinnati the game."[12]

While the team was playing in Cincinnati, the Ohio State second team played a game for the local audience in Columbus. Their opponent was the Chillicothe Athletic Club, featuring new member Renick Dunlap. The O.S.U. team defeated Chillicothe 10 to 8.[13] A highlight of that game was the playing of the fullback Julius Tyler. Tyler's father, James Seneca Tyler, was the first African-American to serve as clerk for the Ohio House of Representatives. Everyone could see that Julius Tyler was faster than James Westwater and Eddie French made the decision that week to add Tyler to the first team. Westwater was moved to the line.

The game the following Saturday was played in Canton, Ohio. It served as a fundraiser for Governor William McKinley in his campaign that year for President. Their opponent was Otterbein. The *State Journal* noted, "O. S. U. rooters were in the majority, the red and gray being conspicuous on many coats and canes."[14] Ohio State won the game 12 to 0, with halfbacks Nichols and Richt each scoring touchdowns and Howard making both kicks.

With the improving play of the backfield, confidence for the remainder of the season was growing. A *Lantern* writer commented, "Homer Howard distinguished himself several times by his fine tackling. He passed the ball in faultless style and kicked both goals very easily."[15] The writer then went on to praise "our trio of backs, who have not an equal on any team in the State. The way that Nichols, Richt and Tyler hit the line was certainly fine."[16]

✻

At about this time the faculty discovered a problem involving Eddie French. Because he was a senior, French was not concerned about his football eligibility the following fall, and he began missing classes. The faculty was worried that other schools would consider French a ringer. Making the issue even more embarrassing, French's brother Thomas had just that year joined the Ohio State faculty. The faculty announced that French was not a full-time student and ineligible to play on the team.

Among the students the feeling was almost universal that the decision to remove French had been ad hoc and arbitrary. The team filed a petition for French's reinstatement on the grounds that the dismissal came without fair notice. Another petition, from the campus as a whole, was signed by six hundred students. A few days later the team travelled to Oberlin for a game. French was not able to enter the field but the team still officially listed him as their captain while his appeal was pending. They lost 16 to 0 and the *Lantern* asked, "Who defeated the O. S. U. team? The Oberlin team or the O. S. U. faculty?"[17]

The faculty met to discuss the petitions on Monday, October 28. Afterward they released a statement:

> Your petitions have been received, and have been duly and carefully considered by the President and Faculty of the University. It would be much more easy and pleasant to grant them at once than to refuse; but we are bound to consider the welfare of the University (which is always in all things the welfare of the students themselves) and we have in mind also the future of athletics in this institution. Under all the conditions it seems unwise and even impossible to grant your request, that Mr. French be reinstated—especially that he be reinstated to continue his connection with the football team.

The faculty response continued, "It is difficult to conceive of a more willful and positive violation of a trust, even when all possible mitigating circumstances are considered. The bearing of this upon athletics ought to be clear to every student. One so negligent of all work cannot possibly be considered a student even though for any reason his nominal connection with the institution has not been severed."[18]

The students had long hoped that their football team would bring their school national attention and the faculty's ruling on Eddie French achieved that goal. Caspar Whitney wrote in *Harper's Weekly*:

> Nothing has been done at any college in this country that more truly shows the spirit of sport for the sake of the playing and not necessarily for the winning, than this action of the Ohio State University faculty and its reception....It is a splendid victory for wholesome university sport; a notable example of genuine sportsmanship.[19]

The students still strongly disagreed, and felt that the faculty had needlessly sabotaged the season. A few days later their anger grew stronger as they discovered that President Canfield continued to advocate the harsh eligibility rules proposed at the meeting of the presidents the previous winter. The *Lantern*'s new editor-in-chief was a student named John E. Sylvester, Jr., and in the November 4 issue Sylvester wrote that Canfield, and the faculty generally, had a fundamental misunderstanding of the relationship between student activities and the school:

> In every rule pertaining to individual players the erroneous idea is at the bottom that to engage in athletics is a privilege which is granted by the great generosity of the Faculty....The notion that a student must have, as a sort of compensation for the right to engage in athletics, some especially high scholarly attainments, is hideous in the extreme, and should be dismissed as soon as possible.[20]

✻

Ohio State's next game was against Case. Lineman Billy Reed took over as captain. Ohio State won 30 to 10, with five different players scoring touchdowns. Homer Howard made all five goals. "Howard's tackling was a feature as well as his never-failing passes. His goal kicking was perfection."[21] Especially notable was Julius Tyler. "Tyler played a strong game, breaking through the line every time."[22]

The team next played three games within the span of a week. The first was on Friday, against Ohio Wesleyan, which Ohio State lost 10 to 4.[23] The second was on Saturday, against the barracks soldiers, which they won 10 to 2.[24] On Wednesday that followed the Ohio Medical University team returned for the second game of the two-game series. Ohio State played terribly, giving up several fumbles, and the game ended tied at 0.[25]

In those three games Howard made the only goal that he attempted, and the *Lantern* began taking note of his achievement: "Howard has kicked 13 goals without a failure. Where is there a team that has an equal?"[26] Two more games were played the following week. On Saturday the team played Wittenberg and lost 24 to 6.[27] The Ohio State players again accused Wittenberg of using ringers—one was a Wittenberg graduate, another was a graduate of Notre Dame, and third was a student at a Springfield business school. The *Lantern* claimed that the fault was no longer with Wittenberg, because everyone knew how Wittenberg played, but rather with Ohio State management for continuing to schedule them.[28] Howard made his only goal attempt of the game, and for many fans the focus of the season had become his perfect record.

The following Saturday, the weekend before Thanksgiving, had originally been an open slot on the schedule, but Ohio Medical University sent a new challenge. They had anticipated a game again that year with their rival Starling Medical College, but the expectation of a game had turned out to be a misunderstanding. Caesar Morrey had received his M.D. the previous spring and Star-ling no longer had a team. Arthur Madden agreed that Ohio State could play a third game with O.M.U. that season. Ohio State won 12 to 0. The *Lantern* trum-peted: "Howard Kicks His 16th Consecutive Goal."[29]

✻

Nearly five thousand spectators arrived for the Thanksgiving game. Vendors worked the crowd, selling candy, popcorn, and peanuts, and flowers for men to buy for their dates. Despite the record crowd the Athletic Association barely broke even that year, an outcome that the *Lantern* blamed on "gross mismanage-ment and reckless extravagance."[30]

The Ohio State players showed up for the game confident of a win. Kenyon had struggled that season, including their worst defeat ever—a 60 to 0 loss to Oberlin. The Kenyon players were also confident, however, because they showed up with a plan.

The Kenyon manager/coach had scouted Ohio State's game with Wittenberg and saw that the light Ohio State backfield had trouble with the heavier Wit-tenberg backs. The Kenyon captain replaced his backfield with heavy linemen with a plan to make slow, steady gains throughout the game. After the game the *Lantern* would claim that "O. S. U. was out-generaled, out-played, out-classed."[31]

Kenyon scored twice early in the game and took a 12 to 0 lead. Soon after-ward the inexperienced Kenyon quarterback made a sloppy mistake and was penalized for a forward pass and turned the ball over to Ohio State at the two-yard line. Richt ran the ball in and Howard made the kick. The score was 12 to 6. Kenyon then scored three more touchdowns before the end of the half. The score at halftime was 28 to 6.

The second half the game became more even as Ohio State learned to counter Kenyon's offensive plan. Near the start of the half Harry Hawkins, who had taken over for Eddie French at right end, took the ball and ran around the left side of the line. A block from Edward Crecelius cleared a path and Hawkins ran 50 yards for a touchdown. Howard made the kick. The score was 28 to 12. Kenyon scored only once more to make the score 34 to 12. Then, as time in the game was running out, Richt scored again for Ohio State.

By then the sun had set and the sky was turning dark. The fans surrounding the field watched with anticipation as Howard prepared his try. He caught the inbound kick, dropkicked the ball, and it sailed over the goal. The score was 34 to 18 with only a few minutes left on the clock. The Kenyon captain requested that the game be called on account of darkness. Billy Reed agreed and Howard officially completed his perfect season.

The next issue of the *Lantern* featured an illustration of Howard splashed across the entire front page. He had arguably the most successful season as a kicker in the entire country, and the caption for the illustration read, "Howard's record of kicking nineteen successive goals this season without a failure is not only marvelous but without an equal."[32] Howard would hold the Ohio State record for consecutive points-after-touchdown until 1969.

After Howard graduated that spring he would remain a fan of the Ohio State football team for the next sixty-five years. Like many alumni he rarely missed a game. He followed on the radio when he finally grew too old to jump and shout with the other fans in the stadium.[33] By the time he died in 1962, football had changed in many ways but the emotional connections remained the same. He never gave up his copy of that old student newspaper from 1896.

✻

After the season many of the students remained angry with the faculty. Many still felt that President Canfield was treating them like children, and the *Makio* addressed that feeling satirically. They offered a beginners' reader, designed specifically for the Ohio State student:

This is the college,
Pride of the Buckeye state.
    These are the Profs,
    That bow to the Prexie,
    That killed the football team,
    That runs the college,
    Pride of the Buckeye state.
    These are the students,
        That run the *Lantern*,
        Light of the U.,
        That vexed the Profs,
        That bow to the Prexie,
        That killed the football team,
        That runs the college,
        Pride of the Buckeye state.[34]

The front page of the Ohio State Lantern following the 1896 Kenyon game. (Photo courtesy of The Ohio State University Archives)

Chapter Twenty-Five

The same crowd of leather-lunged Buckeyes

I n the spring of 1897 the university began construction of an attractive brick
building on campus. It was designed to look like a fortress or castle, with
giant turrets reaching to the sky. In addition to being a gymnasium, the
building also housed the Department of Military Science. The university called
it the Armory, and it cost $115,000.[1]

At the end of that year the *Lantern* wrote, "The new gymnasium which is
rapidly nearing completion will do much to develop athletes from among the
students, and under the care of a competent instructor O. S. U. will place foot
ball, base ball and track teams on the athletic field able to cope with almost any
team in the West."[2] The *Dispatch* sounded even more ambitious, stating that "the
students will now have a chance to better develop athletics, so that in time Ohio
State University athletics may be on a par with those of the students of some of
the eastern colleges."[3]

*

As classes began again that fall the conversations on campus returned to the
topic of football. As the *Lantern* noted, "As much, if not more time is devoted
each day during the first part of the school year to the discussion of our prospects in football than to each one's individual prospects in the class room."[4] The
students seemed most concerned that fall with the fact that so many of the start-
ers from the 1896 team were gone.

The *Lantern* focused on the team's new recruits as their writers tried to reestablish a sense of hope, highlighting the reputations that the newest football

The Armory, home of the first Ohio State gymnasium. (Photo courtesy of The Ohio State University Archives)

players had earned before they entered the university. "It is understood even at this early date that recruits for the team will not be lacking. A number of men who have successfully played upon the high school teams of their homes have entered college and will be seen very soon on the athletic field in their football garb."[5] The potential contribution of those recruits fell into doubt, however, as the faculty debated whether or not freshmen should be allowed to play.

Charles Hickey's contract as coach had not been renewed. Hickey's complicated offensive system, which had seemed so exciting and modern when he was first hired, eventually came to be regarded as merely unintelligible. In place of Hickey, the Athletic Association hired David Edwards, a recently graduated halfback from Princeton. Edwards got the job based primarily on the strength of his recommendations. "The reports concerning him which reached the athletic board were of such a flattering nature, that they determined to bring him to the O. S. U. for the fall season."[6]

The fans also looked forward to some exciting changes to the schedule. Manager Earl Enos scheduled a game that year at Michigan. The teams from

Cleveland—Oberlin, Adelbert, and Case—all regularly played Michigan, which was still the most formidable team west of the Appalachians, and this year Ohio State was finally getting a similar opportunity. In addition, Ohio Wesleyan had challenged Ohio State to a Thanksgiving game, on the Ohio State campus, and Enos accepted.[7] The Kenyon rivalry, growing since 1890, had been fun but reviving the rivalry with Wesleyan made sense, both emotionally and financially.

*

The season opened on October 2 against Ohio Medical University. The Ohio State fans noted sourly that Eddie French, who was dismissed from the Ohio State team as not a legitimate student, was now a medical student and playing with O.M.U.[8] In the second half Ohio State was leading 6 to 0 when Harry Hawkins, the Ohio State halfback and new Ohio State captain, leapt across the goal line for another touchdown. An O.M.U. player then jumped on Hawkins and began biting him. Coach Edwards ran onto the field to pull Hawkins to safety. At that point the O.M.U. player claimed that Edwards had helped push Hawkins over the goal line. The O.M.U. captain backed his player's claim but the referee did not. The O.M.U. captain then took his team off the field, forfeiting the game.[9]

Despite the ugly incident, Ohio State considered the game a promising start to the season. The *Lantern* commented, "Coach Edwards is to be congratulated on the excellent showing the team has made under his care and instruction."[10] The article added that "with a little more practice the team will be ready to give the sturdy athletes from Case School a strong argument on the university field next Saturday."[11]

A week later the Ohio State team lost to Case 14 to 10, and the team now looked to Coach Edwards to turn the situation around. The loss was blamed on the team's failures in tackling and, following Edward's recommendation, the Athletic Association bought a tackling sled. The *Lantern* now commented, "O. S. U.'s offensive work is good and last week a tackling machine was purchased and set up so that Coach Edwards will remedy the defective tackling."[12] Again the newspaper looked with hope to the game the following week: "O. S. U. will be in much better shape for our game with the University of Michigan at Ann Arbor next Saturday, and our chances are very good."[13]

While Ohio State had been playing Case, Michigan had been playing Ohio Wesleyan. The Michigan-O.W.U. game ended in scoreless tie, and after the game it was discovered that the O.W.U. coach, Fielding Yost, had put himself in the game in place of his brother, who was a legitimate O.W.U. player. The Michigan faculty condemned Coach Yost and banned future games between the two schools.[14] The Ohio State students, following the controversy from a distance, were amused by the spectacle. The next week Ohio State lost to Michigan 34 to 0, but the *Lantern* wrote, "There is one consolation for the followers of O. S. U., and that is that although we were beaten we were not disgraced by playing professional foot ball."[15]

Three days after losing to Michigan, the team suffered a potentially embarrassing loss to the soldiers from the Columbus barracks. The campus discounted the loss, however, attributing it to fatigue from the Michigan game.[16] Fans were more interested in the fact that the faculty had finally cleared the freshmen to play.[17]

On October 23 the team played Otterbein and tied 12 to 12—the *Lantern* praised the "brilliant work" of the team—but immediately afterward the team began a losing streak.[18] They were "crippled" in a loss to Oberlin, 44 to 0, followed by a "crushing defeat" by West Virginia, in Parkersburg, West Virginia, 28 to 0.[19] Then came a "bitter defeat" at Cincinnati, 24 to 0.

Everyone was forced to recognize that the O.S.U. team was in bad shape. Their record going into the Thanksgiving game was 1–6–1. Their finances were equally poor. The Athletic Association had barely been able to scratch together the funds for the trips to West Virginia and Cincinnati. The *Lantern* said that for the Thanksgiving game the team had "determination to do or die in the attempt to uphold the noble old colors of scarlet and gray," but begged the students as a whole to be equally driven: "Now is the trying time which proves the loyalty of each student. Lend your every effort to encourage and assist the boys in their last great struggle to uphold the honor of O. S. U."[20]

Attendance at the Thanksgiving game was less than one thousand spectators—the lowest Thanksgiving attendance in six years. Ohio State lost the game to Ohio Wesleyan 6 to 0 but some claimed a moral victory that the score was even that close.[21] The Athletic Association finished the season $1,400 in debt.[22]

On December 8 the *Lantern* gave a final look back on the season. Opinion had consolidated by then that the blame belonged to Coach Edwards: "In looking back over the games played by the foot ball team for the season of 1897 it cannot be said that the team was composed of poor material, as it was evident that the team work against their opponents was miserable." With a better coach they "had a team which would have probably been one of the best that O. S. U. has ever had and a credit to the University." The article continued, "The experience that the Ohio State University has had during the past two years with high salaried eastern coaches who were supposed to know the game, but who did not, has taught a lesson not to be forgotten soon."

The *Lantern* writer concluded, "The foot ball season of 1897 has come to an end and the followers of athletics in the University will look forward to the balmy spring days when base ball, tennis and track athletics will hold sway."[23]

✻

By January the gymnasium was complete, and almost immediately a student named Melville Karshner formed a basketball team to play there.[24] Karshner had been trained in the sport through the Columbus Y.M.C.A.[25] On Tuesday, February 8, the basketball team played its first game, against the team from Columbus North High School.[26] The high school had the more experienced team but Karshner's team won 13 to 3.[27] His team then played more games on Wednesday and Thursday.[28]

The new sport quickly became popular among the students, and some began to wonder whether it could replace football on campus. New *Lantern* editor-in-chief Ivy Kellerman argued that basketball was "more graceful and less destructive" than football,[29] and the female students began talking about forming a team of their own.[30] Meanwhile the Athletic Association focused on whether the new sport could help relieve their debt.[31]

✻

The faculty had instituted another rule that year, requiring sports teams to submit their schedules for the faculty to approve. The students considered the rule a meaningless demonstration of faculty authority. In mid-February Rufus Patchin, the baseball manager, submitted the baseball schedule. He was surprised when the faculty denied it.[32]

In January the faculty had learned of the Athletic Association's $1,400 debt, and they were angry. The university was preparing to build the new athletic field on campus and the students, operating under the name of the university, were potentially putting the credit rating of university at risk. When Rufus Patchin submitted the proposed baseball schedule, the faculty took the opportunity to show their displeasure. They resolved that, until the debt was paid and a plan

Ohio State's first basketball team. (Photo courtesy of The Ohio State University Archives)

put in place to prevent new debt in the future, the faculty would "decline to receive or consider any petitions concerning athletics."[33]

Professor Joseph Denney, the secretary of the faculty, wrote a stern letter to Patchin. He pointed out that when "those representing college athletics" fail to meet their debts they put at risk "the good name of the university."[34] The *Lantern* called the letter "humiliating" and called on all the students to help come up with a solution.[35]

Other schools were watching the humiliation at Ohio State. Denison still remembered the problems created when Wooster's teams were lost and they did not want to see Ohio State's teams similarly disappear. The *Denisonian* published an editorial of support: "O. S. U. has held an honored position in Ohio collegiate contests in the past, and we sincerely hope that the efforts of the students will be successful and that she will be represented in the coming contests."[36]

The Athletic Association requested a meeting with the Advisory Board to be held on March 8. The *Dispatch* publically expressed doubt that anything would come of it because they suspected that the administration had its own plan to take control of student athletics.[37] At the meeting President Canfield and the other faculty members remained unyielding but sounded more sympathetic toward the students' plight.[38] President Canfield recommended that the Association form a Ways and Means Committee, with that committee representing "every society and fraternity and the alumni" and accepting guiding input from the faculty.[39]

Over the next few weeks the students held a series of fundraisers, with the proceeds targeted toward paying off the debt. The Glee Club, the Banjo Club, and the University Quartet offered a combined concert.[40] The Drama Club staged William Dean Howells's farce "The Mouse-Trap."[41] The basketball team donated all the proceeds from their games.[42] In addition, a dance band held a fundraising "hop," although the event had to be held off campus because, in another appeasement to traditional attitudes, the administration still forbade dancing on campus.[43] Meanwhile, representatives of the Athletic Association knocked door-to-door begging for donations. In late April the Ways and Means Committee announced that the debt was down to $191.75.[44]

Dorothy Canfield, the president's daughter, helped as best she could. She was talented, and after her graduation she would become a noted author and social reformer. That spring she played violin in the University Quartet, and she played a lead role in the Drama Club production.

By early May the debt was paid.[45] The baseball team was permitted to begin its season. Work continued on the new athletic field. The students offered to put up the fence themselves with a fence-raising, and at the end of May the athletic field, which would soon come to be known as Ohio Field, was nearly complete.[46] It hosted the spring field day as its inaugural event, despite the fact that a running track had not yet been prepared.[47]

The students had not, however, developed a plan to the administration's satisfaction to prevent debt in the future. The faculty now required new oversight. The Athletic Association was told that it was to report to a new Athletic Board.[48] The Athletic Board included representatives from the students, the alumni, and the faculty, but everyone understood that the faculty held final say. The plan was essentially identical to one that the faculty had proposed among themselves in January and that the board of trustees had approved in March.[49]

Students pitch in to build Ohio Field in 1898. (Photo courtesy of The Ohio State University Archives)

Following the creation of the new Athletic Board, the control of the faculty over student athletics continued to increase, and the role of the students correspondingly decreased. In October 1906 the faculty hired a man named Harry Shindle Wingert to serve as Director of Physical Education,[50] and his responsibilities were the hiring and firing of all coaches—football, baseball, basketball, and track. By the time he took the position at the start of 1907 his title was called "Athletic Director."[51] By the time the university finally established an "Athletic Department" in 1912, the change was mostly a matter of the surrounding bureaucracy and by then had little direct meaning to the students.[52]

Soon after Dr. Wingert took his position in 1907 he announced that female students would no longer be permitted to play varsity basketball. The *Lantern* reported that Wingert found varsity sports to be "detrimental to women, both physically and morally."[53] The women were told that they could earn Varsity "O" letters by playing intramural games between the classes, but not in front of the leering eyes of any male spectators.

❊

When football returned in the fall of 1898, three men applied for the position of coach. The Athletic Board preferred to rehire Fred Ryder. Ryder was by then known as Jack Ryder because he had begun to work as a sportswriter. Ryder, the faculty members of the Athletic Board said, "has been the only man who has ever coached our teams to victory."[54]

Kenyon requested a Thanksgiving game but Ohio State decided to face Ohio Wesleyan again instead.[55] Ohio State finished 1898 with a 3–5–1 record. The highlight of the year was defeating Wesleyan on Thanksgiving 24 to 0.[56] The most disappointing moment was a loss to Kenyon 29 to 0.[57] After the season coach Ryder enlisted to fight in the Spanish-American War, and the Athletic Board hired Kenyon's coach, John B.C. Eckstorm.

After the football season the basketball team was ready for its second season. Mel Karshner was unanimously reelected captain.[58] The university did not recognize the season played before the formation of the Athletic Board, however, and the games before December 1898 do not appear in the official record of Ohio State basketball history.[59]

At the beginning 1899 football season the *Lantern* wrote, "Never since the days of Snedecker, Howard, Crecilius and Nichols have the prospects for a good foot ball team at O. S. U. been better."[60] That prediction proved accurate, as the team finished the season with a 9–0–1 record and was universally regarded as the champion of the state.[61] The season ended with a hard-fought[62] 5-to-0 victory on Thanksgiving, against Kenyon.[63]

In 1900, Coach Eckstorm's second year at Ohio State, the team finished 8–1–1. The only loss was an upset by Ohio Medical University by a score of 11 to 6. The margin of victory for O.M.U. was a 5-point field goal.[64] Kenyon had earlier defeated O.M.U. 10 to 5, and Ohio State defeated Kenyon that Thanksgiving 23 to 5, so the three schools declared themselves to be co-champions of the state.[65]

An even more memorable highlight of that year was the game played with Michigan in Ann Arbor. Before the game Ohio State students held a series of meetings to organize a delegation to send to the game. Nearly one thousand attended and, despite rain and snow during the game, they loudly cheered their team.[66] The *Lantern* commented, "All were decked in the Scarlet and Gray, in fact, it seemed that our College colors out-shown the yellow and blue....Everyone was in high spirits, singing College songs and giving the College yell."[67] The game

Ohio Field as it looked in the first decade of the twentieth century. (Photo courtesy of
The Ohio State University Archives)

ended tied at 0. After the game the Michigan team agreed to come down to
Columbus the following year, starting an annual tradition that would come to
be important to both schools.

In the spring of 1901 the Ohio State baseball team played a game with Michigan in Ann Arbor. The *Lantern* was disappointed that the enthusiasm of the fans
did not match the earlier football game. "One would hardly have believed that
this was part of the same crowd of 'leather lunged Buckeyes' that took Ann Arbor
by storm last fall."[68]

*

Ohio State's next trip to Ann Arbor was in the fall of 1902. Every week of
the 1902 football season was treated as a countdown to the Michigan game,[69] and
every outcome was assessed in terms of how well prepared the team seemed to
play Michigan.[70] Despite the Michigan faculty's condemnation of Fielding Yost

in 1897, Michigan team had hired Yost to coach for them beginning in 1901.[71] That year Yost had assembled Michigan's best team to date.

Ohio State lost the game 86 to 0, a score that would remain its worst loss ever. The *Lantern* lamented, "The Buckeyes were clearly and undeniably out-classed."[72] Afterward the *Lantern* would use that nickname—"Buckeyes"—for the team even when the team was not playing Michigan.

On the train ride back to Ohio the players were pensive. The right end, Fred Cornell, struggled to gather his thoughts and feelings. Cornell was also a member of the Ohio State baseball and basketball teams, and he was also a member of the glee club. A year later the glee club asked Cornell to compose a song for them to perform about their school, and he was inspired by his thoughts from that sad train ride home.[73]

Titled "Carmen Ohio," the song portrayed the university as a reflection of everything that is good and noble about the state that founded it, and it was quickly adopted as the university's alma mater:

Oh come let's sing Ohio's praise
  And songs to Alma Mater raise
While our hearts, rebounding, thrill
  With joy which death alone can still
Summer's heat or winter's cold
  The seasons pass the years will roll
Time and change will surely show
  How firm thy friendship, Ohio

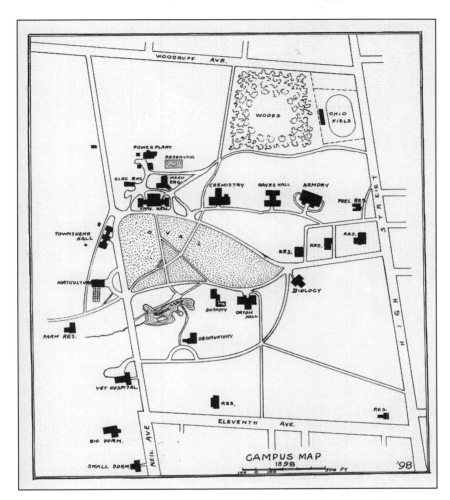

The Ohio State campus as it looked at the turn of the twentieth century. (Photo courtesy of The Ohio State University Archives)

Part Six

But campus work is unchanged—
It goes on forever

Chapter Twenty-Six
The father of football at Ohio State

On December 1, 1909, the *Lantern* published an article explaining how football had begun at Ohio State twenty years earlier. It described the campus students casually exploring "the fundamentals of the new American college game" until eventually a "formal challenge was sent to the students of Ohio Wesleyan University, who had also organized a football team."[1] The writer of the article claimed that the game with Wesleyan had been played on April 1, 1890, and that Caesar Morrey had scored the game-winning touchdown, but aside from those two details the story told in the article was mostly accurate.

The information in the article may have come from Charles Foulk. Foulk had graduated from Ohio State in 1894 but he continued his studies at the University of Leipzig in Germany. There he became an expert in quantitative chemical analysis, and in 1899 he returned to Ohio State as a professor of analytic chemistry.[2]

It seems more likely, however, that the information in the article came from Caesar Morrey himself. Morrey had also become a member of the Ohio State faculty. After his graduation from Starling Medical College in 1896, he had continued his studies in biology. First he attended the University of Vienna and then the Pasteur Institute in Paris, and in 1899 he returned to Ohio State and established the university's Department of Bacteriology.[3] He continued to keep an eye on the Ohio State football team, and he always made himself available as a first-hand source of information about the early days.[4]

George Cole read that article in the *Lantern* and he felt compelled to supply some missing details. Cole had graduated in 1891. In 1909 he was working as a mechanical engineer in New York, but he wrote a letter to the *Lantern* to remind everyone about his own role in the birth of the team. He described how he had helped Jesse Lee Jones take up the collection to buy a football for the team. He then ended his letter by referencing his role in bringing the team a coach, stating, "Mention should also be made of our first football coach, Al S. Lilley, and of the fact that 'Snake' Ames, of Princeton, came out one afternoon to show us how to kick."[5]

✳

In 1916 the Ohio State campus was anticipating a special football season. Over the first fifteen years of the twentieth century the team had continued, through fits and starts, to grow in stature. During those years the team's schedule came to include some of the better college teams in the nation, and as a result Walter Camp, Caspar Whitney, and other football sportswriters had begun to consider Ohio State's best players for their various "All America" lists. The 1916 team lineup included promising new recruits and the campus hoped to see the team's reputation take another step.

The season opened on October 7 with the latest game against Ohio Wesleyan. The *Lantern* commented, "Little fear is being felt as to the team that will trot from the field victorious....Ohio State has a machine this year that looks fit to withstand all that Ohio Wesleyan can offer."[6] The Ohio State team won 12 to 0, but they were just warming up.

The team played Oberlin the following week, and they won that game 128 to 0. At the time it was the highest score by one team in a game in the history of college football. Ohio State coach Jack Wilce had to empty his bench in the second half to try to keep the game from getting even farther out of hand.[7] The Ohio State team's dominance in that game over their once-feared rival could barely have been imagined twenty years earlier.

On the following Saturday, October 21, the conference season began. In 1912 Ohio State had joined the Western Conference, also known as the Big Nine, later renamed the Big Ten. The first game on the Western Conference schedule in 1916 was against the University of Illinois, who had entered the season as the favorite to win the championship. Ohio State upset Illinois 7 to 6 with a last minute touchdown from Ohio State's new halfback Charles "Chic" Harley.[8]

The homecoming game was played on November 4 against the University of Wisconsin. Wisconsin had been another conference favorite that year but

Chic Harley carries the ball against Northwestern in 1916. (Photo courtesy of The Ohio State University Archives)

Ohio State upset them as well, 14 to 13. Harley was again the hero of the game, scoring both of his team's touchdowns and making both extra-point kicks.[9] The community lionized Harley that year, building up his legend, a ritual repeated for decades afterward for Ohio State players with names such as Fesler, Janowicz, Cassady, Griffin, and George, among many others.[10]

The next two wins of the 1916 season came easier. On November 11 Ohio State defeated Indiana University 46 to 7. That game was followed with a non-conference game on November 18 against the Case School, which Ohio State won 28 to 0. Those games set up a finale on November 25 against Northwestern University.

Northwestern was also undefeated that year and this game would determine the conference champion. In the days before the game the *Lantern* wrote, "The campus is today the center of absorbing football interest…wherever football is talked in the United States. When Northwestern and Ohio State clash on Ohio Field Saturday, it will not be a mere football game as football games go—that fight will be a classic."[11] A crowd of 15,000 spectators set a new campus attendance record. Ohio State won the game 23 to 3. The *Lantern* afterward declared it "the most important game of school's history."[12]

After the game the *Oberlin Review* wrote, "We take our hats off to the Ohio State team that won the Western Conference championship and so put Ohio football on the map....Here's to you, Ohio State. We're sorry we could not do it, but we are glad you did it for us."[13]

✻

Demand for tickets had reached a new high that year, and far more spectators came for the games than could fit into Ohio Field. After the season the university began considering how to accommodate them in the future. The most audacious plan came from Thomas French, Edward French's brother, who had since become the chairman of the university's Department of Architecture and Drawing. He was also the president of the Athletic Board. Out of his plan came a massive horseshoe-shaped coliseum, sitting on the west side of the campus, known as Ohio Stadium. The stadium, completed in 1922, originally seated nearly 70,000 fans.[14]

Alumni fundraising for the stadium project was led by Paul Lincoln.[15] After his graduation in 1892 Lincoln had become an electrical engineer. He eventually became the director of the School of Engineering at Cornell University, but he also maintained a close relationship with Ohio State. In the early 1920s he was the president of the Ohio State University Alumni Association.[16]

As part of the fundraising efforts, Lincoln asked George Cole to write an article for the alumni magazine. Cole had always remained eager to discuss his early involvement with the football team, and the article that he wrote early in 1920 expanded on the narrative that he had previously written in 1909. He continued to emphasize his own role—writing of helping Jesse Lee Jones buy a ball and rulebook and of bringing a coach to campus—although he conceded that he had never actually played and that he had found both the rulebook and the shape of the ball confusing.[17]

✻

In 1924 the Ohio State homecoming game had offered fans a special event. The game that year was played against the University of Michigan, which had by then succeeded Ohio Wesleyan University and Kenyon College as Ohio State's primary rival. The 1924–25 school year was the thirty-fifth anniversary of the team that defeated Ohio Wesleyan in 1890, and the university invited the

The spring 1890 football team returned to campus in 1924. (Photo courtesy of The Ohio State University Archives)

members of that first team to a special halftime ceremony. The *Lantern* trumpeted, "First Football Heroes Will Be at Homecoming."[18]

Seven members of the first team returned. They were Charles Foulk, Dave Hegler, Herbert Johnston, Jesse Lee Jones, Paul Lincoln, Caesar Morrey, and Ham Richardson. Dick Ellis was in the U.S. Army, stationed in the Canal Zone in Panama, and unable to return, and Walter Miller could not be located. Jack Huggins, Mike Kennedy, Jo Jo Large, and Hiram Rutan had all since died.[19]

After his graduation in 1890 Jesse Lee Jones had found a successful career in metallurgy. He originally found a job as a metallurgist at a factory in the town of Mingo Junction, near Martins Ferry, but he eventually took a job at Westinghouse in Pittsburgh where he rose to the position of Chief Chemist. By 1924 he was the President of the American Institute of Metals. At Westinghouse he had developed new alloys that were used to build the American warships of World War One.[20]

At halftime of the 1924 homecoming game the members of the 1890 team each ceremonially received varsity letters.[21] In 1903 the university had formed the Varsity "O" Association, which began awarding varsity letters to the athletes on the university's teams and which maintained a list of the letter winners.[22] In 1924 the Association decided to begin recognizing the athletes from before 1903, and they chose to begin the commemorative process with the team that had done so much in 1890 to build the reputation of the school. The Varsity "O" Association told the members of that team that their names would to be added to the list for posterity.[23]

The *Lantern* published an article a few weeks later that considered the school's expanding place in college football. The writer wrote of discovering a story that had originally been published in the *Makio* in 1902. That story forecasted life in the distant future of 1950, where an elderly O.S.U. alumnus returned to campus and discovered that Ohio State football had achieved every goal of its founders. The football team routinely defeated the best teams in the nation, and the campus gymnasium needed an entire room to house the team's trophies. The *Lantern* writer noted that the *Makio* prediction had come true a quarter century ahead of schedule. The *Lantern* writer then noted how the *Makio* story ended. The alumnus walking across the campus falls into a state of reverie:

> 'Everything is not strange,' he says, 'there are new buildings, and new customs, and little that I knew here when the century was young. But campus work is unchanged. It goes on forever'.[24]

By the time that 1950 actually arrived, however, some of the founders of Ohio State football had been forgotten. When the Varsity "O" Association added the names of the members of the first team to the list of letter winners, three members of that team were somehow left off the list. One was the prep student Jack Huggins, and another was Herbert Johnston, the last player added to the original lineup. The third forgotten man was Jesse Lee Jones.[25]

✳

Some of Ohio State's football pioneers have always been left out of the story. The football players from before 1890 were never recognized for their role in developing the team. Jumbo Hedges, Chester Aldrich, Fred Ball, and C.C. Sharp had all lived to see their own contributions forgotten.

C.C. Sharp had invested in mines after his graduation in 1888, and he made a fortune. In 1922 he gave back to Ohio State with an $18,000 donation. With that money the university built the "Charles Cutler Sharp Library of Chemistry,"[26] which stood until all of the O.S.U. science libraries were merged in 1993.[27] After that donation, Paul Lincoln asked Sharp if he had any more money to spare. Sharp then donated $5,000 to the Athletic Department[28]—one of the largest private contributions toward the building of Ohio Stadium.[29]

Fred Ball had become a prominent lawyer in Montgomery, Alabama. In 1911 he argued a landmark case before the United States Supreme Court, successfully representing a sharecropper against the state of Alabama for civil rights violations.[30] Ball also held a position on the Y.M.C.A. National Council, and was a trustee of the Cramton Bowl, the home field of the University of Alabama football team.[31]

In Ulysses, Nebraska, Chester Aldrich also became a lawyer and built a reputation for fighting for the rights of the underprivileged. That fight pulled him into Nebraska politics and he was elected to the state legislature as a Progressive Republican. His regular stump speech was "Our National Permanence—Its Strength and Its Dangers."[32] In the legislature he wrote laws that upset the power of the national railroad trusts, and in 1910, with support from the Populist Democrat William Jennings Bryan, he was elected Nebraska's governor.[33] In 1912 the Progressive wing of the Republican Party considered Aldrich as a possible candidate for U.S. President.

During the time that Chester Aldrich was governor, the University of Nebraska held its first homecoming game. Aldrich involved himself in those football festivities. In the tradition of politicians at a baseball game throwing out the first pitch, Governor Aldrich arranged to "kick out the first ball."[34]

In 1914 the city of Columbus had completed an internal improvements project. The city had finished paving High Street, the primary route connecting the Ohio State campus to downtown. To welcome visitors driving up High Street from the city the university planned to build a "Gateway" at the southern end of campus.

If High Street had been paved in 1887 the Ohio State football team could have played the game that they had scheduled against Columbus Buggy. When Jumbo Hedges heard about the Gateway project he sent word from Iowa that he wanted to make a donation. He wrote, "I trust the committee will have no trouble in raising sufficient funds to carry the project to completion. I stand ready to do my full share in bringing '88's proportion of the cost up to the limit."[35] Ultimately Hedges personally provided half of the funds to build the downtown Gateway.

*

As the twentieth century continued, the Ohio State football team continued to consolidate their new stature as a national power. A game between O.S.U. and Notre Dame University in 1935 would be known for years afterward as "the Game of the Century."[36] That 1935 game helped inspire the Associated Press to begin a poll of sportswriters the following year to name the best teams in the nation, and that poll would be used to determine a college football national champion. From this beginning in 1936 until the present, the Ohio State team would routinely be in contention for the title.[37]

The growing success on the field of Ohio State football was accompanied by similar success off the field. The support given the team by the students on campus had quickly been matched by support from throughout the city of Columbus, and the support of the city was afterward matched by support from throughout the state. Fans could be found in the liberal northeastern corner of the state as well as in the conservative strongholds of its western plains. Traditional Appalachian communities gave their hearts to the team, as did larger multi-ethnic, multi-cultural cities. No other topic seemed to bind the people of Ohio as tightly, even among those who attended other colleges.[38]

In the following decades Ohio Stadium was often filled to capacity with fans shouting at the top of their lungs. Seating would need to be expanded frequently to try to keep up with demand. In 1973 a visiting professor of psychology attended a game at the stadium and he was stunned by the emotional intensity displayed for such an objectively unimportant event. He was inspired to develop a model to explain fan behavior, rooted in social-identity theory, stating that fans build their sense of self from the success of their teams and display their identities through the symbols of the team.[39] His model, called "Basking in Reflected Glory," remains the standard of the field.

Support for the O.S.U. team has continued to grow in recent years. In 2008, the Delaware County Historical Society put a marker on the campus of Ohio Wesleyan University, and that marker proudly commemorating the "Site of the first Ohio State football game" and Wesleyan's role in the event.[40] In 2011 the *New York Times* statistician Nate Silver estimated that Ohio State football had developed the largest fan base in the nation.[41]

*

Growing prominence also led to changes in how the university administration managed the Ohio State football team. The university's board of trustees no longer worried about farming and religious interests in the state government taking away their funding, but they did hope to keep the major donors in the state happy, and those donors were fans of the football team. The donors came to be called the called "the downtown coaches" and as early as the 1920s they were considered the true power behind the scenes. In 1934 the University of Michigan alumni magazine wrote, "Down in Columbus, Ohio, so rumor has it, there is some kind of association commonly designated as the 'Downtown Coaches.' If one were to judge from all the reports emanating from the Ohio capital, this organization exists for the chief purpose of firing Ohio State University football coaches'."[42]

To keep these outside patrons of the university satisfied in the early years of the twentieth century, the administration introduced an unofficial policy banning African American students from the campus sports teams. The ban was especially rigid for the popular football team. More racially-progressive football coaches, such as Sam Willaman, Paul Brown, and Woody Hayes, fought back against the racial restrictions, but there was a limit to what they could do.[43]

It is tempting to wonder how the rise of the football team's national reputation might have played out if the university administration had not taken over campus sports in 1898. How might history be different if the publicly-owned Athletic Company had been successful? The students had traditionally been recklessly idealistic in their opposition to bigoted and reactionary power in the state, and they had been racially tolerant in their management of the football team. The administrative takeover, however, was probably inevitable. It was part of a larger trend at the university in which faculty and administrative oversight increased in all parts of student life. In 1913 the *Lantern*, the voice of the students, officially became a product of the O.S.U. School of Journalism.[44] In 1906 the university closed the North Dorm, and in its place they built dormitories that were not administered by a student governing body.

Forty-five years after Fred Patterson had considered Ohio State's environment to be a cocoon from the world's prejudices, the university did not allow their greatest athlete, the track star Jesse Owens, to live on campus in one of the university-administered dormitories.[45]

✳

As George Cole grew older the more central his own role in the beginnings of Ohio State football seemed to become in his memory. In a 1938 interview with the *Columbus Citizen* many of the details of his story had become reversed. It was now the others on campus who had been confused by the rulebook that Cole had given them, and it was now the others on campus who had been bewildered by the shape of the ball until Cole had set them straight. More than ever, Cole seemed to suggest that Al Lilley had led the team up to Delaware to defeat Ohio Wesleyan. Jesse Lee Jones had disappeared from Cole's story entirely.[46]

By then Cole had begun to refer to himself as the "daddy" of Ohio State football, and the *Alumni Monthly* referred to him by that term in his obituary in 1941.[47] In 1938 the university placed a plaque in Ohio Stadium to honor Alexander Spinning Lilley for, according to the *Lantern*, "laying the foundation for football at the University."[48] That same year the athletic department presented Cole with a special award—a scroll thanking him for his contributions, and an honorary varsity letter, the only football letter ever given to a student who did not play a single down in a game.[49]

Ten years later the *Lantern* introduced a new version of the story. In this telling the students had originally ordered the Spalding rugby ball by accident, and it was to make the best of a bad situation that Cole ordered them a football rulebook because he "figured they might as well get some use out of the ball."[50] This *Lantern* writer went on to claim, "With Cole still pushing things the boys bought some football uniforms," but noted with sad irony that Cole, "the father of football at Ohio State," was never able to wear one himself.[51]

Cole's version of the story has become the accepted history of Ohio State football. An overview of Ohio State Football history published in 2013 stated that "Sports at Ohio State University (OSU) were pretty informal until 1890. In that year, George Cole talked some of his fellow students into forming a football team."[52] In 2014, an article on the NCAA website claimed, "They've been playing football in Columbus, Ohio for a long time—125 years to be exact. George Cole and Alexander S. Lilley introduced the game to the university in 1890."[53] *The Official Ohio State Football Encyclopedia*, "officially endorsed and licensed by the Ohio State University," explains, "George N. Cole, class of '91, is credited with helping develop Ohio State's first official football team."[54]

The true story of the early days of football at Ohio State, however, is much more interesting. Football originally grew at the university because the students, working with little to no supervision, made football their priority. It was only after a small group of students foolishly took on enormous debts that the faculty and administration took over the governance of football at Ohio State. By that time, however, the students had proven to all authority that football was a significant way to develop and promote their school's reputation.

*

Perhaps George Cole's most important contribution to the history of the Ohio State University was his courageous and principled act of civil disobedience, which led to the end of the university's policy mandating chapel attendance. That policy had threatened to change the early character of the campus and to undermine Rutherford B. Hayes's vision of a broadly-welcoming, ecumenical university with no sectarian barriers to education. In the twentieth century the racial tolerance and gender fairness of the university were sometimes tested, but it remained an institution open to Jews, Muslims, Buddhists, Hindus, non-believers, and Christians of every stripe.

Hayes had believed that a policy of toleration would allow his Land-Grant University to unite his diverse and fractured state. To a large extent he was correct. What Hayes could not have foreseen was that the Ohio State University would also unite the state behind its football team.

Acknowledgments

I would like to thank the following archivists and librarians for the assistance that helped launch the research for this project: Tad Bennicoff (Princeton University), Dawne Dewey (Wright State University), Karen Fischer (Mansfield/Richland County Public Library), Stephen Grinch (Otterbein College), Jacqueline Haun (the Lawrenceville School), Eileen Keating (Cornell University), Heather Lyle (Denison University), Doris Oliver (the Stevens Institute of Technology), Linda Showalter (Marietta College), Elaine Smith Snyder (the College of Wooster), Tim Sprattler (the Phillips Academy), Jill Tatem (Case Western Reserve University), and the staff at the Delaware County Historical Society. I would especially like to thank Bertha Ihnat and Michelle Drobik from the Ohio State University Archives.

I would also like to thank the following friends and family members for their comments that helped to navigate the writing of the manuscript: Frank Alexander, Jim Colegrove, Leonor Costa, Mark Dintenfass, Ronda Eisenberg, John Millard, Gordon Moskowitz, Jody Peck, Don Roman, Katherine Roman, and Matthew Schneeberger.

Finally, I would like to thank Jon Miller and the rest of the staff at the University of Akron Press for their vital assistance in bringing the book in for a landing.

Notes

Chapter One

1. Hedges was referred to as "Jumbo" in print throughout his time at Ohio State and beyond. The first time was "College Organizations: Alcyone," *The Fortnightly Lantern*, October 1, 1884, 116. See also "Catalogue of Students," *Fifteenth Annual Report of the Board of Trustees of the Ohio State University*, 1886, 125–31; "Quotations," *The Makio*, 1888, 138; "Class of '88," *The Makio*, 1886, 45.

2. "Students At Play," *Ohio State Journal*, April 29, 1886, 4; "A College 'Rush'," *Columbus Dispatch*, April 28, 1886, 4; "Class Rush," *The Lantern*, May 6, 1886, 104–5.

3. "Local Notes," *The Fortnightly Lantern*, October 15, 1885, 172.

4. Dyer was from the unincorporated community of Georgesville, Ohio. "Catalogue of Students." *Fifteenth Annual Report of the Board of Trustees of the Ohio State University*, 1886, 125–31. His father is stated to have been a farmer in Joseph Smith, "Joseph H. Dyer," *History of the Republican Party in Ohio and Memoirs of its Representative Supporters, Volume II*, (Chicago: Lewis Publishing Company, 1898), 192–98; Dyer began attending Boston Law School in 1887. "Personal," *The Fortnightly Lantern*, October 6, 1887, 169.

5. "Catalogue of Students," *Fifteenth Annual Report of the Board of Trustees of the Ohio State University*, 1886, 125–31.

6. *Ibid.*

7. "Ohio State's First 100 years," *The Lantern*, April 1, 1970, 7.

8. The freshman voting-bloc plot was discussed in the fall of 1885: "Local Notes," *The Fortnightly Lantern*, November 5, 1885, 188. The specific roles of the various class conspirators was finally laid out almost four years later: A. B. Rickey, "Class History," *The Fortnightly Lantern*, June 28, 1889, 229–232.

9. "Local Notes," *The Fortnightly Lantern*, November 5, 1885, 188.

10. "The Sophomores, with traditional boldness, have challenged…the Freshmen to a game of foot ball." Reported in "Local Notes," *The Fortnightly Lantern*, November 5, 1885, 188.

11. "Local," *The Lantern*, April 1881, 47.

12. "The warm weather has laid foot ball upon the shelf, and base ball now fully takes its place." This observation was reported as the opening words of the May 1881 issue of the *Lantern*: "Editorials," *The Lantern*, May 1881, 49. Ten pages later, however, was an observation that "Foot ball is still the favorite game at the Dorm," noted in "Local," *The Lantern*, May 1881, 59.

13. Allison Danzig, *The History of American Football: Its Great Teams, Players, and Coaches* (Englewood Cliffs, NJ: Prentice-Hall, 1956).

14. "Dorm Notes," *The Fortnightly Lantern*, November 19, 1885, 207.

15. Walter Camp, *American Football* (New York: Harper & Brothers, 1891).

16. "O. S. U. vs Broad Treads," *The Fortnightly Lantern*, November 1, 1884, 144.

17. The *Makio*, the Ohio State University yearbook, regularly reported membership of all university athletic teams, and there is no record of Hedges participating with any team prior to the spring 1886 football team.

18. Walter Camp & Lorin F. Deland, *Football* (Boston: Houghton, Mifflin and Company, 1896).

19. "Lawn Tennis Club," *The Makio*, 1886, 70.

20. "Foot Ball Team," *The Makio*, 1886, 72.

21. "Local Notes," *The Fortnightly Lantern*, October 15, 1885, 172.

22. "Young Men's Christian Association," *The Makio*, 1886, 76.

23. "Local Notes," *The Fortnightly Lantern*, October 28, 1886, 205.

24. "Chester Hardy Aldrich," the Hillsdale Collegian, November 23, 1910, 8.

25. J. Howard Galbraith, "The Incognitus et Agnos," *The Ohio State University Monthly*, January 1918, 39–42.

26. "Mr. Aldrich C. F. got mad at Jumbo, and said he wouldn't play which detracted much from the meeting." Reported in "Incognitus et Agnos," *The Fortnightly Lantern*, June 26,1886, 141–42.

27. Sharp was consistently referred to as "C.C." by the *Lantern* and *Makio*, but it is difficult to highlight a first occurrence because those publications occasionally referred to everyone by their initials.

28. "Base Ball Association," *The Makio*, 1885, 78.

29. "Catalogue of Students," *Fifteenth Annual Report of the Board of Trustees of the Ohio State University*, 1886, 125–31.

30. "Personal," *The Fortnightly Lantern*, October 6, 1887, 169.

31. "Personal Mention," *Electrical Review and Western Electrician*, October 23, 1915, 781.

32. "Class of '89," *The Makio*, 1886, 48.

33. "Personal," *The Fortnightly Lantern*, October 28, 1886, 206.

34. "Personal," *The Fortnightly Lantern*, October 6, 1887, 170.

35. 1880 United States Census.

36. "Personal," *The Fortnightly Lantern*, April 15, 1885, 76.

37. "Jumbo in his autumnal peramulambulations took in several of our more prominent colleges, among which was Johns Hopkins University." From "Local Notes," *The Fortnightly Lantern*, December 10, 1885, 221.

38. "History of '88," *The Makio*, 1886, 46–47.

39. "Local Notes," *The Fortnightly Lantern*, December 10, 1885, 220.

40. "General College Notes," *The Fortnightly Lantern*, February 24, 1886, 45; "General College Notes," *The Fortnightly Lantern*, February 4, 1886, 29; W. K. Cherryholmes, "A Communication," *The Fortnightly Lantern*, January 21, 1886, 7.

41. "General Literature," *The Fortnightly Lantern*, March 18, 1886, 71.

42. *Ibid.*

43. "Local Notes," *The Fortnightly Lantern*, February 24, 1886, 42.

44. "Local Notes," *The Fortnightly Lantern*, March 18, 1886, 73.

45. "Local," *The Lantern*, May 1881, 60.

46. "Local," *The Lantern*, November 1882, 108.

47. "Editorials," *The Lantern*, November 1883, 118.

48. "Base Ball," *The Makio*, 1982, 76–77; "Bicycle Club," *The Makio*, 1985, 79; "O. S. U. Rifle Club," *The Makio*, 1984, 77; "Bully Buoy Club," *The Makio*, 1884, 75.

49. "Cricket," *The Lantern*, June 1, 1882, 70; "Local," *The Lantern*, May 1, 1883, 64; "Pony Club," *The Makio*, 1884, 74.

50. "Editorials," *The Fortnightly Lantern*, October 15, 1884, 123; "Athletics," *The Fortnightly Lantern*, March 18, 1885, 53.

51. "College spirit as it is known now can hardly be said to have existed at all." From J. H. Galbraith, "The First Gleams of the Lantern," *The Ohio State University Monthly*, October 1914, 29–35.

52. "Local Notes," *The Fortnightly Lantern*, February 4, 1886, 26.

53. "Personal," *The Fortnightly Lantern*, January 21, 1886, 10.

54. Joseph Smith, "Joseph H. Dyer," *History of the Republican Party in Ohio and Memoirs of its Representative Supporters, Volume II*, (Chicago: Lewis Publishing Company, 1898), 192–98; Alexis Cope, *History of the Ohio State University, Vol. I: 1870–1910* (Columbus, OH: Ohio State University Press, 1920), 377.

55. "Local Notes," *The Fortnightly Lantern*, Vol. VI, No. 13, 28 October 1886, 207; "Personal," *The Fortnightly Lantern*, May 6, 1886, 107.

56. "Local Notes," *The Fortnightly Lantern*, March 18, 1886, 73.

57. "Local Notes," *The Fortnightly Lantern*, May 20, 1886, 121.

58. "Personal," *The Fortnightly Lantern*, March 18, 1886, 74.

59. *Ibid.*

60. "Although the warm weather days have produced symptoms of 'spring fever,' the loyal O. S. U. student is awake." From "Ohio State University," *Columbus Daily Press*, April 23, 1890, 9.

61. "Home a Hard Place to Find for Past OSU Women Undergrads," *From Woody's Coach*, March 7, 2013, Accessed February 5, 2016 from https://library.osu.edu/blogs/archives/2013/03/07/home-a-hard-place-to-find-for-past-osu-women-undergrads/.

62. "Students At Play," *Ohio State Journal*, April 29, 1886, 4.

63. "The Clashing Classes," *The Lantern*, March 1884, 43–44.

64. "A College 'Rush'," *Columbus Dispatch*, April 28, 1886, 4.

65. "Class Rush—'87 vs '88," *The Lantern*, May 6, 1886, 104–5.

66. "Personal," *The Fortnightly Lantern*, October 7, 1886, 192.

67. "A College 'Rush'," *Columbus Dispatch*, April 28, 1886, 4.

68. "Personal," *The Fortnightly Lantern*, May 6, 1886, 107.

69. "A College 'Rush'," *Columbus Dispatch*, April 28, 1886, 4.

70. *Ibid.*

71. "Personal," *The Fortnightly Lantern*, May 6, 1886, 107.

72. "A College 'Rush'," *Columbus Dispatch*, April 28, 1886, 4.

73. "Local Notes," *The Fortnightly Lantern*, May 6, 1886, 106.

74. "A College 'Rush'," *Columbus Dispatch*, April 28, 1886, 4.

75. *Ibid.*

76. "Students At Play," *Ohio State Journal,* April 29, 1886, 4.

77. "Local Notes," *The Fortnightly Lantern,* May 6, 1886, 106.

78. *Ibid.*

79. "The Latest Scheme—Class '89 to the Front," *The Fortnightly Lantern,* May 20, 1886, 119–20.

80. "History of '88," *The Makio,* 1886, 46–47.

81. "O Freshie how brilliant was thy scheme," quoted in: "Local Notes," *The Fortnightly Lantern,* May 20, 1886, 120.

82. "Editorials," *The Fortnightly Lantern,* May 6, 1886, 99; "Local Notes," *The Fortnightly Lantern,* May 6, 1886, 105.

83. "Foot Ball Team," *The Makio,* 1886, 72.

84. "Personal," *The Fortnightly Lantern,* May 6, 1886, 107.

85. "Editorials," *The Fortnightly Lantern,* October 7, 1886, 183.

Chapter Two

1. Hedges and Aldrich remained friends at least until 1894, when the *Lantern* reported that Hedges had recently visited Aldrich in Nebraska. "Our Alumni," *The Lantern,* October 10, 1894, 4.

2. "Local Notes," *The Fortnightly Lantern,* October 28, 1886, 206.

3. "Personal," *The Fortnightly Lantern,* October 28, 1886, 206.

4. "Dormitories," *The Makio,* 1985, 86–87.

5. Nikki M. Taylor, *America's First Black Socialist: The Radical Life of Peter H. Clark* (Lexington, KY: University Press of Kentucky, 2013).

6. "Editorials," *The Lantern,* May 1884, 65.

7. Coy F. Cross II, *Justin Smith Morrill: Father of the Land-Grant Colleges* (East Lansing: Michigan State University Press, 1999).

8. Alexis Cope, *History of the Ohio State University, Vol. I: 1870–1910* (Columbus, OH: Ohio State University Press, 1920).

9. "Base Ball," *The Makio,* 1883, 72; "Foot Ball Team," *The Makio,* 1886, 72.

10. "Class and Field Day," *The Fortnightly Lantern,* June 26, 1885, 141.

11. "History of '88," *The Makio,* 1885, 52–53; "Base Ball Association: Second Team," *The Makio,* 1886, 69.

12. "Personal," *The Fortnightly Lantern,* October 7, 1886, 191.

13. Alexis Cope, *History of the Ohio State University, Vol. I: 1870–1910* (Columbus, OH: Ohio State University Press, 1920).

14. "Universities of the World," *The College Transcript,* May 15, 1890, 233; "General College Notes," *The Fortnightly Lantern,* December 1, 1884, 180.

15. Timothy L. Smith, "The Ohio Valley: Testing Ground for America's Experiment in Religious Pluralism," *Church History,* December 1991, 461–79.

16. Roger L. Geiger, *The American College in the Nineteenth Century* (Nashville, TN: Vanderbilt University Press, 2000).

17. H. J. Eckenrode, Rutherford B. Hayes: Statesman of Reunion (New York: Dodd, Mead & Company, 1930).

18. James Quay Howard, *The Life, Public Services and Select Speeches of Rutherford B. Hayes* (Cincinnati: Robert Clarke & Co., 1876).

19. William A. Kinnison, *Building Sullivant's Pyramid: An Administrative History of the Ohio State University, 1870–1907* (Columbus, OH: Ohio State University Press, 1970).

20. James E. Pollard, *History of the Ohio State University: The Story of Its First Seventy Five Years, 1873–1948* (Columbus, OH: Ohio State University Press, 1952).

21. Alexis Cope, "Remarks on the Occasion of the Public Reception of a Portrait of President Rutherford B. Hayes," *The Fortnightly Lantern*, November 15, 1889, 53–54.

22. "An O. S. U. Song," *The Lantern*, March 10, 1892, 305.

23. "Geological Excursion," *The Fortnightly Lantern*, November 11, 1886, 218–19; "Local Notes," *The Fortnightly Lantern*, March 20, 1886, 120.

24. "History of '88," *The Makio*, 1886, 46–47.

25. "Local Notes," *The Fortnightly Lantern*, November 5, 1885, 190.

26. "Fred Ball to the Preachers," *The Ohio State University Monthly*, March 1915, 11.

27. "Editorials," *The Lantern*, March 1884, 33.

28. George B. Kirsch, *Baseball in Blue and Gray: The National Pastime during the Civil War* (Princeton, NJ: Princeton University Press, 2003); "Local Notes," *The Fortnightly Lantern*, October 15, 1885, 173.

29. Dave Stilwell, "A Century of Sports," *The Lantern*, May 29, 1881, 10.

30. "Local," *The Lantern*, April 1881, 48.

31. "Base Ball," *The Lantern*, June 1881, 68.

32. "Exchanges," *The Lantern*, May 1882, 58.

33. Thomas Nathanael Hoover, *The History of Ohio University* (Athens, OH: Ohio University Press, 1954).

34. Quoted in "Editorials," *The Fortnightly Lantern*, January 21, 1886, 4.

35. "Editorials," *The Fortnightly Lantern*, January 21, 1886, 4.

36. "Local Notes," *The Fortnightly Lantern*, February 17, 1887, 40.

37. "The University," *The Fortnightly Lantern*, June 11, 1885, 127.

38. "Editorials," *The Fortnightly Lantern*, March 18, 1885, 51; "Editorials," *The Fortnightly Lantern*, October 11, 1889, 18.

39. "Editorials," *The Fortnightly Lantern*, October 17, 1890, 17–18.

40. "There is a greater number of colored students every year. The O. S. U. is broad in its principles." In "Local Notes," *The Fortnightly Lantern*, September 27, 1889, 11.

41. "General College Notes," *The Fortnightly Lantern*, March 5, 1886, 60.

42. "Curses and oaths are often heard on the way; As we marched, marched, marched to play baseball," quoted in "Song of the Franklins," *The Ohio State University Monthly*, April 1916, 28.

43. "Makio," *The Makio*, 1906, 9.

44. "Dedicated to the Divil," *The Makio*, 1887, 6.

45. "Symposium on the O. S. U.: The O. S. U. and the Past," *The Makio*, April 1897, 21–26.

46. "Base Ball," *The Lantern*, June 1882, 69; "Base Ball Notes," *The Lantern*, Vol. II, No. X, December 1882, 118.

47. "Base Ball Notes," *The Lantern*, November 1882, 107.

48. "College Rows," *The College Transcript*, 24 May 1879, 241–42.

49. "Editorials," *The Lantern*, February 1883, 13–14.

50. *Ibid.*

51. *Ibid.*

52. "The Chimes of the Campus," *The Ohio State University Monthly*, April 1915, 15.

53. Alexis Cope, *History of the Ohio State University, Vol. I: 1870–1910* (Columbus, OH: Ohio State University Press, 1920).

54. *Ibid.*

55. *Ibid.*

56. "Deaths," *The Ohio State University Monthly*, February 1916, 49.

57. "Editorials," *The Fortnightly Lantern*, 1 March 1889, 131–32.

58. "Religion in Public Schools," *The Lantern*, March 1883, 28–29.

59. *Ibid.*

60. "Local Notes," *The Lantern*, June 1884, 101.

61. "Base Ball Association," *The Makio*, 1885, 77.

62. "Local Notes," *The Fortnightly Lantern*, No. XI, October 15, 1885, 172.

63. "Base Ball Revived," *The Fortnightly Lantern*, October 15, 1884, 129; "O. S. U. vs Broad Treads," *The Fortnightly Lantern*, November 1, 1884, 144.

64. "Local Notes," *The Fortnightly Lantern*, June 3, 1886, 139.

65. "Local Notes," *The Fortnightly Lantern*, October 7, 1886, 192.

66. "Local Notes," *The Fortnightly Lantern*, October 28, 1886, 207.

67. "Personal," *The Fortnightly Lantern*, December 9, 1886, 239.

68. "Personal," *The Fortnightly Lantern*, January 20, 1887, 11.

69. Carmi A. Thompson, "Golden Age of the Dorm," *The Ohio State University Monthly*, June 1915, 19–23.

70. "History of the Class of '88," *The Makio*, 1887, 50–51.

Chapter Three

1. "Our Students," *The Lantern*, February 1884, 27.

2. "Personal," *The Fortnightly Lantern*, June 26, 1885, 144.

3. J. Arnold Norcross, "Stevens in Gas," *Stevens Indicator*, November 30, 1923, 130.

4. Betty Garrett, *Columbus, America's Crossroads* (Tulsa, OK: Continental Heritage Press, 1980), 80.

5. "Personal," *The Fortnightly Lantern*, October 27, 1887, 186.

6. "Class and Field Day," *The Fortnightly Lantern*, Vol. V, No. IX, 26 June 1885, 141.

7. Athletics," *The Stevens Indicator*, November 1885, 127.

8. "Foot Ball Team, 1885," *The Eccentric Revolution*, May 1886, 69.

9. Allison Danzig, *The History of American Football: Its Great Teams, Players, and Coaches* (Englewood Cliffs, NJ: Prentice-Hall, 1956).

10. "Foot Ball Team," *The Makio*, 1886, 72.

11. "Local," *Marietta College Olio*, November 27, 1886, 44.

12. Allison Danzig, *The History of American Football: Its Great Teams, Players, and Coaches* (Englewood Cliffs, NJ: Prentice-Hall, 1956).

13. *Ibid.*

14. John J. Miller, *The Big Scrum: How Teddy Roosevelt Saved Football.* (New York: Harper-Collins, 2011).

15. "Personalia," *Marietta Olio*, November 14, 1885, 35.

16. *Ibid.*

17. "Local Notes," *The Fortnightly Lantern*, March 18, 1886, 73.

18. "Personalia," *Marietta Olio*, November 14, 1885, 35.

19. Allison Danzig, *The History of American Football: Its Great Teams, Players, and Coaches* (Englewood Cliffs, NJ: Prentice-Hall, 1956).

20. Football at Minnesota: The Story of Thirty Years' Contests on the Gridiron," *Minnesota Alumni Weekly*, November 9, 1914.

21. Will Perry, *The Wolverines: A Story of Michigan Football* (Huntsville, AL: Strode Publishers, 1974).

22. Nat Brandt, *When Oberlin Was King of the Gridiron: The Heisman Years* (Kent, OH: Kent State University Press, 2001).

23. John Kiesewetter, "Civil unrest woven into city's history," *Cincinnati Enquirer*, July 15, 2001. Accessed March 21, 2016 from http://www.enquirer.com/editions/2001/07/15/tem_civil_unrest_woven.html.

24. "Athletics," *The Eccentric Revolution*, May 1885, 63.

25. "Foot Ball: Record of Games," *The Eccentric Revolution*, May 1886, 70.

26. "Slugs," *The Eccentric Revolution*, May 1886, 79.

27. Walter Camp, *American Football* (New York: Harper & Brothers, 1891).

28. "Athletics," *The Stevens Indicator*, June 1886, 96.

29. "Stevens Institute Athletic Association," *The Eccentric Revolution*, May 1886, 62.

Chapter Four

1. "Personal," *The Fortnightly Lantern*, November 11, 1886, 222.

2. Personal communication with former Caldwell High football coach Mike DeVol.

3. "Local," *The Lantern*, July 1882, 87.

4. "State University," *Ohio State Journal*, April 24, 1890, 4.

5. Morris Bishop, *A History of Cornell*, (Ithica, NY: Cornell University Press, 1962), 48.

6. "Local," *The Lantern*, July 1882, 87.

7. "Local Notes," *The Fortnightly Lantern*, May 20, 1886, 120.

8. "Local Notes," *The Fortnightly Lantern*, November 5, 1885, 1890.

9. "Damon and Pythias." *The Makio*, 1886, 87.

10. William R. Lazenby, "Report of the Superintendent of Grounds," *Fifteenth Annual Report of the Board of Trustees of the Ohio State University*, 1886, 48–50.

11. "Res Gestae," *The Lantern*, June 1881, 68.

12. "Prize Drill: O. S. U. vs Wooster," *The Fortnightly Lantern*, June 28, 1886, 149–50.

13. "Bleeds Scarlet and Gray: Joseph Bradford," Ohio State University: University Libraries, *OSU.EDU*, August 5, 2011, accessed July 5, 2016, https://library.osu.edu/blogs/archives/2011/08/05/bleed-scarlet-and-gray-joseph-bradford/.

14. Lauren Yapalater, "This Is Why Ohio State University's Marching Band Is Actually The Best Damn Band In The Land," BuzzFeed, October 3, 2013, accessed July 5, 2016, http://www.buzzfeed.com/lyapalater/this-is-why-ohio-state-universitys-marching-band-is-actually.

15. "College Organizations," *The Fortnightly Lantern*, October 6, 1887, 171.

16. "Alcyone," *The Makio*, 1887, 63; "Alcyone Literary Society," *The Makio*, 1885, 59; "Alcyone Literary Society," *The Makio*, 1884, 50; "College Organizations," *The Fortnightly Lantern*, October 6, 1887, 171.

17. "O. S. U. Oratorical Association," *The Makio*, 1887, 67.

18. "The Lantern," *The Makio*, 1887, 145.

19. "The Contest," *The Fortnightly Lantern*, February 11, 1885, 26.

20. "The Contest Friday Evening, Feb. 4, '87," *The Fortnightly Lantern*, February 17, 1887, 37–38.

21. Chester A. Aldrich, "Our National Permanence—Its Strength and Its Dangers," reprinted in *The Fortnightly Lantern*, March 17, 1887, 71–73.

22. "The Contest Friday Evening, Feb. 4, '87," *The Fortnightly Lantern*, February 17, 1887, 37–38.

23. *Ibid.*

24. "Mob and Law," *Winning Orations of the Inter-State Oratorical Contests* (Topeka, KS: 1891), 171–76.

25. K. Austin Kerr, *Organized for Prohibition: A New History of the Anti-Saloon League* (New Haven: Yale University Press, 1985).

26. "The Contest Friday Evening, Feb. 4, '87," *The Fortnightly Lantern*, February 17, 1887, 37–38.

27. *Ibid.*

28. "Local Notes," *The Fortnightly Lantern*, February 17, 1887, 40.

29. "Editorials," *The Fortnightly Lantern*, March 3, 1887, 50.

30. "Nebraska's Chief is Orator for Commencement," *The Ohio State Lantern*, April 12, 1911.

31. "Local Notes," *The Fortnightly Lantern*, February 17, 1887, 40.

32. "Personal," *The Fortnightly Lantern*, March 3, 1887, 61.

33. "Local Notes," *The Fortnightly Lantern*, February 17, 1887, 39.

34. "A Prize Fight," *The Makio*, 1887, 96–97.

35. "Editorials," *The Lantern*, March 1884, 33.

36. "Editorials," *The Fortnightly Lantern*, May 5, 1887, 99.

37. "Class and Field Day," *The Fortnightly Lantern*, June 26, 1885, 141.

38. "Field Day," *The Fortnightly Lantern*, June 23, 1887, 154.

39. "Local Notes," *The Fortnightly Lantern*, May 8, 1885, 97.

40. Alexis Cope, *History of the Ohio State University, Vol. I: 1870–1910* (Columbus, OH: Ohio State University Press, 1920).

41. "Local Notes," *The Fortnightly Lantern*, May 26, 1887, 122.

42. Alexis Cope, *History of the Ohio State University, Vol. I: 1870–1910* (Columbus, OH: Ohio State University Press, 1920).

43. "Editorials," *The Fortnightly Lantern*, May 26, 1887, 115.

44. "Local Notes," *The Fortnightly Lantern*, April 21, 1887, 89.

45. "Personal," *The Fortnightly Lantern*, May 26, 1887, 122.

46. "Personal," *The Fortnightly Lantern*, April 21, 1887, 90.

47. "Local Notes," *The Fortnightly Lantern*, April 21, 1887, 88.

48. *Ibid.*

49. "Damon and Pythias." *The Makio*, 1886, 87.

50. "Local and Personal Notes," *The Fortnightly Lantern*, February 2, 1888, 23.

51. "Club Notes," *The Fortnightly Lantern*, December 1, 1887, 219.

52. "Club Notes," *The Fortnightly Lantern*, April 21, 1887, 93; "Another Alumnus," *The Lantern*, May 24, 1899, 1.

53. "Club Notes," *The Fortnightly Lantern*, April 21, 1887, 93; "Field Day," *The Fortnightly Lantern*, June 23, 1887, 154–55.

54. "Base Ball Association," *The Makio*, 1885, 78.

55. "Lawn Tennis Club," *The Makio*, 1886, 70–71.

56. "Stickers for Our Country Teachers to Drop into the Institute Question Box," *The Makio*, 1989, 137.

57. O. S. U. Victorious," *The Fortnightly Lantern*, October 7, 1886, 188.

Chapter Five

1. "Personal," *The Fortnightly Lantern*, October 6, 1887, 170.

2. Quentin R. Skrabec, Jr., *Rubber: An American Industrial History* (Jefferson, NC: McFarland, 2013).

3. "Class of 1888," *The Makio*, 1888, 45.

4. "Dorm Doings," *The Fortnightly Lantern*, June 10, 1887, 140.

5. James Ellsworth Boyd, "A Note on the Old North Dormitory," *The Ohio State University Monthly*, October 1910, 36–37.

6. "The Lantern: Board of Editors," *The Fortnightly Lantern*, October 6, 1887, 162.

7. "Aldrich is Popular," *The Lantern*, June 16, 1911, 7.

8. "Personal," *The Fortnightly Lantern*, October 6, 1887, 169.

9. "Editorials," *The Fortnightly Lantern*, October 27, 1887, 179; "Local Notes," *The Fortnightly Lantern*, October 27, 1887, 185.

10. "Local Notes," *The Fortnightly Lantern*, October 6, 1887, 167.

11. "Ohio State University," *Ohio State Journal*, October 19, 1887, 8.

12. *Ibid.*

13. "State University," *Ohio State Journal*, October 11, 1887, 5.

14. "Personal," *The Fortnightly Lantern*, October 6, 1887, 169.

15. "Local Notes," *The Fortnightly Lantern*, October 6, 1887, 168.

16. "Personal," *The Fortnightly Lantern*, December 10, 1885, 225.

17. "University Trustees," *Ohio State Journal*, November 24, 1887, 8.

18. "Ohio State University," *Ohio State Journal*, October 19, 1887, 8; "Editorials," *The Fortnightly Lantern*, October 27, 1887, 179.

19. "Personal," *The Fortnightly Lantern*, October 27, 1887, 186.

20. "State University," *Ohio State Journal*, October 25, 1887, 8.

21. "Dorm Notes," *The Fortnightly Lantern*, November 10, 1887, 204.

22. "State University," *Ohio State Journal*, October 25, 1887, 8.

23. "Editorials," *The Fortnightly Lantern*, October 27, 1887, 179.

24. *Ibid.*

25. "State University Matters," *Columbus Dispatch*, November 8, 1887, 4.

26. "University Notes," *Columbus Dispatch*, November 2, 1887, 4.

27. "State University," *Columbus Dispatch*, October 25, 1887, 4; "The University," *Columbus Dispatch*, October 28, 1887, 4;

28. "Foot Ball Team," *The Makio*, 1888, 103.

29. *Ibid.*

30. Chas. B. Morrey, "Beginnings of Football at Ohio State," *Football Program: Princeton University vs. The Ohio State University, Ohio Stadium*, November 3, 1928, 60–61.

31. "Local Notes," *The Fortnightly Lantern*, November 10, 1887, 201.

32. "Personal," *The Fortnightly Lantern*, November 10, 1887, 202.

33. "Foot Ball Team," *The Makio*, 1888, 103.

34. *Ibid.*

35. "University News," *Columbus Dispatch*, November 12, 1887, 4.

36. "Editorials," *The Fortnightly Lantern*, May 5, 1887, 99.

37. "Thanksgiving Day," *Columbus Dispatch*, November 23, 1887, 4.

38. "University Trustees," *Ohio State Journal*, November 24, 1887, 8.

39. "All-Time Scores," *Cincinnati Bearcats: 2015 Football Media Guide*, 109, accessed July 5, 2016, http://grfx.cstv.com/photos/schools/cinn/sports/m-footbl/auto_pdf/2015-16/misc_non_event/15_fb_guide.pdf.

40. "Blue and Crimson," Ohio State Journal, November 25, 1887, 4.

41. "Dorm Notes," *The Fortnightly Lantern*, December 1, 1887, 219.

42. Information about the life of Fred Ball courtesy of Richard J. Ball of Ball, Ball, Matthews & Novak, P.A., who mailed me photocopies of undated newspaper clippings describing the work founding the Montgomery Y.M.C.A. football team in 1890.

Chapter Six

1. "Editorials," *The Fortnightly Lantern*, April 23, 1888, 84.

2. "The Engineer and Critic," *The Makio*, 1888, 153.

3. "Engineers' Association," *The Makio*, 1888, 95.

4. "Student Publications of the O. S. U.," *The Makio*, 1888, 87.

5. "Class of '89," *The Makio*, 1886, 48.

6. "Class of '89," *The Makio*, 1886, 52; "College Organizations: Horton," *The Fortnightly Lantern*, May 26, 1887, 123.

7. "Y. M. C. A.," *The Makio*, 1888, 88.

8. "Local and Personal Notes," *The Fortnightly Lantern*, May 8, 1888, 105.

9. "Men of the Iron Trade," *The Iron Trade Review*, October 21, 1915, 779.

10. *Record of Studies: Ohio State University Collegiate Department*, Vol. III: 1890–1894. Courtesy of the Ohio State University Archives.

11. "Local and Personal Notes," *The Fortnightly Lantern*, October 26, 1888, 24.

12. "Personal," *The Fortnightly Lantern*, June 3, 1886, 140.

13. "Local and Personal Notes," *The Fortnightly Lantern*, June 26, 1888, 154.

14. "Brief School History," Ulysses High School Alumni Association, *rootsweb*, accessed July 5, 2016, http://www.rootsweb.ancestry.com/~nebutler/ulyssesgrads3.htm.

15. J. H. Galbraith, "Choosing the University Colors," *The Ohio State University Monthly*, Dec. 1914–Jan. 1915, 11–13.

16. *Ibid.*

17. "Editorials," *The Fortnightly Lantern*, April 23, 1888, 83.

18. "Athletic Association," *The Makio*, 1888, 99.

19. "Local: Field Day," *The Fortnightly Lantern*, June 6, 1888, 134.

20. "Fencing Club," *The Makio*, 1888, 109.

21. "Base Ball Club," *The Makio*, 1888, 101.

22. "Local and Personal Notes," *The Fortnightly Lantern*, May 8, 1888, 105.

23. "Lantern: Board of Editors," *The Fortnightly Lantern*, April 23, 1888, 84.

24. "South Dorm Boys, May 1886," *The Ohio State University Monthly*, March 1922, 20.

25. "Local and Personal Notes," *The Fortnightly Lantern*, March 1, 1888, 54.

26. "The Ball Game," *The Fortnightly Lantern*, April 8, 1888, 87.

27. "'Five Brothers' Celebrate 50-Year Stand on the Oval," *The Lantern*, October 22, 1951, 7.

28. "Local: Field Day," *The Fortnightly Lantern*, June 6, 1888, 134.

29. "Local and Personal Notes," *The Fortnightly Lantern*, May 8, 1888, 105.

30. *Ibid.*

31. "The Ball Game," *The Fortnightly Lantern*, April 8, 1888, 87.

32. *Ibid.*

33. *Ibid.*

34. "Editorials," *The Fortnightly Lantern*, May 8, 1888, 99.

35. "Missionary Society," *The Makio*, 1888, 89.

36. "Weekly Account of an O. S. U. Student," *The Makio*, 1888, 105.

37. "A College Joke to Cure the Dumps," *The Makio*, 1886, 6.

38. "Local and Personal Notes," *The Fortnightly Lantern*, May 22, 1888, 120.

39. "Dorm Notes," *The Fortnightly Lantern*, May 8, 1888, 107.

40. E.g., "Toussaint L'Overture, the Black Hero," *The College Transcript*, January 12, 1884, 102–4.

41. "Local and Personal Notes," *The Fortnightly Lantern*, May 22, 1888, 121.

42. "Base Ball: The O. S. U.–K. M. A. Game," *The Fortnightly Lantern*, June 6, 1888, 135–36.

43. "Editorials," *The Fortnightly Lantern*, June 6, 1888, 131.

44. "Base Ball: The O. S. U.–K. M. A. Game," *The Fortnightly Lantern*, June 6, 1888, 135–36.

45. "Editorials," *The Fortnightly Lantern*, May 22, 1888, 116.

46. "Dorm Notes," *The Fortnightly Lantern*, May 22, 1888, 124.

47. "Military Department," *The Fortnightly Lantern*, June 6, 1888, 138.

48. "Class of '90," *The Makio*, June 1889, 27.

49. "Editorials," *The Fortnightly Lantern*, March 17, 1888, 67–68; "Editorials," *The Fortnightly Lantern*, May 22, 1888, 116–17.

50. "Local and Personal Notes," *The Fortnightly Lantern*, May 8, 1888, 105.

51. "Local: Base Ball," *The Fortnightly Lantern*, June 6, 1888, 135.

52. "Locals," *The College Transcript*, June 16, 1888, 312.

53. "Editorials," *The Fortnightly Lantern*, June 6, 1888, 131.

54. "Editorials," *The Fortnightly Lantern*, June 6, 1888, 131; "Local: Notes," *The Fortnightly Lantern*, June 6, 1888, 135.

55. "Local and Personal Notes," *The Fortnightly Lantern*, June 26, 1888, 154.

56. "Weybrecht, Charles Christopher," *The National Cyclopædia of American Biography* (New York: James T. White & Co., 1922) 18:371.

57. "Brief School History," Ulysses High School Alumni Association, *rootsweb*, accessed July 5, 2016. http://www.rootsweb.ancestry.com/~nebutler/ulyssesgrads3.htm.

58. "Dorm Notes," *The Fortnightly Lantern*, June 6, 1888, 138–39.

Chapter Seven

1. "Go As You Please," *The Makio*, June 1889, 129.

2. "Local and Personal Notes," *The Fortnightly Lantern*, April 26, 1889, 186.

3. "Dorm Notes," *The Fortnightly Lantern*, October 13, 1888, 12.

4. "Dorm Notes," *The Fortnightly Lantern*, June 6, 1888, 138.

5. "Observations," *The Fortnightly Lantern*, December 7, 1888, 69.

6. Dick Forbes, "Football Country," *Cincinnati* 5, no. 1 (October 1971), 38–43.

7. "A Challenge," *Columbus Daily Press*, October 1, 1889, 9.

8. Peter Schweizer & Rochelle Schweizer, *The Bushes Portrait of a Dynasty* (New York: Doubleday, 2004).

9. "A Challenge," *Columbus Daily Press*, October 1, 1889, 9.

10. *Ibid.*

11. "Here You Are People!" *Columbus Daily Press*, October 11, 1889, 8.

12. "Local and Personal Notes," *The Fortnightly Lantern*, October 13, 1888, 9.

13. "Local: Lawn Tennis," *The Fortnightly Lantern*, October 13, 1888, 6.

14. "Lawn Tennis Club," *The Makio*, 1889, 49.

15. "Local and Personal Notes," *The Fortnightly Lantern*, October 13, 1888, 10.

16. "Local and Personal Notes," *The Fortnightly Lantern*, October 26, 1888, 23.

17. "Local and Personal Notes," *The Fortnightly Lantern*, November 9, 1888, 38.

18. "Local and Personal Notes," *The Fortnightly Lantern*, April 23, 1888, 89; "Local and Personal Notes," *The Fortnightly Lantern*, April 26, 1889, 186.

19. "Local and Personal Notes," *The Fortnightly Lantern*, January 11, 1889, 89.

20. "Editorials," *The Fortnightly Lantern*, February 8, 1889, 115–16.

21. *Ibid.*

22. *Ibid.*

23. *Ibid.*

24. "Base Ball Club," *The Makio*, June 1889, 48.

25. Julie Des Jardins, *Walter Camp: Football and the Modern Man* (New York: Oxford University Press, 2015).

26. Walter C. Camp, "Hints to Football Captains," *Outing*, January 1889, 357–60.

27. "Athletic Association," *The Denison Collegian*, February 28, 1889, 72–73.

28. *Ibid.*

29. *Ibid.*

30. "Constitution of Denison Athletic Association," *The Denison Collegian*, February 28, 1889, 80–82.

31. *Ibid.*

32. "Local," *The Fortnightly Lantern*, April 26, 1889, 185.

33. "Athletics," The Fortnightly Lantern, April 12, 1889, 170–71.

34. *Ibid.*

35. *The Ohio State University Monthly*, November 1947.

36. "Athletics," The Fortnightly Lantern, April 12, 1889, 170–71.

37. "Local: Base Ball," *The Fortnightly Lantern*, April 26, 1889, 185.

38. "Local: Base Ball," *The Fortnightly Lantern*, May 10, 1889, 201.

39. "De Nunciis," *The Denison Collegian*, April 30, 1889, 113.

40. "Local: Base Ball," *The Fortnightly Lantern*, May 10, 1889, 201.

41. "Editorials," *The Fortnightly Lantern*, May 9, 1890, 186–87.

42. "Athletic Association," *The Makio*, June 1889, 48.

43. "Observations," *The Fortnightly Lantern*, March 15, 1889, 148.

44. "General College Notes," *The Fortnightly Lantern*, February 17, 1887, 43.

45. "Our College Yell and Colors," *The Denison Collegian*, January 25, 1890, 68.

46. "Local and Personal Notes," *The Fortnightly Lantern*, March 15, 1889, 155.

47. "Ohio College Yells," *The Makio*, 1890, 132.

48. "Wah Hoo! A Base-Ball Game at Delaware Winds Up in a Wrangle," *Ohio State Journal*, May 6, 1889, 8.

49. "O. W. U. vs. O. S. U.," *The Practical Student*, May 10, 1889, 2.

50. *Ibid.*

51. "Locals," *The College Transcript*, May 10, 1889, 220.

52. "Wah Hoo! A Base-Ball Game at Delaware Winds Up in a Wrangle," *Ohio State Journal*, May 6, 1889, 8.

53. *Ibid.*

54. *Ibid.*

55. James R. Tootle, *Baseball in Columbus* (Mount Pleasant, SC: Arcadia Publishing, 2003).

56. *Ibid.*

57. "Tears of Woe," *Columbus Daily Press*, May 1, 1890, 4; "Toledo Takes the First Game from the Buckeyes," *Columbus Post*, May 2, 1890, 4.

58. "History of Physics at Clark: The Michelson Era (1889–1892)," Clark University Department of Physics, *Clark University*, accessed July 5, 2016, https://www.clarku.edu/departments/physics/history/history2.cfm.

59. "F.L.O. Wadsworth," *Google Patents*, accessed July 5, 2016, https://patents.google.com/?q=F.L.O.+Wadsworth.

60. Donald E. Osterbrock, *Yerkes Observatory, 1892–1950: The Birth, Near Death, and Resurrection of a Scientific Research Institution* (Chicago: University of Chicago Press, 2008).

61. "Tennis," *The Cap and Gown*, 1896.

62. "Lawn Tennis," *Outing*, August 1899, 544.

63. Zane Grey, *Betty Zane* (New York: Grosset & Dunlap, 1903).

64. "Elizabeth Zane: Pioneer Heroine," *YesterYear Once More*, September 29, 2009, accessed March 29, 2016, https://yesteryearsnews.wordpress.com/2009/09/29/elizabeth-zane-pioneer-heroine/.

65. Levi Jones's occupation is listed as "cooper" in the 1880 United States census.

66. "Jones, Jesse Lee," *The National Cyclopædia of American Biography*, Vol. XXI, (New York: James T. White & Co., 1931) 431.

Chapter Eight

1. "Local and Personal Notes," *The Fortnightly Lantern*, June 28, 1889, 234.

2. *Record of Studies: Ohio State University Collegiate Department*, Vol. III: 1890–1894. (Courtesy of the Ohio State University Archives).

3. "Got a Dime for a Football?" *The Lantern*, August 12, 1947, 3.

4. "1887," *Heritage–Spalding*, accessed February 21, 2016, http://shop.spalding.com/info/Heritage.

5. "John Wahl Queen," *The Fortnightly Lantern*, September 27, 1889, 8.

6. "Them Were the Happy Days Back in 1890," *Football Program: Michigan vs. Ohio State, Ohio Stadium*, November 15, 1924, 53.

7. "That First Football," *The Ohio State University Monthly*, February 1920, 29–30.

8. Information courtesy of Hamilton Richardson's grandson, David, who has said that copies of those letters were maintained for generations and may still be held by someone in the family.

9. "Some Athletic Chat," *The Fortnightly Lantern*, September 27, 1889, 8–9.

10. "Editorials," *The Denison Collegian*, October 26, 1889, 15.

11. *Ibid.*

12. Edward C. Arn, *Black and Gold: A History of Athletics The College of Wooster 1870–1945* (The College of Wooster, 1995).

13. "The Wooster Game," *The Denison Collegian*, November 30, 1889, 40.

14. Nat Brandt, *When Oberlin Was King of the Gridiron: The Heisman Years* (Kent, OH: Kent State University Press, 2001).

15. "De Nunciis," *The Denison Collegian*, December 16, 1889, 53–54.

16. "Editorial," *The Denison Collegian*, December 16, 1889, 45–46.

17. Edward C. Arn, *Black and Gold: A History of Athletics The College of Wooster 1870–1945* (The College of Wooster, 1995).

18. "To Akron," *The College Transcript*, Vol. XXII, No. 11, 28 February 1889, 171; "The State Contest," *The Denison Collegian*, February 28, 1889, 82.

19. "Editorials," *The Fortnightly Lantern*, February 14, 1890, 117.

20. "Editorial," *The Denison Collegian*, February 28, 1890, 73.

21. "Ohio College Yells," *The Makio*, June 1890, 132.

22. "College Oratory," *Ohio State Journal*, February 21, 1890, 2.

23. "X," *The College Transcript*, February 13, 1890, 153.

24. W. H. Clark, "Monopoly and Communism," *The Fortnightly Lantern*, March 7, 1890, 133.

25. *Ibid.*

26. "Local: The State Contest," *The Fortnightly Lantern*, March 7, 1890, 137–39.

27. "Editorials," *The Fortnightly Lantern*, March 7, 1890, 133.

28. *Ibid.*

29. "Local: The State Contest," *The Fortnightly Lantern*, March 7, 1890, 137–39.

30. "Local and Personal," *The Fortnightly Lantern*, March 7, 1890, 143.

31. "Editorials," *The College Transcript*, February 27, 1890, 161–62.

32. *Ibid.*

33. "Editorials," *The Fortnightly Lantern*, March 7, 1890, 133.

34. *Ibid.*

35. Quoted in "Editorials," *The Fortnightly Lantern*, May 9, 1890, 186.

36. *Ibid.*

37. "Editorials," *The Fortnightly Lantern*, May 9, 1890, 186.

38. *Ibid.*

39. *Ibid.*

40. "Editorials," *The Fortnightly Lantern*, February 14, 1890, 117–18.

41. "State University," *Ohio State Journal*, February 13, 1890, 8.

42. "Editorial," *The Denison Collegian*, February 28, 1890, 73–74.

43. "Editorials," *The Fortnightly Lantern*, March 7, 1890, 133–34.

44. "The Athletic Association," *The Fortnightly Lantern*, March 7, 1890, 142.

45. "State University," *Columbus Post*, March 1, 1890, 3.

46. "State University," *Ohio State Journal*, March 4, 1890, 6.

47. "State University News," *Columbus Dispatch*, March 3, 1890, 4.

48. "The Athletic Association," *The Fortnightly Lantern*, March 7, 1890, 142.

49. "Athletics," *The Fortnightly Lantern*, March 21, 1890, 159.

Chapter Nine

1. "State University," *Columbus Post*, March 8, 1890, 1.

2. "Alumni Notes," *The Fortnightly Lantern*, February 8, 1889, 124.

3. "The Kenyon Game," *The Fortnightly Lantern*, May 9, 1890, 196.

4. "John Buchanan (Jack) HUGGINS," 16th Generation Family of William Beers HUGGINS (7081) & Elizabeth Pridham TAYLOR, accessed February 21, 2016 from http://www.curtsanders.info/k3urt/Kilborn/rr04/rr04_110.html.

5. *Ibid.*

6. Chas. B. Morrey, "Beginnings of Football at Ohio State," *Football Program: Princeton University vs. The Ohio State University, Ohio Stadium*, November 3, 1928, 60–61.

7. Walter Camp republished his book many times for various publishers with only slight alterations of text across four decades. I am quoting here from an 1891-published version, the earliest available, with confidence that it matches the version that Jesse Lee Jones studied in 1890: Walter Camp, *American Football* (New York: Harper & Brothers, 1891), 93.

8. "Class of '90: Officers," *The Makio*, June 1890, 17.

9. "Base Ball," *The Fortnightly Lantern*, 1 November 1889, 40.

10. "Senior Biographies," *The Makio*, June 1890, 20–22.

11. "Seniors," *The Makio*, June 1890, 163.

12. *Ibid.*

13. Walter Camp, *American Football* (New York: Harper & Brothers, 1891), 111–12.

14. "Sophomores," *The Makio*, June 1890, 167.

15. Walter Camp, *American Football* (New York: Harper & Brothers, 1891), 81.

16. *Ibid.*

17. Walter Camp, *American Football* (New York: Harper & Brothers, 1891), 69.

18. Walter Camp, *American Football* (New York: Harper & Brothers, 1891), 55.

19. Walter Camp, *American Football* (New York: Harper & Brothers, 1891), 29.

20. *Ibid.*

21. "Local and Personal," *The Fortnightly Lantern*, November 7, 1890, 42.

22. "A Few Things We Advocate," *The Makio*, June 1890, 155.

23. "Local and Personal," *The Fortnightly Lantern*, April 25, 1890, 175.

24. "Anybody and Anything," *The Makio*, June 1890, 174.

25. "Freshmen," *The Makio*, June 1890, 170.

26. "Local and Personal," *The Fortnightly Lantern*, April 25, 1890, 176.

27. Walter Camp & Lorin F. Deland, *Football* (Boston: Houghton, Mifflin and Company, 1896).

28. "State University," *Ohio State Journal*, April 2, 1890, 2.

29. "Personals," *The Kenyon Collegian*, May 1890, 19.

30. "Where is the O. W. U.?" *The College Transcript*, February 27, 1890, 169.

31. "Delaware," *Columbus Daily Press*, April 16, 1890, 2.

32. "Editorials," *The College Transcript*, March 13, 1890, 177.

33. "Editorials," *The Practical Student*, May 9, 1890, 3.

34. "O. S. U. Notes," *Columbus Daily Press*, April 16, 1890, 7.

35. "Athletics," *The Fortnightly Lantern*, April 25, 1890, 178.

36. "State University," *Ohio State Journal*, April 19, 1890, 5.

37. "Local and Personal," *The Fortnightly Lantern*, April 25, 1890, 176.

38. "State University Sports," *Ohio State Journal*, April 21, 1890, 8.

39. "State University," *Ohio State Journal*, April 24, 1890, 4.

40. "Local and Personal," *The Fortnightly Lantern*, April 25, 1890, 175.

41. "Ohio State University: Thirteenth Annual Commencement, Degrees Conferred and Thesis Subjects," *Annual Reports for 1890 Made to the Sixty-Ninth General Assembly of the State of Ohio*.

Chapter Ten

1. "Delaware: College Boys are Sowing Their Wild Oats," *Columbus Post*, April 26, 1890, 1.

2. "Notes," *The Practical Student*, May 2, 1890, 2.

3. "Editorials," *The Fortnightly Lantern*, May 9, 1890, 185.

4. "Foot Ball Team," *The Makio*, 1890, 78.

5. "Collar Bone Broken," *Columbus Daily Press*, April 29, 1890, 8.

6. "Local and Personal," *The Fortnightly Lantern*, November 7, 1890, 43.

7. Walter Camp, *American Football* (New York: Harper & Brothers, 1891), 95.

8. Walter Camp, *American Football* (New York: Harper & Brothers, 1891), 12.

9. "Local and Personal," *The Fortnightly Lantern*, May 9, 1890, 194.

10. "Foot Ball Team," *The Makio*, 1890, 78.

11. "Rugby," *The Practical Student*, May 9, 1890, 3.

12. "Foot Ball," *The Fortnightly Lantern*, May 9, 1890, 195.

13. "Phil Saylor," *Baseball-Reference.com*, accessed January 21, 2016 from http://www.baseball-reference.com/register/player.cgi?id=saylor001phi.

14. Chas. B. Morrey, "Beginnings of Football at Ohio State," *Football Program: Princeton University vs. The Ohio State University, Ohio Stadium*, November 3, 1928, 60–61.

15. "Editorials," *The College Transcript*, May 15, 1890, 225–26.

16. "Editorials," *The Fortnightly Lantern*, May 9, 1890, 185.

17. "Foot Ball," *The Fortnightly Lantern*, May 9, 1890, 195.

18. David M. Nelson, *The Anatomy of a Game: Football, the Rules, and the Men who Made the Game* (Newark, DE: University of Delaware Press, 1994).

19. *Ibid.*

20. Walter Camp, "Inter-Collegiate Foot-Ball in America," *St. Nicholas*, November 1889, 36–44.

21. Chas. B. Morrey, "Beginnings of Football at Ohio State," *Football Program: Princeton University vs. The Ohio State University, Ohio Stadium*, November 3, 1928, 60–61.

22. Walter Camp, *American Football* (New York: Harper & Brothers, 1891), 168.

23. Walter Camp, *American Football* (New York: Harper & Brothers, 1891), 172.

24. "Foot Ball," *The Fortnightly Lantern*, May 9, 1890, 195.

25. "Editorials," *The Makio*, June 1890, 18.

26. "Rugby," *The Practical Student*, May 9, 1890, 3.

27. "O. S. U. Wins," *Columbus Daily Press*, May 3, 1890, 1.

28. "Delaware," *Ohio State Journal*, May 5, 1890, 1.

29. "Foot Ball," *Delaware Gazette*, May 3, 1890, 5.

30. "Rugby," *The Practical Student*, May 9, 1890, 3.

31. "Editorials," *The Fortnightly Lantern*, May 9, 1890, 185–86.

32. *Ibid.*

33. "Strong Rivalry: Challenge from Delaware," *Columbus Dispatch*, May 9, 1890, 7.

34. "Locals," *The College Transcript*, May 15, 1890, 235.

35. "The Base Ball Trip," *The Fortnightly Lantern*, June 13, 1890, 224–25.

36. "Editorial," *The Practical Student*, May 30, 1890, 3.

37. "Local: Field Day," *The Fortnightly Lantern*, May 23, 1890, 208–09.

38. "College Athletes," *Ohio State Journal*, May 24, 1890, 2.

39. "State Field Day," *The Fortnightly Lantern*, June 13, 1890, 223.

40. "Tennis Association," *The Makio*, June 1890, 74.

41. "Editorials," *The Makio*, June 1890, 18.

42. *Ibid.*

Chapter Eleven

1. "State University," *Ohio State Journal*, March 11, 1890, 8.

2. "Report of the President," *Twentieth Annual Report of the Board of Trustees of the Ohio State University*, 1891, 27–41.

3. *Ibid.*

4. *Ibid.*

5. *Ibid.*

6. *Ibid.*

7. "University Athletic Club," *Ohio State Journal*, September 25, 1890, 2.

8. "Local and Personal," *The Fortnightly Lantern*, October 3, 1890, 11.

9. "Local: Horton," *The Fortnightly Lantern*, October 17, 1890, 23.

10. James Ellsworth Boyd, "A Note on the Old North Dormitory," *The Ohio State University Monthly*, October 1910, 36–37.

11. "Editorials," *The Fortnightly Lantern*, October 3, 1890, 3.

12. "That First Football," *The Ohio State University Monthly*, February 1920, 29–30.

13. *Ibid.*

14. *The M.C. Lilley & Co., Manufacturers of Military Clothing and Equipments* [catalog] (New York: Manor Publishing Company, 1882).

15. "Local Notes," *The Fortnightly Lantern*, October 11, 1889, 30.

16. Lawrenceville School archives.

17. "Knowlton 'Snake' Ames," *National Football Foundation*, accessed February 17, 2016 from http://www.footballfoundation.org/Programs/CollegeFootballHallofFame/SearchDetail.aspx?id=88001.

18. Princeton University archives.

19. "The Foot Ball Schedule," *The Kenyon Collegian*, September 1890, 41.

20. *Ibid.*

21. "On Their Muscle," *The Wooster Voice*, September 20, 1890, 26.

22. Kinley McMillan career timeline courtesy of Kenneth Woodrow Henke, Princeton Theological Seminary Library, Archives and Special Collections.

23. "On Their Muscle," *The Wooster Voice*, September 20, 1890, 26.

24. "Foot Ball," *The Fortnightly Lantern*, October 17, 1890, 25.

25. *Ibid.*

26. *Ibid.*

27. *Ibid.*

28. Wayne L Snider, *All in the Same Spaceship: Portions of American Negro History Illustrated in Highland County, Ohio, U.S.A.* (New York: Vantage Press, 1974).

29. "Foot Ball Team," *The Makio*, 1891, 77.

30. "Local and Personal," *The Fortnightly Lantern*, October 17, 1890, 26.

31. "That First Football," *The Ohio State University Monthly*, February 1920, 29–30.

32. Doug Griffiths, *Tales From Boilermaker Country: A Collection of the Greatest Stories Ever Told* (New York: Sports Publishing, 2003).

33. Chas. B. Morrey, "Beginnings of Football at Ohio State," *Football Program: Princeton University vs. The Ohio State University, Ohio Stadium*, November 3, 1928, 60–61.

Chapter Twelve

1. "Local: Base Ball," *The Fortnightly Lantern*, October 17, 1890, 24–25.

2. "Local and Personal," *The Fortnightly Lantern*, October 3, 1890, 11.

3. "Editorials," *The College Transcript*, December 19, 1890, 107.

4. "Editorials," *The College Transcript*, October 16, 1890, 40–41.

5. "Dayton Boys Win," *Dayton Herald*, October 27, 1890, 7.

6. "The University Eleven," *Dayton Journal*, October 27, 1890, 4.

7. "Columbus Football Team Whipped," *Ohio State Journal*, October 26, 1890, 2.

8. "Local and Personal," *The Fortnightly Lantern*, November 7, 1890, 43.

9. "Dayton Boys Win," *Dayton Herald*, October 27, 1890, 7.

10. "General Sporting News: Inter-Collegiate Foot Ball," *Columbus Dispatch*, October 29, 1890, 8.

11. "Foot Ball Saturday," *Columbus Post*, 31 October 1890, 3.

12. "University Affairs," *Columbus Daily Press*, November 1, 1890, 7.

13. "Locals," *The Wooster Voice*, October 25, 1890, 108.

14. "O.S.U. Team Shut Out," *Columbus Dispatch*, November 3, 1890, 6; "College Football," *Ohio State Journal*, November 2, 1890, 2.

15. "Foot Ball: Notes," *The Fortnightly Lantern*, November 7, 1890, 40.

16. "Hugh S. Fullerton Reminisces Upon His College Life," *Columbus Dispatch*, November 20, 1916, 1.

17. "Foot Ball: Notes," *The Fortnightly Lantern*, November 7, 1890, 40.

18. "Foot Ball: Notes," *The Fortnightly Lantern*, November 7, 1890, 40.

19. "O.S.U. Team Shut Out," *Columbus Dispatch*, November 3 1890, 6.

20. "College Football," *Ohio State Journal*, November 2 1890, 2.

21. *Ibid.*

22. "The Lantern," *The Fortnightly Lantern*, 7 November 1890, 33.

23. *Ibid.*

24. "Foot Ball: Wooster vs. O. S. U.," *The Fortnightly Lantern*, November 7, 1890, 40.

25. *Ibid.*

26. "Foot Ball: Notes," *The Fortnightly Lantern*, November 7, 1890, 40.

27. "Foot Ball: Notes," *The Fortnightly Lantern*, November 7, 1890, 40.

28. "Local and Personal," *The Fortnightly Lantern*, November 7, 1890, 43.

29. "Local and Personal," *The Fortnightly Lantern*, November 7, 1890, 43.

30. "Our First Foot-Ball Game," *The Kenyon Collegian*, November 1890, 60–61.

31. "State University Trustees," *Columbus Post*, November 19, 1890, 1.

32. "The University Trustees," *The Fortnightly Lantern*, November 7, 1890, 56.

Chapter Thirteen

1. "Editorials," *The Kenyon Collegian*, March 1891, 99.

2. "Case Western Reserve University," *The Encyclopedia of Cleveland History*, November 11, 2014, accessed January 28, 2016 from http://ech.case.edu/cgi/article.pl?id=CWRU.

3. "Editorial," *The Wooster Voice*, March 21, 1891, 384.

4. "Local," *The College Transcript*, November 13, 1890, 76.

5. "Columbus Downs Delaware," *Ohio State Journal*, November 9, 1890, 4.

6. "Not In It," *The Practical Student*, November 18, 1890, 1.

7. "Columbus Downs Delaware," *Ohio State Journal*, November 9, 1890, 4.

8. "University Units," *Columbus Daily Press*, November 12, 1890, 8.

9. "Ben Hur Sale of Seats," *Columbus Dispatch*, November 1, 1890, 6.

10. "Local and Personal," *The Fortnightly Lantern*, November 7, 1890, 41.

11. Virginia P. Dawson, *Lincoln Electric: A History* (Euclid, OH: Lincoln Electric Co, 1999).

12. "America's Golden Opportunity," *School: Devoted to the Public Schools and Educational Interests*, December 3, 1914, 128–29.

13. "Local and Personal," *The Fortnightly Lantern*, December 12, 1890, 77.

14. Robert Neff, "Scandals and Gossip in Joseon Korea," *Transactions of the Royal Asiatic Society: Korea Branch*, Vol. 86, 2011, 61–69.

15. "Our Trip to Wooster," *The Denison Collegian*, November 29, 1890, 36–38.

16. "Fraternity Notes," *The Fortnightly Lantern*, November 21, 1890, 60.

17. The description of the 1890 Ohio State-Denison game offered here is taken from "Foot Ball," *The Fortnightly Lantern*, November 21, 1890, 56–57 and "Columbus Fails to Score," *The Denison Collegian*, November 29, 1890, 38–39.

18. "Foot Ball," *The Fortnightly Lantern*, November 21, 1890, 56.

19. *Ibid.*

20. "Local and Personal," *The Fortnightly Lantern*, November 21, 1890, 58.

21. *Ibid.*

22. "Notes," *The Fortnightly Lantern*, November 21, 1890, 57.

23. "Foot Ball," *The Fortnightly Lantern*, November 21, 1890, 57.

24. "Editorials," *The Fortnightly Lantern*, November 21, 1890, 57.

25. "A Clean Shut-Out," *Ohio State Journal*, November 23, 1890, 4.

26. "Foot Ball," *Columbus Daily Press*, November 23, 1890, 8.

27. "Irving," *The Wooster Voice*, November 17, 1890, 164.

28. "The Wooster Game: 30 to 2," *The Kenyon Collegian*, December 1890, 69–70.

29. "30–0," *The Wooster Voice*, November 17, 1890, 163–64.

30. Daniel Hurley, *Otterbein College: Affirming Our Past/Shaping Our Future* (Westerville, OH: Otterbein College, 1996).

31. Trevor Newland, "A Collage of Interesting Moments in the History of Otterbein Football: First Quarter Century 1889–1914, 1982." Unpublished manuscript supplied by the Otterbein Room, the archives of Otterbein University.

32. Alexis Cope, Sec., *Record of Proceedings of the Board of Trustees of the Ohio State University from November 18, 1890, to June 30, 1900.* (Columbus, OH: Hann & Adair, 1900), 5–6.

33. *Ibid.*

34. *Ibid.*

35. *Ibid.*

36. The description of the 1890 Ohio State-Kenyon game offered here is taken from: "Foot Ball," *The Fortnightly Lantern*, December 12, 1890, 71–72; "The Thanksgiving Game," *The Kenyon Collegian*, December 1890, 70–72; and "Details of the Kenyon-O. S. U. Battle Yesterday," *Columbus Dispatch*, November 28, 1890, 2.

37. "Local and Personal," *The Fortnightly Lantern*, December 12, 1890, 77.

38. "Foot Ball: Notes" *The Fortnightly Lantern*, December 12, 1890, 72.

39. "The Thanksgiving Game: Notes," *The Kenyon Collegian*, December 1890, 72.

40. *Ibid.*

41. *Ibid.*

42. "Foot Ball: Notes" *The Fortnightly Lantern*, December 12, 1890, 72.

43. "Foot Ball," *Columbus Daily Press*, November 28, 1890, 8.

44. "'Rah for Kenyon," *Ohio State Journal*, November 28, 1890, 2.

45. "Foot Ball" *The Fortnightly Lantern*, December 12, 1890, 72.

46. "Local and Personal," *The Fortnightly Lantern*, December 12, 1890, 77.

Chapter Fourteen

1. "Athletics in Ohio Colleges," *Outing*, December 1890, 235–40.

2. "Outing for December," *Harvard Crimson*, December 9, 1890, accessed January 16, 2016, http://www.thecrimson.com/article/1890/12/9/outing-for-december-outing-for-december/

3. "Local and Personal," *The Fortnightly Lantern*, December 12, 1890, 78.

4. "Locals," *The Wooster Voice*, December 9, 1890, 198.

5. Correspondence between Bert Leas and Caesar Morrey provided courtesy of the Otterbein Room, the archives of Otterbein University.

6. "'Rah for Kenyon," *Ohio State Journal*, November 28, 1890, 2.

7. Correspondence between Bert Leas and Caesar Morrey provided courtesy of the Otterbein Room, the archives of Otterbein University.

8. "Washington and Jefferson Downed," *The Wooster Voice*, December 6, 1890, 196–98.

9. "Local and Personal," *The Fortnightly Lantern*, January 21, 1891, 93.

10. "Captain John B. Huggins," *Mansfield News*, December 9, 1901, accessed January 17, 2016 from http://www.curtsanders.info/k3urt/Kilborn/rro4/rro4_110.html.

11. "Locals," *The Wooster Voice*, December 6, 1890, 198.

12. "Editorial," *The Wooster Voice*, November 19, 1890, 156–57.

13. "Editorials," *The Fortnightly Lantern*, December 12, 1890, 65–66.

14. "Editorial," *The Wooster Voice*, January 10, 1891, 224–25.

15. *Ibid.*

16. "Editorials," *The Fortnightly Lantern*, January 21, 1891, 86.

17. "The State Contest," *The Fortnightly Lantern*, February 20, 1891, 124.

18. "Editorials," *The Fortnightly Lantern*, March 6, 1891, 135.

19. "A Rousing Reception," *Ohio State Journal*, February 21, 1891, 5.

20. "Editorials," *The Fortnightly Lantern*, March 6, 1891, 135.

21. "Editorials," *The Fortnightly Lantern*, March 6, 1891, 136.

22. "Press Comment," *The Fortnightly Lantern*, March 20, 1891, 164.

23. Francis Stewart Kershaw, "We've an Orator at Last," *The Fortnightly Lantern*, March 6, 1891, 145.

24. "Nothing in It for Wooster," *The Wooster Voice*, February 21, 1891, 325–26.

25. *Ibid.*

26. "Editorials," *The Lantern*, November 5, 1891, 84.

27. "Athletics," *The Lantern*, April 17, 1891, 184.

28. "Dorm Notes," *The Fortnightly Lantern*, February 6, 1891, 112.

29. "Editorial," *The Wooster Voice*, 21 February 1891, 320.

30. "Editorials," *The Kenyon Collegian*, March 1, 1891, 99.

31. *Ibid.*

32. *Ibid.*

33. "Local and Personal," *The Fortnightly Lantern*, October 3, 1890, 10.

34. "The Inter-Collegiate Athletic Association," *The Wooster Voice*, February 28, 1891, 339.

35. *Ibid.*

36. "Editorials," *The Kenyon Collegian*, March 1, 1891, 99.

37. "Athletics," *The Lantern*, April 17, 1891, 184.

38. "Local: Base Ball," *The Lantern*, May 13, 1891, 231.

39. "Base Ball," *The Makio*, 1891, 76.

40. "Editorials," *The Lantern*, June 10, 1891, 292.

41. "Local: Base Ball," *The Lantern*, June 10, 1891, 297.

42. "Local: Field Day," *The Lantern*, May 20, 1891, 247–48.

43. "Local and Personal," *The Fortnightly Lantern*, March 20, 1891, 162.

44. "Local and Personal," *The Lantern*, October 7, 1891, 28.

45. "Local and Personal," *The Fortnightly Lantern*, March 20, 1891, 162.

46. "Editorials," *The Lantern*, May 27, 1891, 259–60.

47. "State Field Day," *The Lantern*, June 10, 1891, 295.

48. "Denison Wins the Day," *Ohio State Journal*, June 6, 1891, 6.

49. "Athletic Notes," *The Lantern*, June 19, 1892, 452.

50. Frank William Rane, "Report from Massachusetts," *Proceedings of the Third National Conservation Congress* (Kansas City, MO: National Conservation Congress, 1912), 281–83.

51. "Janet Esselstyn Rane," *Geni*, accessed February 12, 2016, http://www.geni.com/people /Janet-Esselstyn-Rane/6000000001650881398.

52. Charles Winecoff, *Anthony Perkins: Split Image* (Los Angeles: Advocate Books, 2006).

53. "Athletics," *The Adelbert*, July 1891, 83.

54. *Ibid.*

55. *Ibid.*

56. "Convention of Athletic Delegates," *The Lantern*, June 10, 1891, 296.

57. "Ode to Foot-Ball," *The Makio*, 1891, 112.

Chapter Fifteen

1. "Editorials," *The Lantern*, October 15, 1891, 35.

2. C. W. F., "Local: Foot Ball," *The Lantern*, October 22, 1891, 54.

3. "City News," *Columbus Post*, November 12, 1891, 4.

4. "Local and Personal," *The Lantern*, October 7, 1891, 28.

5. "Foot-Ball," *Notes of the Young Men's Christian Association, Dayton, Ohio*, June 1890, 5–6.

6. "Foot Ball," *Notes of the Young Men's Christian Association, Dayton, Ohio*, December 1891, 6.

7. "Local: Horton," *The Lantern*, October 22, 1891, 57.

8. *Catalogue of the Ohio State University for 1991–92* (Norwalk, OH: Laning Printing Co., 1891).

9. Eloise Riddle, "W. T. Morrey, '88, in South America," *The Ohio State University Monthly*, April 1915, 14–15.

10. "Board of Editors," *The Lantern*, September 30, 1891, 3.

11. "America's Golden Opportunity," *School: Devoted to the Public Schools and Educational Interests* 26, no. 14 (December 3, 1914): 128–29.

12. "Base Ball," *The Lantern*, October 7, 1891, 23.

13. "Local and Personal," *The Lantern*, October 7, 1891, 26.

14. "Results by Year," *2015 Ohio State Men's Baseball Media Information*, 69–79.

15. "Editorials," *The Lantern*, October 7, 1891, 20.

16. "Local," *The College Transcript*, October 6, 1891, 34.

17. Quoted in "Editorials," *The Practical Student*, June 4, 1892, p2.

18. "Editorials," *The Practical Student*, June 4, 1892, 2.

19. "Local: O. S. U. vs O. U." *The Lantern*, October 22, 1891, 55–57.

20. "University Notes," *Ohio State Journal*, October 16, 1891, 8.

21. Trevor Newland, "A Collage of Interesting Moments in the History of Otterbein Football: First Quarter Century 1889–1914, 1982." Unpublished manuscript supplied by the Otterbein Room, the archives of Otterbein University.

22. Daniel Hurley, *Otterbein College: Affirming Our Past/Shaping Our Future* (Westerville, OH: Otterbein College, 1996).

23. "Local: O. S. U. vs O. U." *The Lantern*, October 22, 1891, 55–57.

24. *Ibid.*

25. *Ibid.*

26. "Kumler's New College Record," *New York Times*, October 17, 1894, accessed January 26, 2016 from http://query.nytimes.com/gst/abstract.html?res=950CE3D81531E033A2575BC1A9 669D94659ED7CF.

27. "O. S. U. Team Defeated by Otterbein in a Foot Ball Game," *Columbus Dispatch*, October 19, 1891, 8.

28. "Football Game," *Ohio State Journal*, October 18, 1891, 3.

29. "O. S. U. Team Defeated by Otterbein in a Foot Ball Game," *Columbus Dispatch*, October 19, 1891, 8; "O. S. U. Defeated," *Columbus Daily Press*, October 19, 1891, 2.

30. *Ibid.*

31. "O. S. U. Practices on O. U.," *Otterbein Aegis*, October 1891, 206.

32. "Local: O. S. U. vs O. U." *The Lantern*, October 22, 1891, 55–57.

33. *Ibid.*

34. *Ibid.*

35. *Ibid.*

36. *Ibid.*

37. *Ibid.*

38. C. F. W., "Local: Foot Ball," *The Lantern*, October 22, 1891, 54.

39. *Ibid.*

40. *Ibid.*

41. *Ibid.*

42. *Ibid.*

43. *Ibid.*

44. *Ibid.*

45. "Local and Personal," *The Lantern*, November 2, 1891, 107.

46. "Hugh S. Fullerton Reminisces Upon His College Life," *Columbus Dispatch*, November 20, 1916, 1.

47. "Local and Personal," *The Lantern*, October 22, 1891, 59–60.

48. "Local and Personal," *The Lantern*, October 15, 1891, 42.

49. "Local and Personal," *The Lantern*, October 22, 1891, 59–60.

50. "Local: Foot Ball," *The Lantern*, October 29, 1891, 72.

51. "O. I. C. A. A.," *Kenyon Collegian*, November 1891, 64.

52. "Local: Foot Ball," *The Lantern*, October 29, 1891, 72.

53. *Ibid.*

54. C. A. N., "Cleveland Letter," *Kenyon Collegian*, November 1891, 57.

55. "Local: Foot Ball," *The Lantern*, October 29, 1891, 72.

56. Nat Brandt, *When Oberlin Was King of the Gridiron: The Heisman Years* (Kent, OH: Kent State University Press, 2001).

57. "Local: Foot Ball," *The Lantern*, October 29, 1891, 72.

58. "Fearfully Frightened," *The Practical Student*, October 24, 1891, 1.

59. *Ibid.*

60. "Locals," *The Practical Student*, October 24, 1891, 4.

61. "Alumni Echoes," *Wahoo*, September 14, 1892, 1.

62. Alexis Cope, Sec., *Record of Proceedings of the Board of Trustees of the Ohio State University from November 18, 1890, to June 30, 1900* (Columbus, OH: Hann & Adair, 1900), 66.

63. "Board of Editors," *The Lantern*, November 19, 1891, 115.

64. "Board of Editors," *The Lantern*, November 5, 1891, 83.

65. "Editorials," *The Lantern*, October 29, 1891, 68.

66. *Ibid.*

67. *Ibid.*

68. *Ibid.*

69. *Ibid.*

70. *Ibid.*

71. *Ibid.*

72. *Ibid.*

Chapter Sixteen

1. Ed Koszarek, *The Players League: History, Clubs, Ballplayers and Statistics* (Jefferson, NC: McFarland & Company, 2006).

2. James R. Tootle, *Baseball in Columbus* (Mount Pleasant, SC: Arcadia Publishing, 2003).

3. "Athletic Stock Company," *The Lantern*, December 17, 1891, 172.

4. "Local and Personal," *The Lantern*, October 15, 1891, 43.

5. "The General Association Control," *The Lantern*, May 11, 1892, 420.

6. "The Creed of Sigma Nu Fraternity," *Sigma Nu Fraternity*, accessed February 9, 2016 from http://www.sigmanu.org/about-us/the-creed-of-sigma-nu-fraternity.

7. "History," *Sigma Nu Fraternity*, accessed February 9, 2016 from http://www.sigmanu.org/about-us/history.

8. "The '93's," *The Makio*, 1892, 85.

9. "Local: The Contest," *The Lantern*, February 4, 1892, 220–21.

10. *Ibid.*

11. "The '93's," *The Makio*, Vol. XII, 1892, 87.

12. "Athletics: Adelbert 50—O. S. U. 6," *Columbus Daily Press*, November 12, 1891, 5.

13. "Local and Personal," *The Lantern*, November 5, 1891, 91.

14. "Athletics," *The Adelbert*, December 1890, 158–59.

15. Bob Newhardt Carroll & Bob Braunwart, *Pro Football, from AAA to '03: The Origin and Development of Professional Football in Western Pennsylvania, 1890–1903* (Professional Football Researchers Association, 1991).

16. Julie Des Jardins, *Walter Camp: Football and the Modern Man* (New York: Oxford University Press, 2015).

17. Bob Newhardt Carroll & Bob Braunwart, *Pro Football, from AAA to '03: The Origin and Development of Professional Football in Western Pennsylvania, 1890–1903* (Professional Football Researchers Association, 1991).

18. Caspar W. Whitney, "Amateur Sport," *Harpers Weekly*, December 12, 1891, 1003.

19. Caspar W. Whitney, "Amateur Sport," *Harpers Weekly*, November 7, 1891, 879.

20. "Adelbert Defeats O. S. U. at Football," *Ohio State Journal*, November 12, 1891, 4.

21. "City News," *Columbus Post*, November 12, 1891, 4.

22. *Ibid.*

23. "Athletics: Adelbert 58—O. S. U. 6," *The Adelbert*, November 1891, 136.

24. "O. S. U. Defeated by Adelbert," *Columbus Dispatch*, November 12, 1891, 2.

25. *Ibid.*

26. "Local: Athletic Association," *The Lantern*, November 19, 1891, 120—21.

27. "Local: Foot Ball," *The Lantern*, November 19, 1891, 124—25.

28. "State University Football," *Ohio State Journal*, November 22, 1891, 4.

29. "A Good Beginning," *The Kenyon Collegian*, November 1891, 62—64.

30. "Local: Foot Ball," *The Lantern*, November 19, 1891, 124—25.

31. *Ibid.*

32. *Ibid.*

33. *Ibid.*

34. "Football: O. S. U. 0, Kenyon 34," *The Kenyon Collegian*, December 1891, 74—75.

35. *Ibid.*

36. "State University Football," *Ohio State Journal*, November 22, 1891, 4.

37. "O. S. U. Athletic Association," *The Makio*, 1892, 63.

38. "Editorials," *The Lantern*, January 21, 1892, 200.

39. "Athletic Stock Company," *The Lantern*, December 17, 1891, 172.

40. "Editorials," *The Lantern*, November 19, 1891, 116.

41. "Victory at Last," *The Lantern*, December 3, 1891, 137—38.

42. Austin "Pete" Gillen, "How We Played the Game," *The Ohio State University Monthly*, March 1917, 33—34; "Base Ball," *The Lantern*, October 7, 1891, 23.

43. "Victory at Last," *The Lantern*, December 3, 1891, 137—38.

44. *Ibid.*

45. "Foot Ball," *Columbus Dispatch*, November 25, 1891, 8.

46. "State University," *Ohio State Journal*, November 26, 1891, 8.

47. "Victory at Last," *The Lantern*, December 3, 1891, 137—38.

48. *Ibid.*

49. "The Dorm Dinner," *The Lantern*, December 3, 1891, 138—39.

50. "Football: Adelbert 42, Kenyon 6," *The Kenyon Collegian*, December 1891, 74.

51. "A Clean Shutout," *Ohio State Journal*, November 27, 1891, 2.

52. "Local and Personal," *The Lantern*, December 3, 1891, 139.

53. "Akron Yearly Results," *College Football Data Warehouse*, accessed January 25, 2016, http://cfbdatawarehouse.com/data/active/a/akron/yearly_results.php?year=1891.

54. "State University Wins," *Ohio State Journal*, December 6, 1891, 4.

55. "Buchtel vs. O. S. U.," *The Buchtelite*, December 14, 1891, 117—19.

56. "Local and Personal," *The Lantern*, December 17, 1891, 174.

57. "Athletic Stock Company," *The Lantern*, December 17, 1891, 172.

58. *Ibid.*

59. *Ibid.*

60. *Ibid.*

Chapter Seventeen

1. "Athletic Notes," *The Lantern*, February 11, 1892, 236.

2. "Are You Aware That," *The Makio*, 1892, 88.

3. "Local: Athletic Association," *The Lantern*, February 18, 1892, 250.

4. "Local: Athletics," *The Lantern*, February 18, 1892, 250–51.

5. Walter J. Sears, "Foot Ball Season of '92," *The Lantern*, December 6, 1892, 1.

6. "Local: Athletics," *The Lantern*, February 4, 1892, 220–21.

7. "The Contest," *The Lantern*, 25 February 1892, 268–69.

8. "Athletic Notes," *The Lantern*, 11 February 1892, 236.

9. "Local and Personal," *The Lantern*, February 18, 1892, 253.

10. "The Story of KitchenAid," *Maker*, 2015, accessed February 12, 2016, http://stories.maker .me/the-maker-story-of-kitchenaid/.

11. "Herbert Lincoln Johnston Fund for the Advancement of Engineering Education," *OSU Media Magnet*, accessed February 12, 2016 from https://mediamagnet.osu.edu/items/15971.

12. "Athletic News," *The Lantern*, March 10, 1892, 305.

13. "Local: Athletics," *The Lantern*, February 18, 1892, 250–51.

14. "Get Understanding," *The Lantern*, March 24, 1892, 340.

15. "Fence Raisin'," *The Lantern*, February 11, 1892, 235–36.

16. "Athletic Notes," *The Lantern*, February 11, 1892, 236.

17. "Get Understanding," *The Lantern*, March 24, 1892, 340.

18. "Local and Personal," *The Lantern*, March 3, 1892, 290.

19. *Ibid.*

20. *Ibid.*

21. "Athletics," *The Lantern*, April 14, 1892, 353.

22. "Athletics," *The Lantern*, April 21, 1892, 370–71.

23. *Ibid.*

24. "Athletics," *The Lantern*, April 14, 1892, 354.

25. "Athletics: The First Victory," *The Lantern*, April 28, 1892, 386.

26. "Athletics: Victory No. Two," *The Lantern*, May 5, 1892, 404.

27. "Athletics: A Day of Folly," *The Lantern*, May 5, 1892, 404–05.

28. "A Day of Glory," *The Lantern*, May 26, 1892, 465.

29. "O. W. U.'s Childishness," *The Lantern*, May 26, 1892, 465–67.

30. "Editorials," *The College Transcript*, May 28, 1892, 331.

31. "Baseball: O. W. U. vs. O. S. U.," *The College Transcript*, May 28, 1892, 338.

32. "The Board is Right," *The Lantern*, June 2, 1892, 489.

33. "Athletics," *The Lantern*, June 2, 1892, 487–89.

34. "Found—One 'Puggy' Shaw," *The Ohio State University Monthly*, April 1917, 38–39.

35. "Athletics: Three Straight Victories," *The Lantern*, June 16, 1892, 516.

36. *Ibid.*

37. "Local and Personal," *The Lantern*, April 28, 1892, 388.

38. J. H. Galbraith, "The First Gleams of the Lantern," *The Ohio State University Monthly*, October 1914, 29–35.

39. "Wahoo," *The Lantern*, 16 June 1892, 516; "Editorials," *The Lantern*, June 16, 1892, 515.

40. "Sears, W. J.," *The Makio* 1892, 109.

41. "Financial Statement of O. S. U. Athletic Stock Company, June 20, '92," *The Lantern*, 23 June 1892, 535.

42. *Ibid.*

43. "Locals and Personals," *Wahoo*, 3.

44. "Untimely," *The Lantern*, April 4, 1894, 1.

45. Robert Neff, "Emily Brown: The American Empress of Korea." (Paper submitted to the Royal Asiatic Society, 2004).

46. "Raymond Edward Leo Krumm," *We Relate*, accessed February 14, 2016, http://www.werelate.org/wiki/Person:Raymond_Krumm_%282%29.

47. "Smoker," *The Ohio State University Monthly*, April 1910, 46–47.

48. Eliot Asinof, *Eight Men Out: The Black Sox and the 1919 World Series* (New York, Henry Holt and Company, 1963).

49. "1964 J.G. Taylor Spink Award Winner Hugh Fullerton," *National Baseball Hall of Fame*, accessed February 14, 2016, http://baseballhall.org/discover/awards/j-g-taylor-spink/hugh-fullerton.

50. "A Remarkable Record," *Wahoo*, September 27, 1892, 1.

51. "Athletic Doings," *Wahoo*, October 10, 1892, 1.

52. "A Remarkable Record," *Wahoo*, September 27, 1892, 1.

53. "Financial Statement of O. S. U. Athletic Stock Company, June 20, '92," *The Lantern*, June 23, 1892, 535.

54. "History," *Knowlton School*, accessed February 8, 2016 from http://knowlton.osu.edu/history.

55. "A Remarkable Record," *Wahoo*, September 27, 1892, 1.

Chapter Eighteen

1. "Editorials," *Wahoo*, September 14, 1892, 2.

2. "Wahoo Board Meeting," *Wahoo*, October 21, 1892, 1.

3. James E. Pollard, *History of the Ohio State University: The Story of Its First Seventy Five Years, 1873–1948* (Columbus, OH: Ohio State University Press, 1952), 120.

4. *A Centennial biographical history of the city of Columbus and Franklin County, Ohio* (Chicago: Lewis Publishing Company, 1901).

5. "The Tables Turn," *The Lantern*, November 29, 1892, 1.

6. Walter J. Sears, "Shall We Win in Foot Ball?" *Wahoo*, September 20, 1892, 1.

7. Nat Brandt, *When Oberlin Was King of the Gridiron: The Heisman Years* (Kent, OH: Kent State University Press, 2001).

8. Walter J. Sears, "Foot Ball Season of '92," *Wahoo*, December 6, 1892, 1.

9. "Locals and Personals," *Wahoo*, October 4, 1892, 3.

10. Dr. Emma Scott began practicing medicine as a missionary in Vrindavan, India, in 1896. *Eightieth Annual Report of the Missionary Society of the Methodist Episcopal Church for the Year 1898* (New York: Cable Address Missions, 1899), 372.

11. "Football Team," *Ohio State Journal,* September 12, 1891, 8.

12. "Athletics: The Banquet," *The Lantern,* June 16, 1892, 518–19.

13. "Locals and Personal," *Wahoo,* September 24, 1892, 3.

14. "An Afternoon of Sports," *Wahoo,* September 24, 1892, 1.

15. "Athletics," *Wahoo,* September 14, 1892, 2.

16. "Financial Statement of O. S. U. Athletic Stock Company, June 20, '92," *The Lantern,* June 23, 1892, 535.

17. "Captain Ellis Says," *Wahoo,* October 1, 1892, 1.

18. *Ibid.*

19. "Our Waterloo," *Wahoo,* November 22, 1892, 1.

20. "Locals and Personal," *Wahoo,* October 4, 1892, 3.

21. Charley Powell, "The Story of One Kenyon Game," *The Ohio State University Monthly,* June 1917, 51–52.

22. Walter J. Sears, "Shall We Win in Foot Ball?" *Wahoo,* September 20, 1892, 1.

23. *Ibid.*

24. *Ibid.*

25. "Athletics," *Wahoo,* September 14, 1892, 2.

26. "An Afternoon of Sports," *Wahoo,* September 24, 1892, 1.

27. "Locals and Personals," *Wahoo,* September 14, 1892, 3.

28. "Athletics," *Wahoo,* September 14, 1892, 2.

29. "Athletic Doings," *Wahoo,* October 10, 1892, 1.

30. "Athletic Notes," *Wahoo,* October 1, 1892, 2.

31. "Food for Reflection," *Wahoo,* September 27, 1892, 1.

32. "How We Stand," *Wahoo,* September 24, 1892, 1.

33. *Ibid.*

34. "Athletic Doings," *Wahoo,* October 10, 1892, 1.

35. Walter J. Sears, "Shall We Win in Foot Ball?" *Wahoo,* September 20, 1892, 1.

36. Lee Allen, *The Cincinnati Reds* (Kent, OH: Kent State University Press, 2006).

37. Walter J. Sears, "Shall We Win in Foot Ball?" *Wahoo,* September 20, 1892, 1.

38. "Athletic Notes," *Wahoo,* October 1, 1892, 2.

39. *Ibid.*

40. Nat Brandt, *When Oberlin Was King of the Gridiron: The Heisman Years* (Kent, OH: Kent State University Press, 2001).

41. "Athletic Doings," *Wahoo,* October 10, 1892, 1.

42. "The Tables Turn," *The Lantern,* November 29, 1892, 1.

43. Walter J. Sears, "Foot Ball Season of '92," *Wahoo,* December 6, 1892, 1.

44. "Athletics," *Wahoo,* September 14, 1892, 2.

45. "Locals and Personals," *Wahoo,* October 8, 1892, 3.

46. "The Schedule," *Wahoo,* October 4, 1892, 2.

47. "Locals and Personals," *Wahoo,* October 21, 1892, 4.

48. "Off to Oberlin," *Wahoo,* October 15, 1892, 3.

49. Nat Brandt, *When Oberlin Was King of the Gridiron: The Heisman Years* (Kent, OH: Kent State University Press, 2001).

50. "Athletic Doings," *Wahoo*, October 10, 1892, 1.

51. "President Scott's Action," *Wahoo*, October 8, 1892, 1.

52. *Ibid.*

53. *Ibid.*

54. *Ibid.*

55. *Ibid.*

56. "Dr. Moore's Opinion," *Wahoo*, October 10, 1892, 1.

57. "President Scott's Action," *Wahoo*, October 8, 1892, 1.

58. "Wahoo and Lantern," *Wahoo*, October 25, 1892, 2.

59. "Class of '93," *Wahoo*, October 8, 1892, 1.

60. "Wahoo and Lantern," *Wahoo*, October 25, 1892, 2.

61. *Ibid.*

Chapter Nineteen

1. "Off to Oberlin," *Wahoo*, October 15, 1892, 3.

2. *Ibid.*

3. "It Was a Defeat," *Wahoo*, October 17, 1892, 1.

4. "Our First Victory—Oberlin 40, O. S. U. 0," *The Oberlin Review*, October 19, 1892, 65–66.

5. Nat Brandt, *When Oberlin Was King of the Gridiron: The Heisman Years* (Kent, OH: Kent State University Press, 2001).

6. "It Was a Defeat," *Wahoo*, October 17, 1892, 1.

7. Jacqueline Goldsby, *A Spectacular Secret: Lynching in American Life and Literature* (Chicago: University of Chicago Press, 2006).

8. "A Word from Pat," *The Lantern*, December 13, 1892, 1.

9. Quoted in "Impartial Praise," *Wahoo*, November 1, 1892, 3.

10. "Impartial Praise," *Wahoo*, November 1, 1892, 3.

11. "An Easy Victory," *Wahoo*, October 25, 1892, 1.

12. "Badly Defeated, Ohio State Journal, October 23, 1892, 4.

13. "Badly Beaten," Columbus Daily Press-Post, October 23, 1892, 1.

14. "Southern Trip," *The Buchtelite*, November 5, 1892, 80.

15. "Snowed Under Again," *Akron Daily Beacon*, October 24, 1892, 1.

16. E. Gus Evans, "A Word of Cheer," *Wahoo*, October 28, 1892, 1.

17. "An Easy Victory," *Wahoo*, October 25, 1892, 1.

18. *Ibid.*

19. *Ibid.*

20. *Ibid.*

21. "Editorials: Advertising Athletics," *Wahoo*, November 4, 1892, 2.

22. "College Football," *Ohio State Journal*, October 30, 1892, 4.

23. "Athletics: O. S. U. 80–Marietta 0," *Marietta College Olio*, December 1892, 88.

24. "Badly Swiped," *Columbus Daily Press-Post*, October 30, 1892, 8.

25. Ibid.

26. "Go to Denison," *Wahoo*, November 8, 1892, 1.

27. "What Does It Mean?" *Wahoo*, November 1, 1892, 1.

28. *Ibid.*

29. *Ibid.*

30. *Ibid.*

31. *Ibid.*

32. *Ibid.*

33. *Ibid.*

34. "Hic Breve Fletur," *The Denison Exponent*, November 5, 1892, 1.

35. "Editorials," *Wahoo*, November 11, 1892, 2.

36. Charley Powell, "The Story of One Kenyon Game," *The Ohio State University Monthly*, June 1917, 51–52.

37. "Kenyon vs Adelbert," *The Kenyon Collegian*, November 1892, 66–68.

38. Nat Brandt, *When Oberlin Was King of the Gridiron: The Heisman Years* (Kent, OH: Kent State University Press, 2001).

39. "Notice Everybody," *Wahoo*, November 4, 1892, 3.

40. "The Oberlin Game," *Wahoo*, November 8, 1892, 2.

41. "The Oberlin Game," *Wahoo*, November 8, 1892, 2.

42. "Heisman! Heisman! Rah! Rah! Rah!" *The Buchtelite*, January 31, 1893, 1.

43. "Akron Coaching Records," *College Football Data Warehouse*, accessed January 25, 2016, http://cfbdatawarehouse.com/data/active/a/akron/coaching_records.php.

44. "Another Victory," *Wahoo*, November 15, 1892, 1.

45. "Pig Skin," *Dayton Daily Times*, 14 November 1892, 2; "Foot Ball," *Notes of the Young Men's Christian Association, Dayton, Ohio*, December 1892, 9.

Chapter Twenty

1. "Editorials: Athletics," *Wahoo*, November 19, 1892, 2.

2. "Our Waterloo," *Wahoo*, November 22, 1892, 1.

3. "Our Waterloo: Notes," *Wahoo*, November 22, 1892, 3.

4. "A Protest," *Wahoo*, November 11, 1892, 1.

5. *Ibid.*

6. "Another Editor-In-Chief Speaks," *Wahoo*, November 15, 1892, 1.

7. *Ibid.*

8. *Ibid.*

9. "Ohio State University, Columbus," *Ohio State Journal*, November 21, 1892, 4.

10. *Ibid.*

11. "The Band," *Wahoo*, November 4, 1892, 2.

12. "'Down,' I Yell," *Columbus Daily Press-Post*, November 25, 1892, 8.

13. "O. S. U. vs. Kenyon," *The Kenyon Collegian*, December 1892, 77.

14. "'Down,' I Yell," *Columbus Daily Press-Post*, November 25, 1892, 8.

15. "The Tables Turn," *The Lantern*, November 29, 1892, 1.

16. "O. S. U. Wins," *Columbus Dispatch*, November 25, 1892, 4.

17. "The Tables Turn," *The Lantern*, November 29, 1892, 1.

18. *Ibid.*

19. *Ibid.*

20. "A Word from Pat," *The Lantern*, December 13, 1892, 1.

21. *Ibid.*

22. *Ibid.*

23. *Ibid.*

24. "Delaware's Disgrace," *The Lantern*, 25 April 1893, 2.

Chapter Twenty-One

1. "Harwood Pool Dead," *The Lantern*, January 13, 1904, 2.

2. "Editorials," *The Lantern*, March 1881, 27.

3. "Local," *The Lantern*, April 1881, 47.

4. "Local," *The Lantern*, May 1881, 60.

5. "Memorial Exercises," *The Lantern*, February 3, 1893, 1.

6. "The Hayes Portrait," *The Lantern*, February 3, 1893, 1.

7. "The Student's Friend," *The Lantern*, February 3, 1893, 2.

8. "Editorials," *The Lantern*, February 14, 1893, 2.

9. *Ibid.*

10. *Ibid.*

11. *Ibid.*

12. "Athletics," *The Lantern*, February 17, 1893, 1.

13. "Resolution of Disapproval," *The Lantern*, February 17, 1893, 4.

14. "Mass Meeting," *The Lantern*, February 17, 1893, 2.

15. "Regulation Passed by the Faculty at Their Last Meeting," *The Lantern*, March 14, 1893, 1.

16. "Editorials," *The Lantern*, March 14, 1893, 2.

17. *Ibid.*

18. "The Lantern," *The Lantern*, September 19, 1893, 2.

19. J. H. Galbraith, "The First Gleams of the Lantern," *The Ohio State University Monthly*, October 1914, 29–35.

20. "Ready for the Struggle," *The Lantern*, September 19, 1893, 4.

21. "Foot Ball Day," *Columbus Dispatch*, 23 November 1893, 2.

22. "Foot Ball Notes," *The Lantern*, September 26, 1893, 4.

23. "Foot Ball," *The Lantern*, October 10, 1893, 1.

24. "Foot Ball Notes," *The Lantern*, September 26, 1893, 4.

25. "Athletics," The Lantern, February 17, 1893, 1.

26. "Captain Richard T. Ellis Silver Star Medal Serial Number 32 #19," *Battlefield Museum*, accessed February 7, 2016, http://www.battlefieldmuseum.org/engine/inspect.asp?Item=19&Filter=US+Groupings.

27. "Foot Ball Notes," *The Lantern*, September 26, 1893, 4.

28. "Locals and Personals," *The Lantern*, October 3, 1893, 3.

29. "The Foot Ball Season," *The Lantern*, October 3, 1893, 1.

30. "Foot Ball," *The Lantern*, October 10, 1893, 1.

31. "Editorials," *The Lantern*, September 19, 1893, 2.

32. "Mitchell D. Howard Dies at Home Sunday," *The Lantern*, November 6, 1922, 1.

33. "The Foot Ball Season," *The Lantern*, October 3, 1893, 1.

34. "Ex-Manager's Views," *The Lantern*, November 8, 1893, 2.

35. "The Foot Ball Season," *The Lantern*, October 3, 1893, 4.

36. *Ibid.*

37. *Ibid.*

38. "Foot Ball," *The Lantern*, October 10, 1893, 1.

39. "Athletic Rules," *The Lantern*, October 17, 1893, 1.

40. "Foot Ball," *The Lantern*, October 10, 1893, 1.

41. "Athletic Rules," *The Lantern*, October 17, 1893, 1.

42. "Locals and Personals," *The Lantern*, October 10, 1893, 4.

43. "O. S. U. Now," *Columbus Daily Press-Post*," October 15, 1893, 7.

44. "O. S. U. Wins," *The Lantern*, October 17, 1893, 1.

45. *Ibid.*

46. "For a Third Time," *The Lantern*, October 24, 1893, 1.

47. "Athletics: Oberlin, 38; O. S. U., 10," *The Oberlin Review*, October 25, 1893, 83–84.

48. "Various Sports," *Columbus Dispatch*, October 23, 1893, 8; "Kicked Out," *Columbus Daily Press-Post*, October 22, 1893, 8.

49. "For a Third Time," *The Lantern*, October 24, 1893, 1.

50. "Oberlin Out Kicks," *Ohio State Journal*, October 22, 1893, 2.

51. "Editorials," *The Lantern*, October 24, 1893, 2.

52. "Kenyon 42, O. S. U. 6," *The Kenyon Collegian*, October 1893, 75–77.

53. "Unbroken," *The Lantern*, October 31, 1893, 1.

54. *Ibid.*

55. "The Faults of Kenyon Foot Ball," *The Kenyon Collegian*, November 1893, 92–93.

56. "Kenyon 42, O. S. U. 6," *The Kenyon Collegian*, October 1893, 75–77.

57. Charles L Wood, "Recalls Football in '90's," *The Ohio State University Monthly*, March 1950, 18.

58. "Editorials," *The Lantern*, October 31, 1893, 2.

59. *Ibid.*

60. "Unbroken," *The Lantern*, October 31, 1893, 1.

61. "Misfortunes," *The Lantern*, November 8, 1893, 1.

62. "Ex-Manager's Views," *The Lantern*, November 8, 1893, 2.

63. "Misfortunes," *The Lantern*, November 8, 1893, 1.

64. "Ex-Manager's Views," *The Lantern*, November 8, 1893, 2.

65. *Ibid.*

66. *Ibid.*

67. "O. S. U. Defeats Buchtel," *The Lantern*, November 15, 1893, 1.

68. *Ibid.*

69. *Ibid.*

70. "Misfortunes," *The Lantern*, November 8, 1893, 1.

71. "Our Third Victory," *The Lantern*, November 22, 1893, 1.

72. "Ex-Manager's Views," *The Lantern*, November 8, 1893, 2.

73. "Our Third Victory," *The Lantern*, November 22, 1893, 1.

74. "Falling Off a Log," *Columbus Daily Press-Post*, November 19, 1893, 2.

75. "Everything Ready," *The Lantern*, November 29, 1893, 1.

76. "Kenyon's Big Game: Notes," *Ohio State Journal*, December 1, 1893, 2.

77. "Kenyon Wins," *The Lantern*, December 6, 1893, 1.

78. *Ibid.*

79. "Kenyon 10, O. S. U. 8," *The Kenyon Collegian*, November 1893, 91.

80. "Kenyon Wins," *The Lantern*, December 6, 1893, 1.

81. "Kenyon 10, O. S. U. 8," *The Kenyon Collegian*, November 1893, 91.

82. "Alumni," *The Lantern*, February 21, 1894, 3.

83. "Field Day," *The Lantern*, May 30, 1894, 1.

Chapter Twenty-Two

1. "Foot Ball Tournament," *The Lantern*, March 28, 1894, 1.

2. "$209.00," *The Lantern*, February 7, 1894, 1.

3. "Foot Ball Tournament," *The Lantern*, September 12, 1894, 1.

4. "Buchtel vs. O. S. U," *The Buchtelite*, September 23, 1894, 1.

5. "Foot Ball," *The Lantern*, September 19, 1894, 1.

6. "Antioch Annihilated," *The Lantern*, October 10, 1894, 1.

7. "They're Off," *The Lantern*, September 26, 1894, 1.

8. "The 'Varsity Eleven," *The Lantern*, October 3, 1894, 1.

9. *Ibid.*

10. "Foot Ball," *The Lantern*, September 19, 1894, 1.

11. "Must Be Good," *The Lantern*, October 17, 1894, 1.

12. "Marietta Did Not Come," *The Lantern*, October 24, 1894, 1.

13. "They're Off," *The Lantern*, September 26, 1894, 1.

14. "Baseball," *The Lantern*, September 12, 1894, 5.

15. "Antioch Annihilated," *The Lantern*, October 10, 1894, 1.

16. "Won in a Walk," *Columbus Daily Press-Post*, October 7, 1894, 7.

17. "Antioch Annihilated," *The Lantern*, October 10, 1894, 1.

18. "O. S. U. Boys Defeated," *Ohio State Journal*, October 14, 1894, 4.

19. "Must Be Good," *The Lantern*, October 17, 1894, 1.

20. "Marietta Did Not Come," *The Lantern*, October 24, 1894, 1.

21. "Adelbert wins," *The Lantern*, October 31, 1894, 1; "Adelbert 24, O. S. U. 4," *Ohio State Journal*, October 28, 1894, 4.

22. "From Bad to Worse," *The Lantern*, November 7, 1894, 1.

23. *Ibid.*

24. "Stolen—O. S. U. 8–Marietta 4," *Marietta College Olio*, November 1894, 21.

25. "Same Old Story," *The Lantern*, November 14, 1894, 1.

26. "From an Alumnus," *The Lantern*, November 21, 1894, 4.

27. *Ibid.*

28. *Ibid.*

29. *Ibid.*

30. "Wahoo! Wahoo!," *The Lantern*, November 21, 1894, 1.

31. "The Crisis Passed," *Ohio State Journal*, November 15, 1894, 4.

32. "University Foot Ball," *Columbus Daily Press-Post*, November 18, 1894, 8.

33. "Wahoo! Wahoo!" *The Lantern*, November 21, 1894, 1.

34. "O. S. U. Forty-Six, Soldiers Four," *The Lantern*, November 28, 1894, 1.

35. "Heike, Heike," *The Lantern*, November 28, 1894, 1.

36. *Ibid.*

37. *Ibid.*

38. *Ibid.*

39. *Ibid.*

40. "O. S. U. 20–Kenyon 4," *The Kenyon Collegian*, December 1894, 164–65.

41. "What's the Score," *The Lantern*, December 5, 1894, 1.

42. "Editorials," *The Lantern*, December 5, 1894, 2.

43. Dessa High, "A Twilight Reverie," *The Lantern*, March 20, 1895, 2.

Chapter Twenty-Three

1. "The Incoming and the Outgoing," *The Lantern*, April 17, 1895, 2.

2. "Football," *The Lantern*, September 25, 1895, 1.

3. "Athletics," *The Lantern*, September 18, 1895, 1.

4. "Football," *The Lantern*, September 25, 1895, 1.

5. "Athletics," *The Lantern*, September 18, 1895, 1.

6. "Athletic Association Election," *The Lantern*, October 16, 1895, 4.

7. "Football Manager Appointed," *The Lantern*, June 11, 1895, 1.

8. "Football," *The Lantern*, September 25, 1895, 1.

9. "Football," *The Lantern*, October 30, 1895, 1.

10. "Football," *The Lantern*, September 25, 1895, 1.

11. "Who's Who in the Ohio State University Association: Charles Bradfield Morrey," *The Ohio State University Quarterly*, Volume Three, April 1912, 172.

12. "Athletic Association," *Columbus Dispatch*, November 14, 1895, 4.

13. Allison Danzig, *The History of American Football: Its Great Teams, Players, and Coaches* (Englewood Cliffs, NJ: Prentice-Hall, 1956).

14. "Locals and Personals," *The Lantern*, September 25, 1895, 3.

15. "Football," *The Lantern*, October 2, 1895, 1.

16. "Victory," *The Lantern*, October 9, 1895, 1.

17. "Defeated," *The Lantern*, October 16, 1895, 1.

18. "Very Good," *The Lantern*, October 23, 1895, 1.

19. "College News: Ohio State University," *Ohio State Journal*, October 21, 1895, 8.

20. "Gymnasium-Auditorium," *Columbus Dispatch*, October 21, 1895, 4.

21. "First Mid-Week Game," *The Lantern*, October 30, 1895, 1.

22. "Denison," *The Lantern*, October 30, 1895, 1.

23. "Football," *The Lantern*, October 30, 1895, 1.

24. *Ibid.*

25. "Delaware," *The Lantern*, November 6, 1895, 1.

26. Kevin Grace, Greg Hand, Tom Hathaway, & Carey Hoffman, *Bearcats! The Story of Basketball at the University of Cincinnati* (Goshen, KY: Harmony House Publishers, 1997).

27. "Victory," *The Lantern*, November 13, 1895, 1.

28. "Passing Show," *The Lantern*, November 13, 1895, 2.

29. "Athletic Association," *Columbus Dispatch*, November 14, 1895, 4.

30. "In Old Kentuck!" *The Ohio State University Monthly*, December 1923.

31. *Evening Bulletin*, November 18, 1895, accessed January 16, 2016, https://archive.org/stream/xt7bnz8on28z/xt7bnz8on28z_djvu.txt.

32. "Even Trade," *The Lantern*, November 20, 1895, 2.

33. *Ibid.*

34. "Defeat," *The Lantern*, November 27, 1895, 1.

35. "Perfect Record," *The Ohio State University Monthly*, March 15, 1948, 11.

36. "Red Hot Game," *The Lantern*, November 27, 1895, 2.

37. "Perfect Record," *The Ohio State University Monthly*, March 15, 1948, 11.

38. "Kenyon Knocked Out," *The Lantern*, December 4, 1895, 1.

39. *Ibid.*

40. *Ibid.*

41. "Board of Directors," *The Lantern*, February 19, 1896, 2.

42. *Ibid.*

Chapter Twenty-Four

1. "Intercollegiate," *The Lantern*, January 15, 1896, 1.

2. "Intercollegiate," *The Lantern*, February 12, 1896, 1.

3. "Football," *The Lantern*, September 23, 1896, 1.

4. *Ibid.*

5. *Ibid.*

6. *Ibid.*

7. *Ibid.*

8. *Ibid.*

9. "They Were Dead Easy," *Ohio State Journal*, October 4, 1896, 2.

10. "New Football Coach," *The Lantern*, October 7, 1896, 1.

11. *Ibid.*

12. "Victory," *The Lantern*, October 14, 1896, 1.

13. "Second Team 10. Chillicothe 8." *The Lantern*, October 14, 1896, 1.

14. "Otterbein Defeated," *Ohio State Journal*, October 18, 1896, 2.

15. "Well, Well!" *The Lantern*, October 21, 1896, 1.

16. *Ibid.*

17. "By Whom?" *The Lantern*, October 28, 1896, 1.

18. "Denied," *The Lantern*, October 28, 1896, 1.

19. Caspar W. Whitney, "Amateur Sport," *Harpers Weekly*, November 14, 1896, 1133.

20. "Editorials," *The Lantern*, November 4, 1896, 2.

21. "Defeated," *The Lantern*, November 4, 1896, 1.

22. *Ibid.*

23. "They Bucked the Center," *Ohio State Journal*, November 6, 1896, 2.

24. "Decisions Were Bad," *Ohio State Journal*, November 8, 1896, 2.

25. "'Varsity Team Was Weak," *Ohio State Journal*, November 12, 1896, 2.

26. "Ignorance: Notes," *The Lantern*, November 11, 1896, 1.

27. "Wittenberg Won Easily," *Ohio State Journal*, November 15, 1896, 2.

28. "Foolish," *The Lantern*, November 18, 1896, 1.

29. "Kenyon: Return of Our Old Rivals Thanksgiving Day," *The Lantern*, November 25, 1896, 1.

30. "Editorials," *The Lantern*, December 2, 1896, 2.

31. "Kenyon, 34; O. S. U., 18," *The Lantern*, December 2, 1896, 1.

32. "Kenyon Lands the Thanksgiving Prize," *The Lantern*, December 2, 1896, 1.

33. Frank Evans, "Former Ohio State Football Player Discusses Gridiron Games of 1896," *The Lantern*, August 6, 1959, 1.

34. "Pride of the Buckeye State," *The Makio*, 1897, 296–97.

Chapter Twenty-Five

1. James E. Pollard, *Ohio State Athletics, 1879–1959* (Columbus, Ohio: Ohio State University Press, 1959).

2. "A Review," *The Lantern*, December 8, 1897, 1.

3. "O. S. U. Armory," *Columbus Dispatch*, January 11, 1898, 12.

4. "Football," *The Lantern*, September 15, 1897, 1.

5. *Ibid.*

6. *Ibid.*

7. "Notes," *The Lantern*, November 10, 1897, 1.

8. "In Form," *The Lantern*, September 29, 1897, 1.

9. "Football Season in Full Blast," *Ohio State Journal*, October 6, 1897, 2.

10. "New Life," *The Lantern*, October 6, 1897, 4.

11. *Ibid.*

12. "Superb," *The Lantern*, October 13, 1897, 1.

13. *Ibid.*

14. James E. Pollard, *Ohio State Athletics, 1879–1959* (Columbus, Ohio: Ohio State University Press, 1959).

15. "Defeat," *The Lantern*, October 20, 1897, 1.

16. "The Barracks Game," *The Lantern*, October 27, 1897, 4.

17. "Football," *The Lantern*, October 27, 1897, 1.

18. Ibid.

19. "Crippled," *The Lantern*, November 3, 1897, 1; "Again," *The Lantern*, November 10, 1897, 1.

20. "Foot-Ball," *The Lantern*, November 17, 1897, 1.

21. "Completed," *The Lantern*, December 1, 1897, 1.

22. "Athletics" *The Lantern*, March 16, 1898, 1.

23. "A Review," *The Lantern*, December 8, 1897, 1.

24. "Basket Ball," *Columbus Dispatch*, January 7, 1898, 5.

25. "Basket Ball," *The Lantern*, February 2, 1898, 1.

26. "Basket Ball," *The Lantern*, February 16, 1898, 1.

27. "Basket Ball," *Ohio State Journal*, February 9, 1898, 6.

28. "Auditorium Basket Ball," *Columbus Dispatch*, February 10, 1898, 9; "Had a Warm Game," *Columbus Dispatch*, February 11, 1898, 9.

29. "Editorials," *The Lantern*, February 23, 1898, 2.

30. "What the Girls Are Doing in the Gym," *The Lantern*, March 9, 1898, 3.

31. "Athletic Notes," *The Lantern*, February 9, 1898, 1.

32. "No Baseball" *The Lantern*, March 2, 1898, 1.

33. J. V. Denney, Sec., *Ohio State University Twenty Fifth Academic Year 1897–8*, 201–3. Courtesy of the Ohio State University Archives.

34. "No Baseball" *The Lantern*, March 2, 1898, 1.

35. *Ibid.*

36. Quoted in "As Others See Us" *The Lantern*, March 9, 1898, 3.

37. "Students' Mass Meeting," *Columbus Dispatch*, March 8, 1898, 7.

38. "New Athletics," *Columbus Dispatch*, March 9, 1898, 10.

39. "Athletics" *The Lantern*, March 16, 1898, 1.

40. "Concert," *The Lantern*, April 13, 1898, 1.

41. "Dramatic Entertainment," *The Lantern*, April 27, 1898, 2.

42. "Notice" *The Lantern*, March 16, 1898, 3.

43. "University Hop," *The Lantern*, May 4, 1898, 2.

44. "Athletic Affairs," *The Lantern*, April 27, 1898, 4.

45. "Editorials," *The Lantern*, May 11, 1898, 2.

46. "Athletics," *The Lantern*, May 18, 1898, 4.

47. "Field Day," *Columbus Dispatch*, May 21, 1898, 7.

48. "Editorials," *The Lantern*, May 11, 1898, 2.

49. J. V. Denney, Sec., *Ohio State University Twenty Fifth Academic Year 1897–8*, 201–3. Courtesy of the Ohio State University Archives; Alexis Cope, Sec., *Record of the Proceedings of the Board of Trustees of the Ohio State University from November 18, 1890, to June 30, 1900* (Columbus, OH: Hann & Adair, 1900), 324–26.

50. "Athletics: The New Physical Director," *The Lantern*, October 10, 1906, 2.

51. "The New Athletic Director Who Assumes His Duties This Term," *The Lantern*, January 9, 1907, 2.

52. "Reorganization of Athletics is Under Way," *The Lantern*, January 17, 1912, 1.

53. "Co-Ed Basketball," *The Lantern*, November 27, 1907, 5.

54. "Athletics," *The Lantern*, September 21, 1898, 1.

55. "Foot Ball," *The Kenyon Collegian*, August 1898, 43.

56. "Victory," *The Lantern*, December 7, 1898, 1.

57. "Kenyon," *The Lantern*, November 16, 1898, 1.

58. "Bright Prospects for Basket Ball," *The Lantern*, November 9, 1898, 1.

59. "Results by Year," *2015–16 Ohio State Men's Basketball Media Information Guide*, 186–200.

60. "Foot Ball," *The Lantern*, September 20, 1899, 3.

61. "An Interesting Story: How We Won the Championship of Ohio," *The Lantern*, December 6, 1899, 1.

62. "Editorials," *The Kenyon Collegian*, December 1899, 101.

63. "Kenyon Defeated," *The Lantern*, December 6, 1899, 1.

64. "The Ohio Champions Yield to O. M. U.," *Ohio State Journal*, November 18, 1900, 2.

65. "Still Champions," *The Lantern*, December 5, 1900, 1.

66. "Michigan Played to a Standstill," *Ohio State Journal*, November 25, 1900, 2.

67. "The Ann Arbor Trip," *The Lantern*, November 28, 1900, 1.

68. "Base Ball," *The Lantern*, May 1, 1901, 1.

69. "Outlook for Michigan," *The Lantern*, October 8, 1902, 2.

70. "Ready for Michigan," *The Lantern*, October 22, 1902, 1.

71. F. M. Church, "Fielding H. Yost," *University of Michigan Athletic Annual: An Authoritative Handbook of Athletic Statistics* (Ann Arbor, MI: H. Beach Carpenter, 1914), 11–12.

72. "Four Score and Six," *The Lantern*, October 29, 1902, 1.

73. "Composer of Ohio State's Alma Mater Dies," *Michigan Alumnus*, November 1969, 11.

Chapter Twenty-Six

1. "First 'Varsity Team," *The Lantern*, December 1, 1909, 2.

2. Charles William Foulk, *General Principles and Manipulations of Quantitative Chemical Analysis*, (New York: McGraw-Hill, 1914).

3. *The Ohio State University Board of Trustees: Meeting Minutes*, June 14, 1954.

4. Chas. B. Morrey, "Beginnings of Football at Ohio State," *Football Program: Princeton University vs. The Ohio State University, Ohio Stadium*, November 3, 1928, 60–61.

5. George H. Cole, "The First Football," *The Lantern*, December 8, 1909, 2.

6. "Harley and Karch Made Eligible for Game Tomorrow," *The Lantern*, October 6, 1916, 4.

7. "Largest Score in School's History Made by Varsity," *The Lantern*, October 16, 1916, 1.

8. "Two Field Goals Give Illini Losing End of 7–6 Score," *The Lantern*, October 23, 1916, 1.

9. "Ohio Probably Clinches Championship," *The Lantern*, November 6, 1916, 1.

10. Bob Hunter, *Saint Woody: The History and Fanaticism of Ohio State Football* (Herndon, VA: Potomac Books Inc., 2012).

11. "Championship at Stake in Contest of Season's End," *The Lantern*, November 23, 1916, 1.

12. "Ohio State Wins Conference Title," *The Lantern*, November 27, 1916, 1.

13. "Congrats, Ohio State," *Oberlin Review*, November 28, 1916, 2.

14. "Ohio Stadium: The Men Behind the Stadium," *Birth of Ohio Stadium*, accessed January 28, 2016 from http://wosu.org/archive/horseshoe/men.htm.

15. Paul M. Lincoln, "The President's Page," *The Ohio State University Monthly*, October 1920, 10.

16. "Alumni Affairs," *The Ohio State University Monthly*, February 1945, 8.

17. "That First Football," *The Ohio State University Monthly*, February 1920, 29–30.

18. "First Football Heroes Will Be at Homecoming," *The Lantern*, November 12, 1924, 1.

19. *Ibid.*

20. "Jones, Jesse Lee," *The National Cyclopædia of American Biography*, Vol. XXI, (New York: James T. White & Co., 1931) 431.

21. Albert E. Segal, "Dr. Morrey Awarded His Varsity 'O' for Services on First Grid Team," *The Lantern,* December 20, 1922, 2.

22. "'O' Men Organize," *The Lantern,* May 20, 1903, 1.

23. "1890 Athletes, First Gridders, to Be Honored," *The Lantern,* November 11, 1924, 3.

24. "Class Prophet Was Too Cautious; Predictions for 1950 True Today," *The Lantern,* November 14, 1924, 7.

25. "Letterwinners," *125 Years of Football,* accessed March 20, 2016 from http://grfx.cstv.com /schools/osu/graphics/pdf/m-footbl/all-time-letterwinners-1.pdf.

26. "Two Bookplates Added to Library Collection," *The Lantern,* April 28, 1924, 1.

27. "Newest Library Finally Dedicated," *The Lantern,* October 11, 1993, 3.

28. "C. C. Sharp is Dead," *The Ohio State University Monthly,* February 1934, 164.

29. "New Names Appear on Bronze Tablets Installed in Stadium," *The Lantern,* November 11, 1926, 1.

30. Pete Daniel, *The Shadow of Slavery: Peonage in the South, 1901–1969* (Champaign, IL: University of Illinois Press, 1990).

31. "Fred Ball, Cramton Bowl Trustee," *The Ohio State University Monthly,* February 1922, 30.

32. "Chester H. Aldrich," *The Ohio State University Monthly,* Vol. II, No. 4, January 1911, 14.

33. "The Select Folks: Reputations Who Have Dove Things," *The Luyceumite and Talent* 5, no. 10 (March 1912): 73.

34. J. Hudson, "Nebraska 6, Michigan 6," HuskerMax, October 24, 2012, accessed February 22, 2016 from http://www.huskermax.com/games/1911/08michigan11.html.

35. Wilbur H. Siebert, "Progress of Patriarchs' Gateway Fund," *The Ohio State University Monthly,* April 1914, 36–37.

36. Michael Oriard, *King Football: Sport and Spectacle in the Golden Age of Radio and Newsreels, Movies and Magazines, the Weekly and the Daily Press* (Chapel Hill, NC: University of North Carolina Press, 2004).

37. "Appearances at #1 in the AP Poll: 1936 to 2015," *College Poll Archive,* January 12, 2016, accessed January 28, 2016, http://collegepollarchive.com/football/ap/app_total.cfm?sort=numiapp &from=1936&to=2015#.VsyBItBWfIU.

38. Bob Hunter, *Saint Woody: The History and Fanaticism of Ohio State Football* (Herndon, VA: Potomac Books Inc., 2012).

39. R. B. Cialdini, R. J. Borden, A. Thorne, M. Walker, S. Freeman, and L. Sloan, "Basking in Reflected Glory: Three (Football) Field Studies," *Journal of Personality and Social Psychology* 34, no. 3, 366–75.

40. "Site of the First Ohio State Football Game," *Historical Marker Project,* accessed January 28, 2016, http://www.historicalmarkerproject.com/markers/HMCoJ_site-of-the-first-ohio-state -football-game_Delaware-OH.html.

41. Mike Peticca, "Ohio State Buckeyes Estimated to Have the Most Fans of Any College Football Team in the Country, Study Finds," *Plain Dealer,* September 20, 2011, accessed January 28, 2016 from http://www.cleveland.com/ohio-sports-blog/index.ssf/2011/09/ohio_state _football_take_heart.html.

42. "Conning the Campus," *Michigan Alumnus,* October 27, 1934, 47.

43. Bob Hunter, *Saint Woody: The History and Fanaticism of Ohio State Football* (Herndon, VA: Potomac Books Inc., 2012).

44. Dean Denney, "College of Arts, Philosophy and Science," *The Makio*, 1915, 39.

45. Jeremy Schaap, *Triumph: The Untold Story of Jesse Owens and Hitler's Olympics* (New York: Houghton Mifflin Harcourt, 2007).

46. Lillian Callif, "'Daddy' of Ohio State Football Recalls Players Spurned First Football Pigskin," *Columbus Citizen*, November 19, 1938, 1.

47. "Cole, Swartzel Dead," *The Ohio State University Monthly*, November 1941, 32.

48. "'Key Will Honor First Grid Coach," *The Lantern*, October 28, 1938, 2.

49. "Bucks Name Steve Andrako Captain of 1939 Football Team," *The Lantern*, November 22, 1938, 1.

50. "How a Six Dollar Football Made Millions," *The Lantern*, August 12, 1948, 2.

51. *Ibid.*

52. Ann Byers, *Ohio State Football* (New York: Rosen Publishing, 2013).

53. Craig Thomas, "Ohio State's Greatest Football Players," *NCAA Football*, October 2, 2014, accessed January 28, 2016 from http://www.ncaa.com/news/football/pillars-program/2014-09-30/ohio-states-greatest-football-players.

54. Jack Park, *The Official Ohio State Football Encyclopedia: National Championship Edition* (New York: Sports Publishing, 2002).